Digital Information Ecosystems

Series Editor
Jean-Charles Pomerol

Digital Information
Ecosystems

Smart Press

Dominique Augey

with the collaboration of
Marina Alcaraz

WILEY

First published 2019 in Great Britain and the United States by ISTE Ltd and John Wiley & Sons, Inc.

ISTE Ltd
27–37 St George's Road
London SW19 4EU
UK

www.iste.co.uk

John Wiley & Sons, Inc.
111 River Street
Hoboken, NJ 07030
USA

www.wiley.com

Library of Congress Control Number: 2018964892

British Library Cataloguing-in-Publication Data
A CIP record for this book is available from the British Library
ISBN 978-1-78630-414-8

Contents

Foreword   ix

Introduction   xv

Chapter 1. How Do the Economy and the Press
Influence Each Other?   1

1.1. The concept of media   1
1.2. The concept of information   3
1.3. The economy   7
1.4. A brief history of the media and press economy   7
 1.4.1. The discreet beginnings of the media economy   8
 1.4.2. The renewal of the media economy since the 2000s   10
1.5. The two "meanings" of media economics   17
 1.5.1. Does media have an influence on the economy?   17
 1.5.2. Does the economy influence the media sector?   25
1.6. Summary   32

Chapter 2. Can We Trust the Press?   35

2.1. The credibility of media and journalists   35
 2.1.1. Distrust of the Internet is growing   36
 2.1.2. But criticism of journalists remains strong   37
2.2. Is there an informational or ideological bias in the press?   38
 2.2.1. The measurement of an informational bias   38
 2.2.2. Tests on U.S. media   44
 2.2.3. The case of the Asian and European press   47
 2.2.4. The impact of newspaper owners   48
 2.2.5. Pluralism and competition   50
2.3. Summary of challenges   54

Chapter 3. What are the Links between the Press and Politics?   55

3.1. A diminishing influence   58
3.2. The notion of collusion between the media
and politicians   60
3.3. Do newspapers run elections?   62
3.4. The importance of press freedom   64
3.5. Differences between local and national press   67
   3.5.1. The local press is more influential   67
   3.5.2. The Internet confirms this influence   68
   3.5.3. The case of Japan   68

Chapter 4. Does the Press Need Advertisers?   71

4.1. Advertising-free newspapers?   73
4.2. Pressure from advertisers and readers   74
   4.2.1. When advertisers apply the pressure   74
   4.2.2. When readers put pressure on advertising   76
4.3. Can media say everything?   77
   4.3.1. Seducing advertisers   77
   4.3.2. Can media oppose an advertiser?   81
   4.3.3. The impact of taxation   84

Chapter 5. Is the Printed Newspaper Gamble Crazy?   87

5.1. Is it the end of printed papers in the United States?   88
   5.1.1. Preparing for a change of era?   89
   5.1.2. Digital reading exceeds paper reading   91
   5.1.3. Difficult print launches   93
5.2. Among pure players: the free model is crumbling   95
5.3. The online press mainly chooses the paid model   97
5.4. Managing the model change   99
   5.4.1. Absorbing the negative effects of the Web on print   100
   5.4.2. The copy/paste temptation   101
5.5. The press in start-up mode   104
   5.5.1. Is the future in code?   104
   5.5.2. The hope of finding new resources   106
5.6. Understanding the algorithmic agenda   109

Chapter 6. Are There Dangerous Links between Media and Social Networks?   115

6.1 The indispensable social networks   115
   6.1.1. Strategies to take advantage of social networks   117

6.1.2. Media at the mercy of networks 118
6.1.3. The media brand is fading away behind the
social network brand. 119
6.1.4. The problem of revenue sharing between
media and social networks 120
6.2. The social network eco-system 122
6.2.1. The influence of social networks. 122
6.2.2. The way in which we inform ourselves is not unbiased 125
6.2.3. The influence of social networks on decisions. 128
6.3. Social networks are transforming the information business 131
6.3.1. Journalists in networks. 131
6.3.2. The role of social network algorithms. 133
6.3.3. The impact of social network development on
the quality of information. 136

Chapter 7. Will Fake News Kill Information? 139

7.1. From media and network initiatives to a law 141
7.2. Fake news and post truth. 143
7.2.1. Misinformation circulates very quickly. 145
7.2.2. Fake news and social networks. 146
7.3. Why fake news? 149
7.3.1. The impact of fake news and rumors 150
7.3.2. Fact checking versus fake news 152
7.3.3. Bad news. 153
7.3.4. Fake news and economic expectations 154

Chapter 8. Are Robots and AI the Future of the Media? 161

8.1. Robot journalists are already in action. 162
8.2. What is artificial intelligence? 164
8.3. Research on automatic journalism 165
8.3.1. From quantitative journalism to robot journalism 166
8.3.2. Do readers and advertisers enjoy articles
that have been written automatically? 168
8.3.3. The impact of robotization 168
8.3.4. What do human journalists think about it? 169
8.4. How do these editorial algorithms work? 174

References. 179

Index 205

Foreword

The interest in this book is apparent for two reasons. It provides a rich and comprehensive account of all the challenges that digital technologies have put forward and continue to put forward to news media and journalists. To do this, the two authors use recent statistical data from multiple studies, but above all, they offer an overview of multiple academic works, mostly in English, by economists and social science researchers on these issues. Every reader will therefore learn a lot by reading this book because the works presented are often little or not at all known, given that in France, for example, the academic analysis of the news media is only marginally based on economic theories. It is a real asset of this book that it presents dozens of publications on media economics and related theoretical analyses, such as the application of game theory and "public choice" or the study of "biases" in order to understand the functioning of the media and journalists.

Illuminated by its conceptual contributions, the book thus paints an uncompromising portrait of the current weaknesses of the press in fulfilling its essential democratic mission. All the major issues of the moment are covered, from the destruction of jobs as a result of digitization and the double decline in readers and advertising revenues, to the capture of these revenues by the two giants Google and Facebook, the dangers of poisonous fake news, as well as the links between political power and the press, or the uncertain future created by the introduction of computer-assisted journalism and the weight of algorithms in selecting the information that comes to us.

Based on this book and our own work, we would like to put three major issues facing the press into perspective, ones that briefly outline some key ideas to be retained.

The digitization of the world has an impact on all sectors of activity. It destabilizes acquired situations, and it forces us to rethink economic models and adapt the workforce by promoting new skills. Journalism was affected very quickly, because the Internet opened the doors to competition with new "information producers", whether amateur or semi-professional, and because the citizen's desire to be informed in real time took off as soon as this technology allowed it. The book rightly highlights how difficult it has been for the press to find its bearings in the face of such a reality. There has often been a lack of support for change in editorial offices. The culture of free access on which the Internet has flourished has been an insurmountable challenge for many news media. The notoriety of press brands and the associated financial resources mean that major inequalities in digital adaptation can be seen between the media that have managed to cross the line and are consequently rather profitable, and the others that are still persisting, or even taking a hit in the hope of avoiding ruin.

However, our deep conviction is that this change in the journalistic paradigm is not, as in any revolutionary phase, the transition from a stabilized X state to a stabilized Y state, via a period of turmoil that is linked to the changes to be implemented. No. The digitization of the world is a movement to accelerate technological progress, which means that the new paradigm that is emerging is in fact a paradigm of permanent change. The revolution of "web first" (publishing first online and thinking about the content of one's traditional media in relation to this temporality) is behind us, and we must already master the revolution of the "mobile first" (publishing first for smartphones), while waiting to discover novelties that engineers are creating in their laboratories and soon in their factories. Incidentally, it is regrettable that the Mojo aspect (mobile journalism) is not heavily touched upon in this book.

This revolution for the press is therefore not only an economic challenge, presented in this book from every perspective, but also in the strong sense, it is a cultural challenge. What intellectual and managerial gymnastics must press companies implement in order to become permanently adaptable? The future of media companies is undoubtedly on the side of setting up R&D structures, with research and development becoming a necessity in order to be at the forefront of transformations, rather than being subjected to them in a defensive position, on the back foot. The future also lies in supporting the spirit of initiative and innovation of the employees of these companies, from the editorial staff to the IT development or marketing departments.

The second question we wanted to highlight is that of GAFA. The role of platforms in the information universe is a curious mix of positive aspects and much more negative realities. The positive aspect is undoubtedly the multiplication of meeting points with the journalistic information that they represent. More and more people say they have access to news through these digital social networks, and the phenomenon is even diversifying, since Apple News is now becoming a major provider of traffic for news sites, and since WhatsApp and Snapchat bring new ways to get informed by reaching new, often younger audiences, via its Discover device. However, the other side of the coin is that some of the players in this globalized access market have managed to build up oligopolistic positions. Google and Facebook, for example, capture most of the advertising value, as Marina Alcaraz and Dominique Augey have clearly shown.

Moreover, these players have established themselves thanks to the power of their algorithms, algorithms that become real prescribers of our information choices without us always being aware of them. This is a real democratic challenge. Can we still trust Google to select the information deemed most relevant to our requests? Should we trust Facebook when they prioritize the information posts that come up on our wall, without telling us how? In the name of a legitimate economic interest, these companies refuse to make their algorithms public, since their financial success directly depends on it. However, as soon as these algorithms influence our choices of information, and therefore the functioning of democracy, it is equally legitimate to ask for the transparency of algorithms. Here, the competition of legitimacies is head-on. The interest of companies (secrecy) diverges completely from the interest of citizens (transparency). One thing is certain, we must establish a balance of power with these content providers (since, *de facto*, that is what they are) and stop believing in the "naturalness", the "neutrality", of their dissemination technologies.

A third question, among many others, that we wanted to point out in this foreword, concerns the responsibility of each citizen in the evolution of the press. It would be too simple, too cowardly, to simply accuse the digital players and to point out the weaknesses and inabilities of certain media or journalists in order to explain the current situation. Everyone must be aware that we are all responsible for the media economy, through our information behavior. It is customary to summarize the specificity of information for our democratic societies by saying that if information has a cost, it has no price! And the concept is right. Very right. Not having a price simply means that the day that we lose our ability to enjoy it, will be the day that we realize its value. Thus, let us be careful not to, through our daily practices, produce a world where I will have to write the previous sentence in the past tense, as a reality, rather than in the future tense, as an improbability. Although every democrat easily agrees that press freedom must be cherished, not everyone necessarily draws the result that freedom and the press must be simultaneously cherished. Far from generous statements, we must admit that we have no alternative but to combine a requirement for quality information with the willingness to pay for it. On the condition, of course, that the editorial staff keep their ethical and demanding promises for the quality of what they publish. The culture of free access that the Internet has brought from the outset has shown its limits in all aspects of the creative industries. Consuming content without paying for it and believing that content producers will continue to do so under good conditions is just a whim, a flight of fancy. In the trade-off that some people have to make between quality and free information, they must keep in mind that the quality of information implies human resources, time, investigation and hindsight, which only a solid financial base can provide.

The increased access to democratized information that the Internet and digital social networks have allowed has led to an expansion of (formidable) sources, with, as a dual corollary, a scrambling of the relative value of the various sources and the inexorable weakening of the relationship of loyalty and therefore trust in a press title, or a particular media (or two or three). We are increasingly picking up information, on several media, at different times of the day. It can be an undeniable enrichment, but it is often to the detriment of deepening, and it often encourages questioning as to purpose, easily convincing us that we do not have to pay in order to subscribe to such and such media. If we consider information as a "common good", then everyone must ask themselves whether their own selfish fiscal rationality (as economists say) is enough to arbitrate their relationship to the news media, or whether higher considerations should guide our steps towards accepting funding, not only for receiving information every day, but also for helping to keep the press going.

Arnaud MERCIER

Institut français de presse (IFP), Université Paris 2 Panthéon-Assas

November 2018

Introduction

We come from a world in which the press had a clearly identified place and role. Print editions, teams of journalists, an economic model based on the sale of the newspaper and advertising space and, above all, an essential position on the information market: that of an offer of facts and analyses that was only rivaled by other media (other press titles, radio, television).

The arrival of what we still sometimes call the new information and communication technologies (NICTs), some 20 years ago, changes everything – or almost everything. We like to talk about revolution, an expression that is used in all kinds of ways and yet corresponds to the speed and violence of change. The change modifies the acronym that has now become NBIC (nanotechnologies, biotechnologies, computer science and cognitive sciences), in order to illustrate the heuristic mix of new or renewed disciplines that open up the major change that is artificial intelligence (AI).

It all started slowly, without the press really realizing and caring. A few rare newspapers offered a site to respond to the Internet of the early 2000s. The site was most often poorly made in terms of access when compared to paper format: clumsily duplicated, long to download, without ergonomics designed to facilitate reading or search for information. No one really believed in it and paper format kept its appeal.

Then, very quickly, access to digital networks became easier. Flow rates increased exponentially, as did data storage capacity, and digital tools (tablets, telephones) multiplied. And while technology made huge leaps, the prices of access providers and devices fell. Very quickly, we have all become connected, everywhere, all the time.

Therefore, periodic information is confronted with continuous information. Journalists' information comes up against information from everyone, and already that of artificial intelligence and robots. These are fascinating changes. An economic sector that was based on historical foundations of more than 150 years, and solid practices that had lasted and adapted to the arrival of newcomers such as radio and television in their time, are broken.

We are talking about looking at the current press and wondering about its future. We are not the only ones questioning ourselves. The whole profession is wondering. Journalists, managers and investors. Very good books mark out a path of reflection that began with the arrival of the Internet[1], notably one of the first books on online press, De Laubier (2000). Many researchers have examined the press crisis. Politicians, for their part, regularly update the laws that secure and supervise the press, as well as public financial support policies.

Why did we write this book? Because we are reaching a turning point that is no longer just that of the Internet. All connected, all journalists, all in search of attention, notoriety, 15 minutes of fame. All mobile, all nomads. All in *ultra-modern solitude*, all in networks. All influenced, all influencers. All human, all robots. All personalized assistants. All transformed into data. All objects, all players. All of them, but not really all of them. Not for everyone, not everywhere. Therefore, the question is: how is today's *Smart Press* developing and what are the immense challenges it faces in the digitalization of information?

How did we write this book? We wanted an original approach: to combine the perspective and competencies of two worlds. That of a researcher, university professor and media economist with 20 years' experience and that of a journalist, who follows the media in a major national daily newspaper that knows the field, knows the players and knows their concerns. Their advantage: being immersed in the questions of media decision-makers, both observant of and concerned by the reflections of journalists, his expertise in a profession shaken by change. His analyses will help us to reflect on the "paradox of choices" ranging from everything digital to paper, and from print to web solutions, sometimes within the same press group.

---

1 See section I.1, Recommended reading.

The approach is original: the objective has been to scan all recent economic research on the theme of the media and the press, in order to retain the main points. In a world under constant scrutiny, economists' research sheds light on the possible futures to which the media can turn.

Media economics is a relatively new discipline. The media, and the press in particular, are at the heart of many disciplines. Economic science is the latest arrival.

Political science is the first in this field of analysis: its core target is the questioning of the evolution of political ideas and the position of dissemination of ideas in society. A second issue for political scientists is the position of the media in its role of monitoring public decisions, as Jack Balkin mentioned in a 1999 article (Balkin 1999). For the author, the positive effects of the mass media on political life are threefold: the media explain current events and can therefore help individuals to understand public policies; journalists participate in debates; and the media report on economic policies and thus participate in the assessment and monitoring of public policies.

Philosophers also invite themselves into the debate (Chupin *et al*. 2013; Mulhmann 2017). We need to know if and how the media play a role. The answer is, of course, in favor of freedom of expression, defended by law or even by the constitution. Political scientists mix in with lawyers here (Letteron 2017; Cox and Goldman 1996). A corollary issue is the question of pluralism, which is essential in order to stimulate public debate. Political science is concerned with how to promote and defend it. Media history is also one of the first disciplines that focused on the cradle of media. This very active discipline visits times from the conquest[2] of the media and the press, up to the most contemporary events (Albert 2018; Blandin 2016; Eveno 2017; Jeanneney 2015; Kalifa 2011).

Sociology (Maigret 2015; Neveu 2013) and information and communication sciences (SIC) adopt an indispensable additional path by analyzing the behavior and strategies of information providers and receivers. Alain Rallet (Rallet 2006) proposes an *economy of communication*, in other words, an embedding of economic relations in social relations. Even closer to the media, the practices of journalists and editors are observed, questioned and theorized (Ruellan 2011). By analyzing communication practices, the

---

2 Expression borrowed from the first chapter of Blandin *et al*. (2016).

economic constraints are highlighted, reducing the number of newspapers, journalists and means of investigation.

The socio-economy of the media is taking hold of the press crisis, vigilant about media concentration and the characteristics of press group shareholders, and concerned about information now occurring within media industries. Gérome Guilbert, Frank Rebillard and Fabrice Rochelandet (Guilbert *et al.* 2016) define the socio-economic approach as an emphasis of the first discipline over the second, in other words, emphasizing the position of social interactions rather than the analysis market functioning and individual choices. They justify this approach by the particular nature of cultural property in view of its role in society. Bernard Miege (Miege 2004), a professor at the University of Grenoble, identifies the birth of the political economy of communication and media in the 1970s and, together with Philippe Bouquillon (Bouquillion 2005), a professor at the University of Paris 13, points out the importance of this critical approach, which highlights the weight of the economy on existing media, creating effects of domination and preventing the emergence of alternative culture or media.

A powerful North American movement in the political economy of culture led by Herbert Schiller, Noam Chomsky and Robert McChesney (McChesney and Schiller 2003) stigmatizes the role of finance and major media groups. The cultural studies (Maigret and Rebillard 2015; Mattelart and Neveu 2003; Van Damme 2004) movement, developed at the same time, rejects economic reductionism and focuses on an analysis according to the triptych: class–gender–race.

Economists are the last to enter the arena. As Stuart Cunningham and Terry Flew (Cunningham and Flew 2015) point out, media economics is mainly a neo-classical microeconomic approach: in other words, one which is based on comparing the choices of individuals in a market. What can economics bring to a field of analysis that is already heavily and judiciously crowded by other disciplines? The main interest lies in an additional angle of analysis of the founding disciplines of reflection on media. Nurtured by the conclusions of other disciplines, the economic approach complements that of political scientists, historians, lawyers, sociologists, socio-economists and researchers in information and communication sciences.

Although these founding disciplines sometimes converse with each other because they use common tools, and although researchers mix studies and results, dialog with the economy is rarer. There are two main reasons: the media economy is recent and has taken time to establish itself, as is generally the case for any new field of study; but above all, the economy uses its own methodology and tools. The scientific methodology is based on the analysis of the clash of individuals' behaviors within a complex coordination process, called the *market*. The *market* can be competitive or oligopolistic, or even monopolistic. The goods traded can be public or private, tangible or intangible, with property rights or free (such as software of the same name), regulated by public authorities or rules specific to a profession and by national or international standards. The combinations are almost infinite and it is this profusion of *state of nature* that has pushed researchers to introduce mathematics into the discipline.

The first works of the first economists in the 18th Century were written in literary form with philosophical content, or based on the experience and practice of exchanges. The contemporary economy now mainly uses mathematical tools to model human choices and test individual or collective, private or public policy changes, supposed to lead to more growth, less unemployment, less poverty, less pollution, etc. Thus, mathematics makes it possible to reflect on a balanced or sustainable growth path or to model cooperative, altruistic or predatory behavior in a complex way in order to devise actions designed to stimulate the former and slow down the latter. To achieve this, economics is moving closer to other disciplines in order to develop recent segments of economics, such as *behavioral economics* or *neuro-economics*. However, although the mathematical tool has the advantage of being powerful and proposes to summarize reality in situations that can be modeled and analyzed, it often makes it difficult to access the content of economists' research. A solid education in mathematics and econometrics is now required to navigate this discipline, which is highly invested by engineers and economists. The mathematical tool, although largely used, is also criticized by economists, who are concerned about a modeling deviation whose mathematical complexity does not allow it to grasp the complexity of human choices. Some call for a return to a methodology based on the economic analysis of institutions that are chosen by individuals, rather than continuing to densify models by adding and testing new hypotheses.

This *ivory tower* approach, by limiting access, has the adverse effect of sometimes suggesting that economists contradict themselves. The economy therefore has immense progress to make in disseminating its own scientific results. A peripheral issue is the position of economists in the media. An article written in 1996 by Paul Boltz, entitled *Economics and the media* (Boltz 1996), which takes up the position developed a few years earlier by Harry Wallich (Wallich 1972), questions the place of economic speech and research in the media. He regretted that there was little or no room for complex scientific speech. Economics is a science of the complexity of decision-making that is not compatible with the simplification that is often requested by the media. It is up to economists to make educational efforts, which many of them are now beginning to do, mainly through the implementation of the web and social networks, by multiplying the number of blogs in which they present the state of their research.

What is the method that has been used for this book?

Two approaches are pursued by the two authors simultaneously:

– scanning the press news because since the Internet broke out, solutions have been tested, rejected or adopted: it is important to take stock of 20 years of experience in the world of the press and digital information;

– providing the reader with popularized access to the media economy to see if, on the side of research, solutions are emerging or could provide constructive elements for journalists and investors to build their future.

To do this, we will first take a quick look at the history of media economics in order to see how the economy influences the press and vice versa. Secondly, by combining practice and research, we will answer questions that we think are important in order to think about the digital transformation of information and the press. The book explores eight questions on eight topics of interest to experts, observers or media players.

– Chapter 1: How Do the Economy and the Press Influence Each Other?

– Chapter 2: Can We Trust the Press?

– Chapter 3: What are the Links between the Press and Politics?

– Chapter 4: Does the Press Need Advertisers?

– Chapter 5: Is the Printed Newspaper Gamble Crazy?

– Chapter 6: Are There Dangerous Links Between Media and Social Networks?

– Chapter 7: Will Fake News Kill Information?

– Chapter 8: Are Robots and AI the Future of the Media?

I.1. Recommended reading

English-language texts

Cunningham, S., Flew, T., and Swift, A. (2015). *Media Economics*. Palgrave Macmillan, New York.

Doyle, G. (2013). *Understanding Media Economics*. Sage, London.

Picard, R. and Wildman, S. (2015). *Handbook on the Economics of the Media*. Edward Elgar Publishing, London.

French-language texts

Albert, P. (2018). *Histoire de la presse*. PUF, Paris.

Balle, F. (2017). *Les médias*. PUF, Paris.

Bassoni, M. and Joux, A. (2014). *Introduction à l'économie des médias*. Armand Colin, Paris.

Cagé, J., Hervé, N., and Viaud, M.-L. (2017). *L'information à tout prix*. INA Editions, Paris.

Charon, J.-M. (2014). *Les médias en France*. PUF, Paris.

Charon, J.-M. (2016). *La presse d'information multi-supports*. UPPR Editions, Toulouse.

D'Almeida, F. and Delporte, C. (2010). *Histoire des médias en France*. Flammarion, Paris.

Degand, A. and Grevisse, B. (2012). *Journalisme en ligne*. De Boeck, Brussels.

De Laubier, C. (2000). *La presse sur internet*. PUF, Paris.

Fogel, J.-F. and Patino, B. (2007). *La presse sans Gutenberg*. Points, Paris.

Fotorino, E. (ed.) (2017). *Les Médias sont-ils dangereux ? Comprendre les mécanismes de l'Information*. Philippe Rey, Paris.

Gabszewicz, J. and Sonnac, N. (2013). *L'industrie des médias à l'ère numérique*. La Découverte, Paris.

Le Cam, F. and Ruellan, D. (2017). *Émotions de journalistes : sel et sens du métier*. PUG, Grenoble.

Le Champion, R. (ed.) (2012). *Journalisme 2.0*. La Documentation française, Paris.

Le Flock, P. and Sonnac, N. (2013). *L'économie de la presse à l'ère numérique*. La Découverte, Paris.

Mas, V. and Petit, C. (2014). *La presse sur tablette. Les journaux et magazines de demain*. CFPJ Editions, Paris.

Mathien, M. (2003). *Economie générale des médias*. Ellipses, Paris.

Mercier, A. and Pignard-Cheynel, N. (2018). *#info : Commenter et partager l'actualité sur Twitter et Facebook*. Editions de la Maison des Sciences de l'Homme, Paris.

Schwartzenberg, E. (2007). *Spéciale dernière : Qui veut la mort de la presse quotidienne française?* Calman-Levy, Paris.

How Do the Economy and the Press Influence Each Other?

This question is one of the key topics studied by the press economy that we will be presenting here. In order to do this, let us start by defining the concepts of media and information, before asking ourselves how the media and press economy developed in the early 2000s.

1.1. The concept of media

The dictionary defines media (noun) as "any medium for the dissemination of information constituting both a means of expression and an intermediary transmitting a message". There are also other terms such as medium and news (in this spelling, the name becomes invariable). The word media comes from the Latin words *medialis* and *medians*, the origin of median words. The francization of the word *média* with an acute accent and an *s* in the plural dates back to 1973.

The expression mass media dates back to the 1950s. It was invented in the United States to describe a new phenomenon: the media likely to reach a very large audience (television, cinema). The term mass media is often used with a negative, media-phobic connotation. Mass media are often accused of manipulating minds, misinforming etc.

There is also the acronym MEDIA, which stands for "Measures to Encourage the Development of the Industry of Audiovisual Production", a European program launched in 1991[1].

The word media has given rise to many neologisms: *médiacratie* (mediacracy) – a word popularized in France in 1984 by a political journalist named François Henri de Virieu, who chose it as the title of one of his books.

In addition to the definition mentioned above (media transmits a message), which is described as a narrow definition of media, there is also a definition of media in the broader sense. Media not only conveys a message, but also brings together distinct realities (mainly four): the *technique* – the media uses technology, writing, printing, television, the Internet and so on; the *uses* – uses are sometimes expected (a viewer is expected to watch television), but also deviated or diverted (zapping – the viewer does not necessarily watch a program in its entirety which was probably made with the aim of being viewed from beginning to end); the *public* – it can be limited to one person or be very broad; the reception of the message can be different according to the members of the public; the *genre* – an identifiable or supposed form of expression such as journalism or advertising (we are now talking about hybridization of genres, for example, with infomercials).

Media can also be classified into three types: *autonomous media*, which does not require any connection to a network (the newspaper); *broadcast media*, which allows a wide audience to be reached (television); and *communication media*, which allows two-way communication (telephone, Internet).

Media are classified by advertisers into two categories (Adary *et al.* 2015; De Baynast and Landrevie 2014). The first is mass media/media above the line. There were formerly five types, but there are now six: television, press, radio, display, cinema and Internet. The second is *other media* (media below the line) of which there are eight. In fact, these are promotional operations: direct advertising (direct mail), merchandising, POS advertising (point-of-sale advertising), exhibitions, fairs and salons, sponsorships,

---

1 Since its launch in 1991, the European Union's MEDIA program has invested more than €2.4 billion in European creativity and cultural diversity. It has supported the development of thousands of films in Europe and their international distribution. Source: http://europa.eu.

telephone marketing and public relations (including press relations). This is a global definition because all means of reaching the customer are taken into account. The media is a "raw material" for advertising.

One of the most well-known and popular reflections on media is by Marshall McLuhan. The Canadian Herbert Marshall McLuhan (1911–1980) published *Gutenberg Galaxy* in 1962 and *Understanding Media* in 1964. He gives a new definition of media: *all the technological extensions of man.* McLuhan is best known for his phrase: *the medium is the message.* This means that what matters is not the content conveyed by the media, but how the media influences the reception of the message. It influences the ways of thinking and feeling the message. It transforms the nature of the message through its technical specificities (another expression that can be found is: "the message is the massage"). The media has cultural and historical responsibilities. Continuing with this aphorism, the work of another Canadian researcher and professor named Harold Innis at the University of Toronto (Innis 1942) identifies three stages in the history of humanity:

1) The tribal state characterized by a pre-social state. The human was *total*;

2) The Gutenberg galaxy, based on printed writing that allowed knowledge sharing. However, the tribal subject becomes an individual. The printing industry would therefore have a responsibility for the development of a society based on individualism;

3) The Marconi galaxy, inaugurated with electricity, television and new technologies, brings us into the era of the global village. People are again connected to people. McLuhan's books had a profound impact on their era because they highlighted the importance of the nature of media.

1.2. The concept of information

The Oxford English Dictionary (Pearsall 2002) offers two different meanings of the noun *information* and three different meanings of the verb *to inform.* For *information*:

1) facts or knowledge provided or learned;

2) what is conveyed or represented by a particular sequence of symbols, impulses, etc.

For *inform*:

1) give facts or information to;

2) give incriminating information about (someone) to the police or other authority;

3) give an essential or formative principle or quality to. Both words stem from the Latin *informo*, meaning "to give form".

Information is the core business of journalists. Thus, in an article in *Le Monde* on February 1, 2017, the Decoders[2] questioned what information is and proposed the following answer:

> "Media and journalists are no longer the only ones with effective ways to relay messages – just think of all the permanent posts on social networks such as Facebook, Twitter and Snapchat. However, this multiplication of statements of all kinds, coming from various sources, raises a simple question whose answer is less obvious than it seems: what is information? The word itself, in its media sense, refers to facts brought to the attention of a public. But to be considered as such, an 'information' must meet at least three criteria: it must be of interest to the public, it must be factual, and it must be verified".

Claude Shannon (1916–2001), a researcher at MIT, developed *mathematical information theory* in the 1950s in order to optimize message transmission systems (initially the telegraph and then the telephone). The amount of information or *entropy* of a system is the measure of uncertainty or complexity of the system. An application of this logic can be found in the political will of US Vice-President Al Gore in his 1992 speech on information highways. He promoted an optimistic and proactive vision based on the development of networks so as to create links between individuals and facilitate economic growth.

For economists, the concept of information is essential. It is either used in the Shannonian sense of reducing uncertainty, or as a synonym of

2 The Decoders offer readers around the world the possibility of using the Decodex. "The Decodex is a tool to help you check the information on the Internet and find rumors, exaggerations or distortions". See more at http://www.lemonde.fr/verification/#WErJDU55OlyMYmto.99.

knowledge, as in Friedrich Von Hayek's founding article (Hayek 1945). In the first case, the concept of information is at the heart of decision theory, rational expectations, incentive theory, contract theory and game theory.

Game theory has a strange name. It is in fact a mathematical model that describes the choices of each individual, called a player, as well as the interactions between several players. Each individual assesses the gains and losses of a choice according to their objectives and the information they have about their environment and the choices of others. Depending on the amount of information each player has, the choices of individuals will be very different. A player can be a person, a company, etc.

The information can be complete (the player knows all the rules of the game and the possible strategies for him and the other players), perfect (the decisions previously made are known, as well as the actions of the other players) or imperfect (the opposite of perfect information – the most well-known case: the *prisoner's dilemma*, a case where two bandits are in two interrogation rooms. The police lack evidence and offer each of them a shortened sentence in exchange for betraying the other. If both remain silent, they are free since the evidence is missing; and yet they will both end up in prison because they will make the wrong decision, that of betraying the other).

The model looks like a table or decision tree in which there are at least two players and two actions between which the two players must choose, giving at least four possible combinations of choices, and much more as soon as the number of players increases. Each player makes decisions based on what they imagine their gains and losses to be, which is based on their objectives, their environment and also what they imagine the other player's choice to be. The game can be cooperative or confrontational. The player can be altruistic or selfish. The game can be one shot or repeated. Thereupon, a phenomenon of experimentation and learning can be taken into account.

This rapid definition shows that game theory can describe an infinite number of cases, and reflects the complexity of coordinating individual choices. We also see its limitations and the difficulties encountered in taking into account an ever-increasing number of variables that are likely to influence decisions.

Box 1.1. *Game theory*

In addition, the notion of information must be distinguished from that of expertise or knowledge. Expertise emerges from information that is elaborated, processed, densified and linked to other information or knowledge. The knowledge economy analyzes the processes of knowledge accumulation and how knowledge influences economic growth. Knowledge is distinct from information in its reproductive process. Reproducing information is simple and inexpensive, whereas reproducing knowledge is done through learning and requires collective or personal investment in order to build *human capital.*

Consequently, the knowledge economy should not be confused with the innovation economy, which mainly concerns the conditions for the emergence of new technologies, the role of research and development (R&D) and new forms of enterprise (start-ups, the garage economy, etc., in reference to Apple's early days).

The concept of the information economy was initially confused with that of the media economy. Thus, the first edition of Nathalie Toussaint-Desmoulin's book, the first French researcher to embark on this field of study in 1976, was entitled *Information Economics*, which was transformed into *Media Economics* in the second edition. Now, the information economy is used in a way that has moved far from that of the media economy.

The information economy as defined by Carl Shapiro and Hal Varian (1998)[3], two U.S. researchers who founded the discipline, means the study of networks, information being everything that can be digitalized (Bauer and Latzer 2016). The choice of the term *network economics* would probably have been preferable, as the authors used in the first U.S. edition of 1998, entitled *Information Rules. A Strategic Guide to the Network Economy.* The network economy mainly concerns the consequences of the deregulation of the telecommunications and energy sector. On the side of the *Internet economy* or the net economy, the literature is again abundant, focusing mainly on four aspects: the impact of new technologies on growth, organizational transformations linked to the digitalization of companies, e-business models, mass data (Big Data) and crypto-currencies.

---

3 In their reference work initiating the expression and discipline "network economics".

In summary, as can be seen, whether in the information, network, Internet, knowledge or innovation economy, the media is initially absent.

1.3. The economy

Economics is a social science that studies the reasons and interaction of individual choices, as well as public actions, designed to influence individual choices or modify the outcome of interaction between individuals. Human economic activities are vast and involve monetary or non-monetary choices, such as buying a car or having a child. The methodology generally used is based on the modeling of behaviors by a hypothetical-deductive model, whose robustness is then tested via an econometric study. The hypotheses relate to the behavior of individuals, hence the expression of *methodological individualism*.

Economics is a relatively recent scientific discipline, and its inception is commonly linked to Adam Smith's book *The Nature and Causes of the Wealth of Nations* in 1776. It is a discipline that is deployed in many fields as varied as the economics of health, new technologies, family, economic analysis of law, international economics or circular economics. Like any scientific discipline, it is subject to movements and debates that give rise to intense research and an abundant scientific literature.

1.4. A brief history of the media and press economy

Our brief history of the media economy can be divided into two periods: the early stages in the 1960s, and then, after a period of sleep, a renewal since the 2000s. A longer history of media economics could bring it back to mercantilists and physiocrats, not to mention Marxists, as Alan Albarran suggests in his 2004 article "Media Economics" (Albarran 2002; Albarran 2004; Albarran *et al.* 2008).

1.4.1. *The discreet beginnings of the media economy*

In an article published in 1953, Warner Corden (Corden 1952–1953), a professor at Johns Hopkins University, was one of the first economists to apply economic analysis to the press. The author highlights the originality of newspaper companies in focusing simultaneously on their readers and advertisers. Thus, profitability depends on price elasticity (what the price readers agree to pay is, in order to determine the number of readers buying the newspaper) and circulation elasticity (what the volume of readers targeted by the advertiser is, in order to purchase advertising space in the newspaper). The strategy of media companies is thus based on a fine adjustment between these two objectives.

Several authors have worked on this theme. In the 1960s, James Rosse wondered about the number of press titles there were in the United States: in 1963, only 3.4% of U.S. cities had more than one newspaper, such as New York, where 12 newspapers coexisted. The author explains these local monopolies by the small size of the local market, resulting in a demand for *tailor-made* information that cannot be duplicated to other cities, and by a large amount of investment required at the time in order to produce a paper newspaper.

Ronald Coase, who would receive the Nobel Prize in Economics in 1991, inaugurated a field of research that would become very active, which concerned the influence of media on economic policies and vice versa. He then became more interested in the functioning of the FCC (Federal Communication Commission). His questions on the lack of performance of public decision-makers in media regulation led to an essential article he published in 1974 (Coase 1974) (whose arguments were taken up and developed in a later article in 1977 (Coase 1977)): "the market for goods and the market for ideas", in which he proposed a *First Amendment economy*. This refers to the First Amendment of the U.S. Constitution ratified in 1791[4]. Coase distinguishes between the two types of market. He analyzes the idea, that he believes to be paradoxical, of state intervention that could be justified

---

4 First Amendment: Congress shall make no law that affects the establishment or prohibits the free exercise of a religion, or that restricts the freedom of speech or the press, or the right of the people to assemble peacefully and to petition the government for redress for the wrongs they have to complain about.

on the goods market (because of market failures, negative externalities or specific market situations such as oligopolies), but that would not be justified on the idea market. Coase quotes John Milton, in his *Aeropagitica*, published in 1644, who already warns of possible state interventions to regulate the market of ideas and media. Coase particularly criticizes the licenses granted to the press for publication authorization (which limit the access of new newspapers to this market). He proposes to reverse the paradox by suggesting that the two markets be treated in a similar way, and by duplicating a skeptical view of media interventions based on that of the goods and services market.

As time goes by, a few rare publications mark the youth of the media economy. Most of these publications are in the movement of a new trend called *signal theory*. The industrial economy in the 1970s and 1980s focused on the functioning of markets in *imperfect information*. This means that not all players are equal in a market: some are better informed than others, and some can manipulate information to their advantage.

A reference article is that of George Akerlof (Akerlof 1970), a professor at Berkley, who in 1970 analyzed the functioning of the second-hand vehicle market (*lemons*), where the seller benefits from an *informational asymmetry* compared to the buyer who does not necessarily know whether the vehicle has been damaged or what repairs have been made to it. This asymmetry of information and the resulting lack of trust slows down trading in the market. In order to restore dynamism to trades, the players send signals that they seek to make as credible a trade as possible (e.g. offering a guarantee over a certain period of time, in the event of a vehicle breakdown). Akerlof was awarded the Nobel Prize in Economics in 2001.

In this environment, authors such as Milgrom (Milgrom 1981) are interested in the role played by good and bad information in pricing. However, in this type of problem, the role of the media is barely addressed.

Conversely, it is central to Daniel Orr's analysis in a 1987 article, in which he defined the media as an essential economic institution (Orr 1987). Orr notes that the economy has begun to take an interest in the media since it begun to integrate information asymmetries.

Some economists are concerned about the consequences of concentration in the media sector, such as James Dertouzos and William Trautman (Dertouzos and Trautman 1990), who identify a sustained phenomenon of concentration (at the beginning of the 20th Century, 90% of newspapers were owned by small investors, often family structures, whereas in 1960, 70% of newspapers were integrated into groups). The reason for this is economies of scale. The authors observe sustained competition between local newspapers and local radio stations. The studies they conduct are built against the background of anti-concentration regulations and mainly FCC regulations limiting the number of media per investor, whose economic validity they question.

Articles on media economics have multiplied since the early 2000s, mainly because of the arrival of new modes of distribution in this economic sector (online distribution), and also, above all, because of the digitalization of data, which makes it possible to identify studies that are almost impossible to carry out in advance.

1.4.2. *The renewal of the media economy since the 2000s*

Nathalie Toussaint-Desmoulin (1996) and Patrick Le Flock and Nathalie Sonnac (Le Flock and Sonnac 2000) begin the introductions of their respective works with the same observation:

> "The study of the media, and in particular the written press, has traditionally been addressed by political scientists, sociologists and historians. For a long time, […] the economic approach has been neglected" (Toussaint-Desmoulin 1996).

The authors gave two reasons for this lack of analysis. First, for a long time, the economic media sector was not considered important enough. The turnover remained modest, which did not seem to represent a sufficient stake to be interested in this sector. Second, the studies were made difficult by a long tradition of secrecy and discretion on the part of both management and staff.

Susanne Fengler, professor at the University of Dortmund, and Stephan Russ-Mohl, researcher at the University of Lugano, wrote one of the few articles that attempts to explain the wall between economists and journalism researchers (Fengler and Russ-Mohl 2008). It was published in 2008 in a major scientific journal in economics:

"For several decades, the two disciplines have ignored each other [...]. For many communication researchers, an economic analysis of journalism is unthinkable given the public interest mission of journalism" (p. 521).

The difficulty between the two disciplines comes from the particular nature of economics, which would be of a *fractal nature*, to use the expression used by Tiago Mata (Mata 2011). The economy has a dual nature: on the one hand, it is a social science, but on the other hand, it is a political object claimed daily by political decision-makers as an element contributing to their decision-making. Suzanne Fengler, nevertheless, concludes that the wall is crumbling and Stephan Russ-Mohl (Russ-Mohl 2006) is taking an active approach by proposing a *research manifesto on the economics of journalism*.

The context is changing and the difficulties are fading, which is what made it possible for a media economy to emerge in recent years. Long verified, the assertion of weak development of the media economy seems to be reversing. Indirect evidence suggests a significant number of books and articles in recognized scientific journals or the creation of specific scientific journals.

Let us quote Nathalie Toussaint-Desmoulin (2015, p. 5):

"However, since the early 1980s, a change has taken place. The media have entered the field of economic analysis and the industrial economy, even though statistical sources are still limited. Several factors explain this evolution, as well as the recognition of the concept of merchandise applied to the media. The first is the accelerated changes in media supply and its increasing industrialization. First of all, with deregulation, which, at the beginning of the 1980s, put an end to the public monopoly of the audiovisual sector in France and in other countries, and brought in new competing players. Then, there is the convergence of digitalized data on television, computer, telephone and then on various mobile media, which allows the emergence of new channels and modes of distribution and reception, which are often interactive, particularly via social networks. Lastly, with the intrusion of operators into the media field, such as search engines like Google, which are content aggregators more than they are original content creators, but are nevertheless real competitors of traditional media. The technologies and expertise that characterize these innovations require heavy initial investments that can only be made by large industrial or private financial groups, telecommunications operators or public player: the state, local authorities. Similarly, in order to finance their operations, the media have an increasing need for capital. They use various types of financing: unit sales, subscriptions, sales of derivative products, but also various forms of advertising and assistance. Finally, the high costs associated with the creation of written or audiovisual content lead them to seek increased opportunities, both on the internal and external market, all while multiplying their modes of promotion by the use of the same content on several media. In this way, places of trade are developing that are economic battlegrounds and areas of competition or concentration".

Thus, in the early days of the development of the media economy, many descriptive monographs of a particular media sector can be found. The Turku School around Robert Picard is particularly well known in this area (Picard 1996; Picard 1998).

Scientific peer-reviewed journals specializing exclusively or mainly in media economics are rapidly multiplying. Scientific journals in economics adopt a method of classifying articles that are common to all journals. This classification was created at the initiative of one of the top five international scientific journals in economics: the *Journal of Economic Literature*. Thus, a new category named L82 (*entertainment, media*) was created within category L (*industrial economy*). The emergence of a specific category used by the economic research community symbolizes the recognition of this discipline. Below is a non-exhaustive list of the main journals:

– *Journal of Media Economics* (JME);

– *Journal of Digital Media Management* (JDMM);

– *Journal of Digital and Social Media Management* (JDSMM);

– *Journal of Media Business Studies* (JMBS);

– *Information Economics and Policy* (IEP);

– *International Journal of Media Management* (IJMM);

– *Journal of Cultural Economics* (JCE).

Several journals publish special issues. In 2007, the *Information Economics and Policy* journal published a special issue coordinated by Joel Waldfogel, entitled *Economics of the Media*, in which all the avenues of research in this new discipline are discussed[5].

A key issue is the competition between media to capture the rare attention of Internet users or readers: the rarity of attention opposes the abundance of information, as Dominique Augey, Virginie de Barnier and Nathalie Sonnac point out (Augey *et al.* 2010).

In 2012, the importance of the digital shift was symbolized in a special issue edited by Lapo Filistrucci (University of Florence) and Catherine Truker (MIT), entitled *The Economics of Digital Media Markets*[6].

In the major scientific journals of economics, there have been many articles in the last 15 years or so. This is how economic knowledge progresses. The scientific process involves a permanent debate between researchers via the demand for journals (which select the publications they accept through a process of analysis by two blind referees – referees are recognized researchers who read and comment on an article without knowing who wrote it, and the author does not know who the referees are) and the exchange of points of view or criticism between researchers in these same international journals. A common consequence in almost all disciplines of this scientific method is the widespread use of English in journals and conferences. Moreover, as Jean Tirole points out, economics is a scientific discipline:

"His approach is scientific, in the following sense. The hypotheses are clearly explained, making them vulnerable to criticism. The conclusions and their scope of validity are then

---

5 *Information Economics and Policy*, Economics of The Media, 19(3–4).
6 *Information Economics and Policy*, The Economics of Digital Media Markets, 24(1).

obtained by logical reasoning, in accordance with the deductive method. Lastly, these conclusions are tested using a statistical tool" (Tirole 2016, p. 128).

Reference books specific to this emerging discipline are becoming established in the scientific landscape, such as those by Alan Albarran and Sylvia Chan-Olmsted (Albarran 2002; Albarran *et al.* 2005; Albarran 2016), or Robert Picard (Picard and Wildman 2015) and Lucy Kung (Küng 2008) if we are looking more into the research side of media management, or even the *Handbook of Media Economics* by Simon Anderson, David Stromberg and Joel Waldfogel (Anderson *et al.* 2015) if we are looking into industrial economy.

There are also many international conferences on economics and media management. The main ones are:

– the World Media Economics and Management Conference, established in 1994, is an international conference held every two years in even years (the 2018 conference is being held in South Africa);

– the International Media Management Academic Conference, organized annually by the IMMAA (International Media Management Academic Association), founded in 2003.

Workshops on Media Economics are numerous and generally annual:

– University of Zurich – since 2002;

– Universitat Pompeu Fabra (Barcelona) – since 2002;

– University of Tel Aviv;

– Centre for Studies in Economics and Finance (Universtà Bocconi-Milano) – since 2001;

– Economics of Media Bias Workshop (University of Hamburg) – since 2015;

– Economics of Communication and Media Markets of the Florence School of Regulation – European University Institute[7];

– Annual Media Economics Workshop of Stellenbosch University (South Africa);

7 See http://fsr.eui.eu/communications-media/.

– TILEC (Tilburg Law and Economics Center) Workshop on Competition Policy and Regulation in Media and Telecommunications: Bridging Law and Economics – Tilburg University, the Netherlands.

And while the scientific community is rallying itself, the press crisis is bad. In order to remedy this, professionals and politicians are multiplying meetings, white papers, conventions and reports, etc. Table 1.1 gives an impressive list which, despite its scope, is perhaps not exhaustive, as many can be forgotten, given their proliferation.

Year	Author	Type of publication	Publisher	Title
1999	Jean Miot	Report	CES[8]	Les Effets des nouvelles technologies sur l'industrie de la presse (The effects of new technologies on the press industry)
1999	Claude Chambonnaud	Report	CES	Liberté d'information et protection du citoyen face au développement des médias (Freedom of information and citizen protection in the face of media development)
2001	Maria Teresa La Porte Alfaro and Teresa Sábada	Working paper	European Parliament	Globalization of the media industry and possible threats to cultural diversity
2003	Paul Loridant	Report	French Senate	Jusqu'où aider la presse? (How far do you help the press?)
2004	Bernard Spitz	Report	French Ministry of Culture and Communication	Les jeunes et la lecture de la presse quotidienne d'information politique et générale (Young people and reading the daily press)
2005	Alain Lancelot	Report	Commission for Concentration in the Media (France)	(Rapport sur la Concentration des Médias) Report on media concentration
2005	–	Report	[French] Directorate of Media Development	Etude comparative des règles en matière de propriété des médias et du degré de concentration des médias dans quatre états membres de l'Union européenne et aux Etats-Unis d'Amérique (Comparative study of the rules on media ownership and the degree of media concentration in four member states of the European Union and in the USA)

8 CES stands for the *Conseil Économique et Social* (Economic and Social Council), renamed in 2008 as the CESE, which stands for the *Conseil Economique, Social et Environnemental* (Economic, Social and Environmental Council).

2005	Peter A. Bruck *et al.*	Report	Media Division, Directorate General of Human Rights, Conseil de l'Europe	La diversité des medias en Europe (Media diversity in Europe)
2005	Michel Muller	Report	CES	Garantir le pluralisme et l'indépendance de la presse quotidienne (Guaranteeing the pluralism and independence of the daily press)
2007	Marc Teissier	Report	French Ministry of Culture and Communication	La presse au défi du numérique (The press in the face of the digital challenge)
2007	Louis de Broissia	Report	French Senate	Le modèle économique de la Presse Écrite (The economic model of printed media)
2008	Danièle Giazzi	Report	Report for the [French] President	Les médias et le numérique (Media and digital technology)
2008	Patrick Le Flock	Report	[French] Directorate of Media Development	Les coûts de distribution par abonnement de la presse (Press subscription distribution costs)
2009	Bernard Spitz, *et al.*	Green paper	French Ministry of Culture and Communication	Etats généraux de la presse écrite – Livre vert (The state of the written press)
2010	Bruno Mettling	Report	French Ministry of Economy	La distribution de la presse : la situation de Presstalis (Press distribution: the Presstalis situation)
2015	Jean-Marie Charon	Report	French Ministry of Culture	Presse et numérique : l'invention d'un nouvel ecosystème (Press and digital technology: The invention of a new ecosystem)
2017	Catherine Morin-Desailly	Report	French Senate Culture Committee	Entre stratégies industrielles, soutien à la création et attentes des publics : les enjeux d'une nouvelle chronologie des médias (Between industrial strategies, support for creation and public expectations: The challenges of a new media chronology)
2018	Marc Schwartz and Fabien Terraillot	Report	French Ministry of Economy and Finances and the Ministry of Culture	10 propositions pour moderniser la distribution de la presse (10 proposals to modernize press distribution)

Table 1.1. *Official reports about crisis and evolution of French newspapers*

This endless list of redundant reports would almost make you smile if the press crisis had not remained so bad during this time.

Moving away from traditional reports and exchanges in the form of seminars and conferences, the scientific community is getting closer to economic players in labs designed to bring out innovative ideas and solutions, such as the ObsWeb of the University of Lorraine[9], the NYC Media Lab of New York University[10] and the MIT Media Lab of Columbia University[11]. These labs are positioned towards all digital developments of media, as well as connected objects and forms of visual communication.

These journals, publications and seminars shape a research program based on two main axes. The research is organized around two questions:

– What is the influence of the media on the economy?

– What is the influence of the economy on the media?

1.5. The two "meanings" of media economics

Media   ⟶   Economy
       ⟵

The first meaning of media economics is to question the link between media towards the economy.

1.5.1. *Does media have an influence on the economy?*

Does the information that is disseminated influence individual behavior and collective choices? Does media monitoring of corporate behavior and public policy outcomes stimulate more virtuous or effective behavior? Is press freedom a factor for economic growth?

The study of the influence of the media by economists is based on three seminal articles published at the beginning of the 2000s. Timothy Besley and Robin Burgess (Besley and Burgess 2001; Besley and Burgess 2002), two researchers at the London School of Economics, published an article in

---

9 https://obsweb.net/quest-ce-quobsweb/.

10 http://nycmedialab.org.

11 https://www.media.mit.edu.

2001, entitled *Government responsiveness and the role of media in the European Economic Review*[12]. They analyze public food distribution policy in India, differentiating it according to state, during the period of 1958–1992. This period is interesting because it has seen both long periods of food shortages and important food distribution policies implemented by the authorities. The analysis is based on data from 16 federal states. The results show that the most effective states in supporting populations and distributing food are those in which the press is the most dynamic, free and have a high rate of distribution (Kerala and Rajasthan), and not necessarily the richest states, in other words; those best able to finance a policy aimed at reducing shortages (Punjab and Harayana)[13].

With a similar problem, the second founding article was published by David Stromberg, a professor at Stockholm University, in the same year and in the same journal: the *European Economic Review*. In the article entitled "Mass Media and Public Policy", he analyzes the effects of the introduction of radio in agricultural areas in the western United States during the New Deal period (Stromberg 2001a; Stromberg 2002; Stromberg 2004). The idea tested here is the hypothesis that better-informed voters can influence politicians and direct their policies in their favor. This point was highlighted in Anthony Downs' important book in 1957 (Downs 1957). Here too, David Stromberg introduces his article by noting that research on the influence of the media on economic policy was very limited at the time[14], compared to research in political science. The author examines the allocation of public

---

12 The first sentence of the article illustrates its originality: "The role of mass media in making governments responsive to the needs of citizens is a relatively neglected area in economics" (p. 629). Their starting point is an article by Nobel Laureate Amartya Sen published in 1984, in which he writes: "India has not had a famine since independence, and given the nature of Indian politics and society, it is not likely that India can have a famine even in years of great food problems. The government cannot afford to fail to take prompt action when large-scale starvation threatens. Newspapers play an important part in this, in making the facts known and forcing the challenge to be faced". Sen A. (1984). Food battles: Conflicts in the access to food. *Food and Nutrition*, 10 (1), 81–89.

13 See also Nair (2003), who describes the development of the press since the 1960s, mainly from the English-speaking press which uses roughly 100 regional languages.

14 The article begins with the following observation: "The political influence of mass media is something that policy makers and the public discuss a great deal, but about which economists studying policy making have had little to say. A few recent papers indicate that a change may be taking place, however" (p. 652).

funds in 3000 U.S. counties. The period is interesting because it allows testing *before and after* the expansion of radio stations in rural areas, a time when radio was already well established in urban areas. The conclusion is clear: public financial flows were redirected towards rural areas after the installation of radio.

The third article was published in 2003 by Aymo Brunetti and Béatrice Weder, researchers at the University of Main in Germany. The article is entitled "A Free Press is Bad News for Corruption" (Brunetti and Weder 2003). It appeared in the *Journal of Public Economics*, which subsequently published a large amount of research following this article. The authors justify their approach by the recent results at the time, highlighted by many researchers showing that corruption is a major obstacle to economic development (Mauro 1995). They also follow the formation of the international organization Transparency International in 1993, which developed a corruption perception index that was updated annually and used to rank countries (Balkin 1999). The authors describe two forms of corruption: bribery by extortion (selling an administrative authorization such as an import or building permit) and bribery by collusion (sharing the gains from the award of a public contract). In order to measure press freedom, the authors use Freedom House data available since 1996 for 145 countries[15]. Freedom House calculates a press freedom index based on three elements: the law governing the press, the political environment and the economic environment. A lengthy econometric study[16] shows a strong correlation between press freedom and reduced corruption. Similar results are highlighted by Rudiger Ahrend (Ahrend 2002). Here, the economic analysis confirms the monitoring role of the press. In economic terms, the essential role of the press is to reduce information asymmetry between individuals and to highlight economic choices, actions or outcomes that would have remained hidden or unexplained without the insights and additional information provided by media.

---

15 See https://freedomhouse.org. Another press freedom index is measured by Reporters Without Borders (Martin *et al.* 2016) This article, written by three researchers from NorthWestern University, shows a convergence between the results of the two organizations. https://www.scholars.northwestern.edu/en/publications/the-validity-of-global-press-ratings-freedom-house-and-reporterss.

16 Econometrics refers to statistics applied to the economy (Tirole 2016, p. 147).

In the same year, Ritva Reinikka and Jakob Svensson (Reinikka and Svensson 2003; Reinikka and Svensson 2011) published a study on embezzlement in Uganda between 1995 and 2001. The authors' findings are based on an unusual political experience: a press campaign in Uganda was launched to combat misappropriations by providing parents of schoolchildren with information in order to assess the effectiveness of a major education subsidy program. The results are that public access to information discourages the misappropriation of funds at a local level, and that the reduction in the misappropriation of funds has had a positive effect on children's schooling and learning.

Sebastian Freille, Emranul Haque and Richard Kneller (Freille *et al.* 2007), three English researchers from the University of Nottingham, confirm the results of Brunetti and Weder. They cross-reference Freedom House's press freedom index with Transparency International's corruption perception index for 51 countries from 1994 to 2004. To further ensure their results, they are renewing the test with another corruption index established for 140 countries by the PRS (Political Risk Services[17]), which confirms the link between press freedom and reduced corruption.

Similarly, in 2008, Maria Petrova (Petrova 2008) analyzed 102 countries during the period of 1994–2003, using the Freedom House database and then the RSF (Reporters Without Borders) database. Its angle of analysis is the relationship between economic inequality (income inequality) and media independence. The latter also published a press freedom index based on the number of violations of media and journalists' rights and the pressure on the media, either by the government or by pressure groups. Maria Petrova incorporates the Digital Access Index into her analysis, which is calculated by the International Communication Union (ICU), a UN agency in Geneva that specializes in digital access. As a proxy variable for public action, the author uses the amount of public expenditure on health and education, calculated as a percentage of GDP. The last parameter included in the study is an indicator of democracy or autocracy. The results are similar to the two press freedom indices: first, there is a strong and negative link between social inequalities and press freedom in democracies, due to the investment of high-income individuals in the media to influence their content, so as to avoid overly redistributive policies, and second, the development of the

---

17 See https://www.prsgroup.com. It is a private group that assesses country risks and markets its results to companies and governments.

Internet access goes hand in hand with press freedom, the correlation being stronger in democratic countries – the correlation between press freedom and public spending is positive.

A very different way of looking at the role of media is to measure its impact on a particular economic sector. Martin Boyer (Boyer 2006) of the University of Montreal, for example, is interested in the impact of media on the evolution of automobile insurance prices. The author observed the evolution of automobile insurance prices in 48 countries from 1985 to 1993, and analyzed this period because it corresponded to a strong development in car use. The results show that the states in which the press is most read are also those in which insurance rates are lowest. The press therefore plays an economic role by commenting on price developments. By increasing information, the press improves market results and helps to establish more attractive prices.

These articles are representative of a very active movement of research on the causes of underdevelopment, and propose an approach based on the economics of institutions. The issue that is then raised is not only focused on raw material resources or birth rate dynamics, but on the institutional choices to be made in order to promote development. Among the indispensable institutions, economic and political freedoms are at the forefront, including press freedom and competition between media. This approach is summarized in a reference book written by Islam Roumeen, Simeon Djankov and Caralee McLeish, which was published in 2002, entitled *The Right to Tell: The Role of Mass Media in Economic Development* (Roumeen *et al.* 2002). This book would be quickly followed by an in-depth study within the UNESCO framework, published in 2007, entitled *Press Freedom and Development* (UNESCO 2007).

However, although press freedom plays an essential role in economic development, it retains its full position and usefulness in developed countries, as recalled by a recent seminar on French press regulations. This includes the 1947 Bichet law, which manages the distribution of newspapers throughout the country and which has just celebrated its 70th anniversary, as lawyers Camille Broyelle and Jérome Passa (Broyelle and Passa 2018) point out.

These articles have paved the way for extensive research and publications.

1.5.1.1. *The influence of the press on corporate decisions*

There is a whole field of study on the influence of the press on corporate decisions. Just as the press helps to stimulate effective public decision-making and the fight against corruption, it plays an important role in reporting on decisions taken within companies. Publicly available information on corporate governance affects corporate governance.

As well as Alexander Dyck, a researcher at the University of Toronto, professors Natalya Volchkova and Luigi Zingales (Dyck *et al.* 2008) from the University of Chicago are among the first to highlight the link between the press and corporate management. They study press coverage in the Russian-speaking press and in English. In particular, they analyze the *Vedomosti* newspaper, which is published in Russian and in partnership with the *Wall Street Journal* and the *Financial Times*. This new newspaper benefits from the credibility of its foreign partners. The study covers the period of 1999–2002. The authors conclude that the press had a strong impact. Indeed, executives then discovered the importance of their reputation to manage their business and gain the trust of banks. The three authors concluded that the manager's attitude was guided by a rational calculation that balances the financial gain of a wrongdoing or decision of his or her own interests, with the possible loss constituted by the accumulation of loss of reputation and the financial and/or legal sanction.

This article is in line with other articles published at the same time, such as that of Gregory Miller (Miller 2006), a Harvard professor. It not only highlights the active role of the press in denouncing corporate embezzlement, but also the specific role of the business press. Given the technical nature of the subjects, the business press is more effective than the generalist press, which often reproduces the analyses of the business press or press releases. Miller studies press articles (about 8,000 articles in about ten newspapers) from 1987 to 2002:

> "In a large number of articles, the press supplements the information with additional analyses or investigations that only it alone can provide, given its specific nature, thus playing a major role in the financial markets" (p. 1003).

Baixiao Liu and John McConnel (Liu and McConnel 2013), from the University of Tallahassee in Florida, analyze the impact of the press on managers' decisions, mainly when deciding whether or not to invest in another company. They conducted a study based on 636 business acquisitions between 1990 and 2010. The authors noted that managers are sensitive to press comments, and that this may lead them to modify their investment project. The authors explain this sensitivity of the manager the *capital reputation* through the administration of, whose decisions are highlighted by the press. Press coverage is not the only element influencing the decision, but it plays a significant role. The authors conclude by showing that "managers listen to the market and the media" (p. 4), because they not only calculate the financial risk of an investment, but also the reputation risk.

1.5.1.2. *The influence of the media on stock prices*

This issue concerns the role played by the press and the information it disseminates in the evolution of asset prices and stock prices. This issue has given rise to a study that is still very active today, because it is part of a general research program aimed at a better understanding of the functioning of the securities market. It is divided into two branches: does the information relayed by the media influence stock prices? Is there an informational bias in stock market information and, if so, what is its origin?

Alexander Dyck and Luigi Zingales published an article in 2003, entitled *The Media and Asset Price* (Dyck and Zingales 2003, p. 5)[18]. They studied 600 articles and stock market prices between 1998 and 2000, and highlighted a positive link, all the more clear-cut since the media is credible; in other words, it has a brand known and recognized for the quality of its information. This type of statistical analysis is made possible by the digitalization of data and information, which has been developing strongly since the 2000s. Thus, our two authors use the FACTIVA software, which allows them to select keywords and follow the history of stock prices[19]. The

---

18 "To maintain access to these sources, journalists establish an implicit *quid pro quo*. The source repeatedly reveals valuable information to the journalist in exchange for a positive spin on the news being revealed" (p. 5).

19 FACTIVA is a paid search engine specialized in finance. "Power your decision making with Factiva's global news database of nearly 33,000 premium sources, including licensed publications, influential websites, blogs, images and videos. 74% of Factiva's premium news sources are not available on the free web and thousands more are available via Factiva on or before the date of publication by the source". Source: https://www.dowjones.com/products/factiva/.

authors show the possibility of informational bias among journalists for three reasons: what the authors call the *bias of misunderstanding*, linked to a collusion between a journalist who favors information that is not unfavorable to its source, which is, in this case, the financial director of the company with whom he usually talks to and from whom he obtains interesting information; the sometimes insufficient training of journalists in the field of finance that makes them vulnerable to manipulation by the information disseminated by the companies' communication services; a bias request from readers who are also investors and who would prefer to have positive information on the companies whose securities they offer.

The link between information and the market price of a stock is a central subject in economics. Studies on this are very abundant and show that information plays an essential role, but that the impact depends on how the information is disseminated at two levels: who disseminates it and through what channels? And how does it spread among professional (traders) and amateur investors?

Alexander Dyck and Luigi Zingales describe the influence of the media in three ways: the media chooses the information to be disseminated; by relaying information, the media labels it, and this all the more so as the media is credible in the field of finance; the media creates a *common knowledge* phenomenon. Information known to the greatest number (shared knowledge) makes it possible to obtain a rating that best reveals the information known to all. The concept of *common knowledge* is central to economics. As Lucie Menager points out (Menager 2006, p. 42)[20], economists have strongly questioned the fact that a belief becomes *common knowledge* and therefore can eventually be verified: we are speaking of *self-fulfilling prophecies*.

1.5.1.3. *The influence of the press on court decisions*

A more unusual aspect of media influence on decision-making is the analysis of media influence on court decisions. Claire Lim (Lim 2015), an economist and researcher at Cornell, is interested in the impact of the press

---

20 "A particular interactive state of knowledge is common knowledge. An event is common knowledge in a group of agents if all agents know the event, all agents know that all agents know the event, all agents know that all agents know that all agents know that all agents know the event, etc." (p. 42).

on judgments and, more specifically, on the amount of monetary damages granted in civil justice in the United States. When a county is covered by several newspapers, there is little difference between judgments rendered in a district identified as more Democratic and those rendered in a more Republican county. On the other hand, when press coverage is limited, Democratic districts tend to award higher damages and interest than Conservative districts. Claire Lim, this time with James Snyder and David Stromberg (Lim *et al.* 2015), is also interested in sentencing in criminal cases. To this end, the researchers are studying the press coverage of 9828 judges who handed down 1.5 million sentences between 1986 and 2006. The result here is less clear-cut and depends on how the judge was appointed (whether he is elected or not).

As Marcel Garz, organizer of the Economics of Media Bias Workshop at the University of Hamburg, pointed out in a 2015 article that can be considered as a manifesto for economic research on media bias (Garz 2015):

"The main challenge of research is the credible identification of the causes and effects of bias. The relationship between real-world events and media coverage is theoretically ambiguous. Two questions need to be explored: does media bias change attitudes and behaviors? And do individuals' beliefs and preferences lead to biased coverage?"

Let us now return to the second "meaning" of the media–economy interaction that counteracts the previous causality.

1.5.2. Does the economy influence the media sector?

This second question asked by economists opens up a vast field of research by deploying the economist's tools on a variation of three main questions.

Media are most often private companies. Dominique Augey and Frank Rebillard (Augey and Rebillard 2009) ask: how can this affect the content and profession of journalism? The media are generally in competition with each other. How does this influence the supply of information? The media are marketed to both readers and advertisers. Does this *dual market* influence content?

The first question concerns the structure of the media company in order to identify possible sources of bias or influence.

One of the first articles on this topic was published by Gregory Bovitz, James Druckman and Arthur Lupia in 2002 (Bovitz *et al.* 2002). The article assumes that the editorial line of a newspaper is the result of a confrontation between the actions of the individuals who make up the newspaper company. The authors use game theory to describe all possible combinations of interactions between players. There are four players here: the journalist (reporter), the editor, the owner of the newspaper (owner) and the readers (audience). The purpose of this approach is to answer the question asked in the title of the article: what is at the origin of decisions concerning the editorial line of media: ideology or the market? The hypothesis here is that each player acts according to a personal combination of careerist wishes and ideological goals, ranging from the very careerist to the journalism enthusiast, and all combinations of the two. The result is that ideological bias develops when a specific combination of individual interests occurs. Ideological bias occurs if: (1) the journalist has the same ideology as the public, or if the journalist is a careerist while (2) the writer is independent and pursues ideological goals or is dependent and careerist, and simultaneously (3) the owner has ideological goals and shares the same political interest as the public. Thus, the context of an ideological bias is described, and this article opens the way to an abundant economic study on the theme of bias, as well as to an annual workshop.

Since 2001, Daniel Sutter (Sutter 2001; Sutter 2002) has been laying the foundations for statistical analyses based on the choice of topics covered and the vocabulary chosen within the media, in order to try to identify the existence of ideological biases. Sutter wonders about the source of the ideological bias: is it on the demand side, in other words, the readership side, or is it on the supply side, in other words, the journalist's and/or the owner's side? This question led him to observe the evolution of the number of securities, the number of owners and the nature of the latter (at the beginning of the press, the latter was mostly owned by individuals or families, whereas from the beginning of the 20th Century, the press became the property of industrial groups that were either totally dedicated to the media sector or were focused on various activities)[21].

Sendhil Mullainathan, a professor in the Department of Economics at MIT, and Andrei Shleifer, a professor in the Department of Economics at Harvard, are part of a group of three pairs, all of whom simultaneously published a series of articles in 2002 which formed the basis of a body of research that would later be expanded to include many articles. "Media Bias" (Mullainathan and Shleifer 2002) inaugurates this series of publications. Sendhil Mullainathan and Andrei Shleifer assume that newspaper owners pursue two goals resulting from personal suitability between the two objectives: on the one hand, there is the ideological willingness to disseminate ideas that are important to the owner through the media; on the other hand, there are financial objectives consisting of obtaining a profit as in any other company.

This suitability between the two objectives explains why investors are positioning themselves and investing significant amounts in a sector in crisis, as is currently the case in the press. By doing so, the investor assumes either that a change in the management of the newspaper (reduction of costs, reduction of staff) can restore profitability, or that a change in the editorial line will make it possible to boost the readership, or even that the investor is not motivated by an economic objective but favors the dissemination of ideas and assumes that the dissemination of media will enable him/ her to achieve this objective. As for the readers, they are supposed to have beliefs (committed or non-committed political positioning) and memory (they should identify the credibility of the media according to what they have identified in the past as true or false information provided by the media).

---

21 "Newspaper in the United States typically began as family-owned businesses, but the inheritance laws forced the sale or issuance of stock by most of these companies (Lacy and Simon 1993, Bagdikian 1997). The growth of newspaper groups has been substantial. In 1920, 31 groups owned 7.5 percent of the nation's daily newspapers. By 1986, 127 groups owned 69.9 percent of daily papers. In addition, the size of groups increased, from 4.9 papers per group in 1920 to 9.1 papers per group in 1986. Gannett, the largest newspaper group, owned 90 daily papers in 1986" (Sutter 2001, p. 439).

The authors develop a game theory model with two types of players (the reader and the newspaper). The result of the modeling is that the competition between media weakens the ideological bias, while pushing the media to use more spectacular information to differentiate themselves from their competitors. The authors conclude that for information that is mostly requested by readers, there is strong competition for it between media, and it produces information with little ideological bias, whereas for information that is considered less important, there is competition on what the authors call the *narrative imperative*. Mullainathan and Shleiffer extended the reflection in an article published in the highly prestigious *American Economic Review* in 2004, entitled *Market for News* (Mullainathan and Shleifer 2004). They show an important result: the heterogeneity of readers' points of view encourages information providers to diversify their offer. Thus, heterogeneity would be a more important driver for diversity than competition between suppliers. In other words, a press group, even in a dominant position, can choose a diversification (and therefore pluralism) strategy because it is economically efficient in terms of segmentation of the readership between different ideological demands.

The second pair is Alexander Dyck (Harvard University) and Luigi Zingales (University of Chicago). In an article published in 2002 (Dyck and Zingale 2002) on the ENRON case, they questioned a major financial scandal that had ruined many U.S. pensioners. They comment on both insufficient regulation of the pension fund sector and inefficiency of financial journalists in identifying and covering the crisis. The authors explain that there is a lack of media performance because the media have an ambiguous relationship with their source (the companies on which the media must survey and publish their results). The proximity of the media to the communication or financial managers of companies allows them to have information, and this proximity can be maintained through a certain amount of positive information disseminated about the source in media.

Tim Besley and Andrea Prat are the third pair (Besley and Prat 2006)[22] to use economic analysis of public decisions.

---

22 The first version of their article was published in the form of a working paper in 2002, which would finally be published in 2006 in the very prestigious *American Economic Review* (Besley and Prat 2006).

> *The theory of public choice* or *economic analysis of public decisions* is an axis of economic analysis developed since the 1970s, initially within the School of Virginia (of the U.S. university of the same name), which describes the functioning of the political market and bureaucracy. One of the main founders of this movement is James Buchanan, Nobel Prize winner in Economics in 1986[23].
>
> Here, the political process is described with economic tools. Politicians pursue personal goals that range from optimizing their careers (selfishness) to seeking the common good (altruism), with the full rainbow of possible combinations between these two objectives, depending on the individual. This approach has made it possible to understand why unnecessary or harmful economic decisions are taken by administrations or politicians. These harmful decisions can be made out of ignorance or inability to predict the consequences: they are then the result of an error in analysis or understanding of reality. However, these decisions may come from a more cynical process, especially when a generally ineffective measure may temporarily favor a group of individuals who are supposed to be voters or the potential voters of the politicians making the decision.

Box 1.2. *The theory of public choice*

Here again, the three authors summon a game theory model, this time with three players: the reader, the media and the government. Each media has two possible sources of revenue: commercial resources related to the sale of the media to the reader or advertisers and resources related to collusion with the government. These collusion resources can take various forms, ranging from direct financial payments (the authors refer to the case of Peru under the Alberto Fujimori government) to more subtle forms such as administrative, legislative or fiscal decisions in favor of the media. The distribution between the two forms of profit depends on the structure of the media. Commercial profits outweigh other forms of resources when the media are competitive and independent (in this case, independent means either non-public or non-concentrated media). In addition, by analyzing data from 88 countries, the authors show that the life expectancy in power of politicians (here, the prime minister or the president) is longer when the media are linked to the government.

---

23 See a remarkable presentation and summary in Persson and Tabellini (2000) and in Mueller (2010).

The second question concerns the influence of the structure of the media sector on media content.

Two French economists, Laurent Benzoni and Marc Bourreau, are exploring an important avenue of research by examining the effects of competition between media on the quality of content produced. In 2001, they published an article asking this question in the specific case of television (Benzoni and Bourreau 2001). They apply the analytical framework of a segment that has been very active in economics since the 1980s, that of the *industrial economy*.

The industrial economy studies the behavior of firms in markets according to whether they are competitive or oligopolistic. Companies have multiple strategic choices before them, depending on their economic environment. These choices range from horizontal or vertical differentiation (price or quality competition) to mimicry, cooperative or predatory strategies between competitors. The industrial economy also analyzes the impact on the functioning of markets of rules, regulations or incentives decided by public authorities.

Box 1.3. *The industrial economy*

Although the study of television became very active after the 1980s, especially in France due to the privatization of public channels, the study of the radio economic sector is much older. As early as 1952, Peter Steiner (Steiner 1952) analyzed radio programs and concluded that competition produced mimicry (low program diversity).

In 2003, Lisa George and Joel Waldfogel (George and Waldfogel 2003) focused on the press market segmentation strategy in the United States and editorial diversification in the white and black communities. The study covers 1200 press titles spread over 269 territorial areas differentiated by postal code.

Piet Bakker (Bakker 2002), a professor at the University of Amsterdam, published an article representing a trend of analysis of the brand new, free general-information daily press launched in 2002 (80 newspapers in 26 countries). Robert Picard (Picard 2000a; Picard 2000b), then professor at the University of Turku in Finland, multiplied the publications on this new phenomenon as well as on the emergence of the online press, which were barely visible at the time. Very prolific in this field of research and anticipating the importance of the development of this sector, he created the World Media Economics and Management Conference in 1994, as mentioned above. It is gradually being joined by a large number of researchers who are concerned about the long-term economic viability of newspapers that are financed solely by the sale of advertising space (Mings and White 2000).

The third question concerns the consequences of the particular nature of media financing, which are simultaneously based on the sale to individuals and the sale of advertising space to advertisers.

The joint presence of two funders (or even three in the case of state-subsidized media) raises questions: can content be influenced (ideologically biased, impoverished in terms of content, etc.) by one of two funders and mainly by advertisers who may require content that is favorable to them? Given that this is a crucial question, let us first look at the main lines of research before returning to them more fully later.

The economist here uses a specific segment of the industrial economy: the *two-sided markets*. Brian Reddaway (Reddaway 1963) was one of the first economists to define media by an essential characteristic. They are generally sold twice: once to readers and once to advertisers. Does the presence of advertisers limit the newspaper's editorial freedom? Martin Koschat, professor at the Strategy Department of the University of Vienna, and William Putsis, professor at the London School of Economics, discuss what a "monetizable" audience for advertisers is (Koschat and Putsis 2000), while Jean Gabszewicz, Didier Laussel and Nathalie Sonnac[24] (Gabszewicz et al. 2001; Gabszewicz et al. 2002) show that optimizing advertiser revenues can lead the media to seek consensus (the authors speak of "single-mindedness") in order to attract the widest possible readership, given that advertising revenues largely depend on the characteristics of the readership (number of readers, age, sex, socio-professional category). At the same time, Dell Champlin and Janet Knoedler were wondering about the consequences of the 1996 Telecommunication Act, which accelerated the mergers between media

---

24 Nathalie Sonnac is a member of the CSA (Superior Council of Audiovisual) since 2015.

groups, that led to the emergence of the Big Six (Champlin and Knoedler 2002). Nathalie Sonnac also highlights a kind of "advertising dose" not to be exceeded in media, at the risk of triggering a rejection among readers who might turn away from the newspaper (Sonnac 2000; Sonnac 2001).

1.6. Summary

As a summary of this chapter, let us ask ourselves what we can learn from the early days of media economics. There are three important breakthroughs.

– Information was at the heart of the economy. Now, information producers who were almost forgotten before the 2000s are taken into account.

– The media are information providers. They are not the only ones. Companies, the state and local authorities issue information directly to the general public via their communication service, publish their own newspapers (as almost all town halls, departmental and regional councils now do) and buy commercial inserts to announce their actions. Individuals are also very present via social networks. The specificity of the media is to investigate (in other words, expand and compare sources) and prioritize information. Research in media economics shows that it is a factor for growth and efficiency. Information produced by the media improves firms' strategic choices and public policy decisions. It plays a key role in reducing corruption.

– The media are companies placed in a highly competitive environment, whether to attract a customer or an advertiser. The media compete with each other, that is, between types of media (press, television, etc.), but also within the same category (the national press, for example, or the local press, etc.). Is the *media market* a way of coordinating offers that produces diversified and high-quality information? The early days of media economics, specifically the press economy, showed that information can have an ideological bias and that its origin must either be found on the side of demand (satisfying the opinions of readers *a priori*) or on the side of supply (the influence of the owner, the intensity of competition).

The current media economy, the one we will discover in the following chapters, has grown considerably. It has also focused on the digitalization of information, whether in new media for the dissemination of information (websites or mobile online press applications), social networks that are both a means of disseminating information and a means of collecting it for journalists, or new ways of producing information using robots or artificial intelligence.

2

Can We Trust the Press?

It is only a tremor, but it is going in the right direction. The French are starting to believe in the media again. Despite the proliferation of fake news, and despite repeated violent attacks against journalists, including from journalists themselves but also regularly from politicians, several surveys show that the French have a certain attachment to traditional media.

2.1. The credibility of media and journalists

According to the 31st "media trust barometer", published in 2018 and realized by Kantar/Sofres for *La Croix*, credibility is on the rise[1]: the written press is in the top-ranking list and has improved its score by 8 points (to 52%), ahead of television, which is credited with +7 points (to 48%). Radio remains the most trusted media at 56% (+4 points). This trend comes just after a significant decline in confidence in traditional media in recent years (particularly in the previous survey, which was conducted just before the Fillon "affairs"). The vast majority (90%) of French people expect the media to provide "reliable and verified" information much more than solutions (only 6%) or the expression of partisan choices (2%). In short, the French are asking to be better informed, not influenced.

---

1 Kantar/Sofres barometer: carried out face to face from January 4 to 8, 2018, on a representative sample of 1000 people. The question on trust is: "In general, in terms of the news that these media broadcast, do you think that things happened as they tell it?".

Another study corresponds to this barometer, regarding the renewed credibility of the media. According to a Viavoice[2] survey for the *Assises internationales du journalism* (International Journalism Forum) in March 2018, in partnership with the *Journal du Dimanche, France Médias Monde, France Télévisions* and *Radio France*, 92% of respondents believe that journalism is useful. They expect journalists and the media to check rumors and misinformation (61%), to provide them with practical, useful information on a daily basis (49%) and to identify facts and illegal or offensive practices (48%). This expectation is far more pronounced than their wish to have the media help them to form an opinion (27%).

The general public gives journalists a whistleblower function. The notion of verification of information is therefore raised once more here.

2.1.1. *Distrust of the Internet is growing*

On the contrary, the Internet is continuing to arouse a certain amount of mistrust: only one in four French people (25%) consider the information it contains to be credible, according to the media trust barometer of the *La Croix* newspaper. When the French get information on the Internet, they prefer newspaper sites or applications (28%) rather than social networks (18%). However, more than a third of them do not know how to clearly identify their sources of information (37%).

The study focuses on social networks: distrust here is at its highest. In this study, 66% clearly indicate that they do not trust information from social networks (such as Facebook or Twitter), even when it is published by a friend. Even more surprisingly, 45% do not trust the information, even when it is published by media.

Other studies support this view. An OpinionWay survey conducted for JIN, a public relation agency, was published in the fall of 2017, showing that despite growing consumption of these networks, Internet users do not believe everything they read on them. On a scale of 0 to 5, 74% of French people give a score of 0 to 2 to Twitter in terms of trust, and 69% of people express a similar opinion for Facebook.

---

2 Viavoice: online interviews conducted from February 12 to 15 with a sample of 1008 people.

Another study, the French people's digital technology trust barometer, which was conducted by Harris Interactive for ACSEL (*Association de l'économie du numérique* or the Digital Economy Association) and La Poste[3], and was published at the end of 2017, shows similar results. While 75% of French people say they trust the information on traditional online media sites, this figure drops to 25% for information circulating on social networks.

2.1.2. *But criticism of journalists remains strong*

Despite the renewed trust in traditional media, particularly in the face of social networks, the French still have a poor opinion of journalists, or more precisely of their relations with economic and political power. The media trust barometer for *La Croix* attests it as follows: 68% (+1 point) of French people believe that the latter are not independent of the pressures of political parties and power, and 62% (+4 points) believe that they are not independent of the pressures of money.

Even journalists regularly criticize themselves. Many essays have pointed to the abuses of journalistic practices. Recently, in a vitriolic book, *La pensée en otage* (Lancelin 2018), Aude Lancelin, the former deputy director of *Marianne* and *Obs*, expressed concern about, among other things, the massive investment of CAC 40 companies in the media. The book's subtitle, *S'armer intellectullement contre les médias dominants* ("intellectually arming oneself against the dominant media"), sets the tone: the author criticizes the world of media, targeting both press owners and journalists, reminding the reader in particular that the deteriorating job market in media has destabilized the balance of power between writing and management.

The author tries to disassemble seven ideas that she presents as false (shareholders do not intervene; we cannot do without large private capital; criticizing the media is like attacking people; there is diversity and "media" does not exist; journalists must be neutral; newspapers are by definition democratic forces to be defended no matter what; the media cannot do much) which "prevent the public from becoming aware of the need to take up the media issue and make it a priority political issue".

---

3 Harris barometer for La Post and Acsel on a sample of 1067 people, by questionnaire sent via the Internet at the end of September and beginning of October 2017. See the website: http://www.acsel.asso.fr.

2.2. Is there an informational or ideological bias in the press?

Economic research has investigated this question using the concept of bias. The research focuses on the functioning of a press whose owners are most often private shareholders[4]. Knowing that the press is on a two-sided market, in other words one that derives its income from two markets simultaneously, where the firm's strategy consists of balancing the search for resources from the readership (issue sales, subscriptions) and from the sale of advertising space, which is itself correlated with the volume and characteristics of the readership. The question thus becomes: does a market with private press companies continue to play its role within society by fostering debates of ideas that are useful to the citizen and all individuals? Or does a market with competing media companies drain public debate and deplete the world of ideas so as not to shock anyone, in order to please as many people as possible and optimize advertising revenues by targeting the widest possible audience?

Research provides elements of public policy answers to key questions: should competition between media be reduced or encouraged, should public subsidies be granted or should political power be kept at a distance from media?

Economists are present in this questioning, in which all other major scientific disciplines are called upon and are very active, with a clear precedence on economics. Economists address this issue through their expertise in competitive analysis and product differentiation. Here, the product is the content of the newspaper.

2.2.1. *The measurement of an informational bias*

The first task is therefore to define what differentiated content is in the economic sense of the term, in other words: in relation to an average. We could average a lot of things for example, establishing the mood of an article or newspaper, calling it optimistic or pessimistic, light or serious and so on. The list is long and could be very imaginative. Whatever the criterion that is chosen, in order to establish a qualification in any field, it is necessary to go through the content of articles and newspapers; thus, basically, the words

---

4 One of the owners' motivations is to obtain a return that is at least equal to what they could have obtained by investing in another economic sector. The ROI (return on investment) is calculated by the profit/capital ratio invested.

chosen, and even the layout – which is far from impartial in the way in which information is valued – could also be taken into account. This type of analysis is now made even easier by the digitalization of content, which makes it possible to use appropriate databases that are sorted by country, newspaper, year, etc., and by software that makes it possible to sort through databases using keywords. The approach that is most often adopted by economists is that of political ideas and the ranking of a newspaper in relation to other newspapers.

Why political ideas? Because what interests the economy is economic results, such as changes in unemployment or purchasing power; and because these results are the result of the clash of individual choices, which are derived from raw or non-raw information received, beliefs, convictions and public policies, which are themselves chosen by politicians and bureaucrats driven by raw or non-raw received information, beliefs, convictions, etc.

The approach in terms of content or ideas has long been neglected by economists. Following the seminal article by Jean Gabszewicz, Didier Laussel and Nathalie Sonnac (Gabszewicz *et al.* 2001) published in 2001, many authors are involved in this major subject.

The researchers' method is done in two stages: first, to measure the political bias and then to investigate its causes. The bias is highlighted by an *econometric* analysis of the content and frequency of articles. To do this, the research uses the processing of databases that integrate digitalized articles. Identifying the frequency of words or themes in articles, comparing it with the frequency in other media or in politicians' speeches, is the way to analyze possible bias, whereas the cause of the bias is analyzed using a model, where the objective is to isolate the relative weight of the players involved in direct or indirect decision-making. Depending on the models, the bias is on the demand side, the supply side or a combination of both.

As Matthew Gentzkow, Jesse Shapiro and Daniel Stone pointed out in the second volume of the *Handbook of Media Economics* in 2016 (Gentzkow *et al.* 2016), economic research on press content and the origin of information biases offers two types of explanations for this bias.

2.2.1.1. *Bias and advertising revenues*

First of all, bias originates on the demand side because media maximize their revenues or their audience. Media strategy is based on readers' beliefs and behaviors. The media then segment the market in order to offer readers the product that corresponds to their demand. This can lead the media to choose journalists according to their ideological positions, as Francesco Sobbrio's work shows (Sobbrio 2014). The author constructs a game theory model in which the strategy of press groups is to respond to demand by ensuring editorial cohesion and selecting journalists that are consistent with the chosen editorial line. Each ideological position, if it corresponds to a sufficient number of readers, in other words if the size of the market is sufficient to absorb the costs of creating a specific media, will have a media representing it. Consequently, a press group seeking to increase its market share may deploy media with opposing editorial lines within the same group.

Armando Garcia Pires (Garcia Pires 2013; Garcia Pires 2014) explains this result using the size of the advertising market. If the market is small, media companies choose a single-ideology strategy, while if the advertising market is large, a multi-ideology strategy is useful in order to be present in all market segments and cover the broadest possible ideological spectrum. There is therefore a link between pluralism and the size of the advertising market.

This is all the more true given that readers receive information that is difficult for them to verify. Readers, like all of us, analyze reality through the filter of their *cognitive dissonance*. In other words, we tend to judge information more easily as true when it reinforces our beliefs and to doubt its quality when it offends our beliefs. This cognitive dissonance and our subjective reading of what is *true* and what is *false* makes it easier for us to trust media that is closer to our opinions *a priori*. If a medium seeks to retain and develop its readership, one strategy is to position itself on beliefs corresponding to a group of individuals that is large enough to generate satisfactory revenues. Bias is then the way to generate reader confidence and loyalty. *The concept of cognitive dissonance* was highlighted in 1957 by psychologist Léon Festinger. George Akerlof (Akerlof 1982) described the importance of cognitive dissonance in economic decision-making. We may be surprised at the persistence of bias when we receive a lot of information that should help us to eventually revise our positions. However, this is not necessarily the case, as Wing Suen (Suen 2004) shows for two reasons: the cognitive dissonance we have just mentioned makes us doubt the validity of the information received, even though it is accurate, and also the data or facts themselves, which are sometimes difficult to interpret. Thus, the successive flows of information lead individuals to revise their position, but there is a gap between the evolution of positions and the information received. This delay can lead to a perpetuation of cognitive bias.

Box 2.1. *Cognitive dissonance*

Santiago Oliveros and Felix Vardy (Oliveros and Vardy 2015), researchers at *Berkley*, also show that the ideological bias is on the demand side and more particularly linked to the consequences of the rise in abstention. One of the origins of abstention lies in the voter's prognosis about the future winner of elections. If a Democrat believes that the winner will be a Republican, he or she may be encouraged to abstain. The problem therefore lies in the way in which the voter constructs his or her prognosis. The author takes the case of a Democratic voter. If he reads a newspaper from his side, he will receive information that is favorable to his candidate, but he takes the ideological bias of the newspaper into account and relativizes the information that he ultimately does not consider useful to build his prognosis. If he reads a Republican newspaper, he perceives a symmetrical bias with which he does not think he can establish a solid prognosis. His final choice will therefore be a centrist journal, one that assesses the chances of the two candidates and compares comparative analyses of their program and past results. In summary, for the authors, the rise in abstention leads to a reduction in ideological bias. This result implies, on the one hand, that abstention plays a more important role than cognitive dissonance, and on the other hand, that voters correctly identify the ideological bias of newspapers. Here again, research must be continued and is necessary in order to better understand the editorial strategy of media.

2.2.1.2. *Bias and the editorial line*

The bias can also be a supply-side bias. The bias is then explained by the preferences of media companies. The bias is either due to the convictions of the owners or due to pressure from politicians. Therefore, a change in ownership can change the editorial line of a newspaper. How is the content of newspaper articles determined?

Because it is a fact that a newspaper cannot talk about everything. For example, if a daily newspaper included all of the AFP dispatches (5,000 per day according to the *Agence France Presse* website), it would be very large and would not be read very much. Similarly, when a journalist writes a paper, he or she must make choices: he or she must choose an angle, a way of understanding the subject and the aspects he or she will highlight according to many parameters, including his or her readership.

Economic research translates this into the notion of bias. These ideological biases can take four forms. A media chooses the topics it covers and those it will not cover (issue bias), the way in which it covers a topic with or without certain aspects (fact bias), the way in which it presents the topic (framing bias) and the way in which it comments on it (ideological bias).

The most commonly used approach to highlight the existence of bias is to rely on an econometric analysis of content according to its political positioning. This "political" prism is consistent with the concerns of the economist, who seeks to identify information asymmetries between voters and the impact of these asymmetries on private and political decision-making, and therefore on macroeconomic outcomes.

It resonates research on agenda-setting. This theory, which is emphasized by Maxwell McCombs and Donald Shaw in a founding article published in 1972 (McCombs and Shaw 1972; Bregman 1989)[5], identifies the power of media over the formation and evolution of public opinion through the choice made by media, in order to potentially highlight a theme or information, in other words to organize the information agenda through the possibility of media.

As we have seen, given the large amount of information, the media suggest that readers prioritize this information. The *economic service* that the media provides is therefore to collect, prioritize and disseminate information in place of each and every one of us. The counterpart is that the prioritization of information chosen by media guides public opinion.

Media bias also occurs in media that are not privately owned. With the exception of Brazil, Turkey and the USA, there is a public medium among the top three most influential media, in each country. This raises the question about the independence of government-owned media. This question has been

---

5 Dorine Bregman explains the approach of the two researchers.
McCombs and Shaw formulate the basic assumptions of the agenda function based on the following observations: in an election campaign, voters derive most of their information from the media, and they do learn new information, even though not all are equally able to use it; they learn and inform themselves according to the insistence with which the media speak or report on the issues discussed during the campaign. The methodology used to test this hypothesis is based on a comparison between the issues that are declared to be important to the campaign by voters, and the media content consulted by them during the period. The results can be summarized in three points: 1) Much of the information is devoted to the analysis of the campaign on a day-to-day basis, which U.S. journalists have come to call "the horse race"; 2) a strong correlation appears between the importance given by the media to certain issues and that given by voters to these subjects; 3) voters who are not particularly attached to a candidate at the start are more attentive to all the information (no selective perception on their part) (Bregman 1989, p. 194).

a recurrent issue among economists since the article by Simeon Djankov *et al.*, published in 2003 (Djankov *et al.* 2003), in which the authors study 93 countries and show that the most important media are owned, depending on the country, either by the government or by private family investors. The authors then focus on public media in order to test the two economic theories that are being used when considering public economics: the *common good* theory or the *public choice* theory.

In the first case, public decision-making processes are supposed to be taken with the objective of maximizing the common good, by acting to compensate for market failures. In the second case, public decisions are analyzed in light of the *political market* and the *economic analysis of the bureaucracy*; in other words, they are supposed to be taken by individuals whose primary objective is not necessarily the pursuit of the public good, but their own career or personal interests. In the first case, the existence of one or more public media would be justified in order to better inform individual voters that they are being informed by private media that are subject to market failures like any other company, and thus that are broadcasting information that could be biased or incomplete. In the second case, too strong a link between one or more media and political power is suspected of biasing information in favor of existing politicians. This is either because the state owns media, or because it subsidizes them, or even because it intervenes in their financial balance by buying advertising space. To overcome this difficulty, private and competing media would thus be the guarantors of quality information and play the role of the fourth power.

The economic analysis of bureaucracy, based on a founding article by William Niskanen (Niskanen 1975) in the mid-1970s, highlights two types of ongoing conflicts: the first is between politicians subject to the frequency of elections and bureaucrats that are generally in office over a longer period of time (to be modulated according to the rules specific to each country; bureaucrats may or may not be civil servants); the second is a conflict between the pursuit of effective policies and the pursuit of personal interests, such as election or re-election, or a career development within the administration, or even personal gain (corruption).

The study on freedom of expression and the press links the latter to a better effectiveness of public policies and bureaucracy, because criticism of their failures or mistakes then finds its place in the public eye and forces politicians and bureaucrats to achieve better results, or risk being dismissed or replaced.

Box 2.2. *The economic analysis of bureaucracy*

2.2.2. *Tests on U.S. media*

Much of the research on bias concerns U.S. newspapers. This is essentially for a practical reason: in order to test the hypothesis of an informational bias, it is necessary to have large databases and computer resources. However, the digitalization of the press first took place in the U.S. press.

In 2005, (Groseclose and Milyo 2005), Tim Groseclose, a professor at *George Mason University*, Adam Smith, Head of the Chair, and Jeffrey Milyo a professor at the University of Missouri, were among the first to use content digitalization to measure the number of times keywords, which were chosen for their political representation, were used in certain media. They compared this number with the number of times these same words were used by elected officials in the U.S. Congress, both Republicans and Democrats. By comparing the frequency of keywords used, they ranked the media according to the ideological bias they adopted (in this case, Democrat or Republican). The basis of the test is constituted by all the speeches delivered by the elected representatives between the 103rd and 107th Congresses (between 1993 and 2002). The average frequency of keyword use among Republicans or Democrats is used as a reference base. As a result, newspapers or media are classified as neutral, or with a liberal bias in the Anglo-Saxon (i.e. Democrats) or conservative (i.e. Republicans) sense. The sample selected consists of 20 media outlets. The authors define the concept of bias by:

> "the choice of a journalist to not broadcast information or to
> not give it its rightful place corresponding to its importance"
> (p. 20).

The result of their study is that there is a centrist media group with USA Today, ABC Good Morning America or CNN, a rather Democratic group with CBS, the New York Times or the Washington Post and a rather Republican group with Fox News or the Washington Times.

The analysis is based on the number of times the names of 200 think tanks are mentioned in speeches or articles, all of which are clearly positioned politically. The choice of these keywords was the subject of much discussion. As we will see, other authors taking other references result in a different positioning of some newspapers.

Riccardo Puglisi, a researcher at the London School of Economics, provides an econometric focus on the New York Times during the period 1946–1994 (Puglisi 2011). He counts the subjects covered by the newspaper. He sorts the topics according to themes qualified as Democrats (civil rights, health, labor market, etc.) and Republicans. He deduced that the New York Times has a Democratic editorial line. This positioning is particularly clear during election periods. When the incumbent President is a Republican, there is a 26% increase in papers on Democratic topics in the three months preceding the election. This increase does not occur when the outgoing President is a Democrat.

Puglisi and Snyder, also in 2011 (Puglisi and Snyder 2011), analyzed the contents of 200 U.S. newspapers covering 32 political scandals. Using a semantic keyword search, they identify newspapers with Democratic sensibilities by realizing that they do not discuss the scandals on their side and propagate articles on scandals caused by Republican politicians, and vice versa for the Republican newspapers. Sandra Garcia-Uribe (Garcia-Uribe 2016), for example, bases the measurement of information bias on the editorial choices of the covers or first pages (place given, choice of topics covered) between 2007 and 2012 for the major U.S. newspapers, and comes to similar conclusions.

In a team with two other researchers, Puglisi is continuing this research. Along with Valentino Larcinese, a professor at the London School of Economics, and James Snyder of MIT (Larcinese et al. 2011), Puglisi shows that pro-democracy newspapers tend to propagate articles on unemployment and labor market difficulties when the President is Republican, in order to highlight the latter's poor macroeconomic performance to the public. The results are similar for the trade deficit. On the contrary, partisan behavior does not appear when we look at articles about inflation, no doubt because it is an area of politics that is less divided. The three researchers analyze the press between 1996 and 2005, and more specifically, the Los Angeles Times, owned by a family – the Chandlers – from 1884 to 2000. When Otis Chandler took over the management of the newspaper in 1960, the latter was identified as rather conservative, before then becoming favorable to the Republicans. Otis Chandler wanted to make his newspaper a credible competitor of the New York Times. This concrete case allows the authors to illustrate the weight of an owner's influence. The particularly interesting point of this study is that is not only shows that an editorial line changes over time, but also that the reason behind it is clearly the influence of the owner.

The article and the survey do not say how this change took place within the newspaper, for example if the teams of journalists changed within the political service.

In 2015, Puglisi and Snyder (Puglisi and Snyder 2015) conducted further research on the identification of ideological bias. They classified the research into three categories: research that identifies bias by comparing expressions used by newspapers and those used by politicians; research that analyzes the agenda, in other words, how information is reported in the media (subject, frequency); and lastly, research that focuses on media that support a politician or a party (endorsement). The authors propose a summary of these different approaches by constructing a model that integrates a larger number of variables and simultaneously takes into account the strategies of newspapers, pressure groups, political parties and voters.

The interesting result here is the highlighting of the heterogeneity of biases within the same newspaper that can adopt rather democratic positions on social issues and a more conservative position on economic policy, despite the global position of the newspaper on one side or the other. They conclude that the informational bias is less pronounced than in the analyses conducted by other researchers.

The identification of bias is therefore very complex. The nature of bias is equally important, since it may not be unique and may be heterogeneous within a newspaper or press group.

In 2014, John Lott and Kevin Hassett (Lott and Hassett 2014) developed an econometric analysis based on the Nexis/Lexis database from 1985 to 2004. The database contains 389 press titles. The study mainly focuses on economic articles. The results of the analysis are that the coverage of economic events is presented in a more positive way when the President is a Democrat than when he is a Republican. To do this, the authors examine how the unemployment results are presented. The difference is significant as it is 30% in favor of democrats. This bias itself would lead to a 7% improvement in public opinion regarding the results of the President's economic policy. The result is even clearer if we take the top 10 of the press (40% instead of 30%). The study shows that economic articles play an important role in shaping public opinion and that there is an ideological bias on these subjects in the U.S. press.

2.2.3. *The case of the Asian and European press*

Most of the research on the concept of bias has been conducted from U.S. media. Some authors propose to extend the analysis to other countries, such as South Korea and China (Hang 2006), as well as to some European countries.

Han Yuan, from the University of Hong Kong, studies the Chinese press (Yuan 2016). The author relies on press coverage of the 18th Party Congress in November 2012 in 21 local newspapers in seven provinces, as well as in the national newspaper People's Daily (the People's Daily is the official media of the Chinese Communist Party. Its daily circulation is approximately three million copies[6]). While the first measures of information bias in the United States were based on the existence of a political system with two parties and the media's preference for one of them, the same method cannot be applied in China. The author proposes to extract a matrix of words representative of the journal from the articles of each journal. This does not reveal a bias in the usual sense of the word, since all newspapers are controlled by the Communist Party, which determines the editorial line, but it does reveal significant changes that concern geographical similarities or differences, as well as the proportion of political information in relation to economic information. Concerning geographical areas, newspapers in the same region use very similar vocabulary, which is consistent with the fact that the Communist Party is organized into committees; each committee controls a specific region and therefore the newspapers published there. The author concludes that although the information is controlled by the party, there are nevertheless significant variations between newspapers.

Ralf Dewenter, University of Hamburg, Uwe Dulleck, University of Queensland in Australia, and Tobias Thomas researcher at DICE (*Düsseldorf Institute for Competition Economics*), (Dewenter *et al.* 2016), are building a media bias index by compiling 35 German media outlets (including five daily and 10 weekly newspapers) and over seven million articles from 1988 to 2012. The authors complete the computerized linguistic analysis with the results of *Media Tenor International*[7]. Qualifying the bias

---

6 English version available at: http://en.people.cn.

7 Excerpt from the Media Tenor website (http://us.mediatenor.com/en/about-us). The Media Tenor research team, created in 1993, statistically assessed Media Tenor's own media data in order to determine which reality is reflected (agenda) in the media and which reality is not selected or reflected in the media (Agenda Cutting). Researchers compare these results with external statistics (survey results, consumer behavior reports, consumer confidence index,

during this period is all the easier, as this period can be characterized as bi-party (CDU/CSU vs. SPD). In this recent article, a new element is introduced into the rationale. The media now play a role in people's perception of, for example, economic performance. In other words, the media influences economic sentiment. The results show that political direction evolves over time, but one thing in common is that the media are generally harder on the ruling government than on any opposition party. The authors speak of government malice or anti-government bias.

In a 2015 article, Mark Kayser and Michael Peress (Kayser and Peress 2015) analyzed two million articles in 32 daily newspapers in 16 countries[8]. The period analyzed varies according to the newspapers (due to a problem of access to digitalized archives which allows the identification of an editorial line by keyword counting). It covers the 20-year period before 2014. The study is very complex to conduct given the diversity of languages used. Nevertheless, it shows that the press publishes more positive articles on the economy when there is a period of growth and when the newspaper has a position close to the political team in power, whereas the number of critical articles increases when there is both an economic decrease and a team in power that is not supported by the newspaper.

Content econometrics seems to show that most media adopt an editorial line that includes a choice that is favorable to an ideological movement and/or to politicians. Further research is needed. It remains to be seen whether this trend is increasing or moderating over time and whether this media bias is identified, accepted or rejected by readers.

2.2.4. The impact of newspaper owners

Recent developments in France constitute a particularly rich field of analysis. A whole stream of research is interested in the impact that a newspaper owner can have on a media outlet. This is a fundamental issue

stock prices, tourism statistics, etc.) and investigate the effects of the media on public perception and behavior. Our client studies and reports are not standardized statistical assessments of media results, but instead, each researcher deals with specific cases with individual approaches and deploys multiple analyses and comparative models in order to provide strategic media information and research.

8 Australia, Canada, France (*Le Monde*, *Le Figaro*), Germany, Ireland, Israel, Italy, Japan, Luxembourg, New Zealand, Portugal, Spain, Switzerland and the United States.

that is very often raised in France, where most of the major newspapers are privately owned and often have large companies whose main activity is not in the media sector. In the space of a few years, the media landscape has been opened up with the takeover of major media (*Le Monde*, *Libération*, *L'Express*, *Le Parisien*, etc.) by investors such as Xavier Niel, Patrick Drahi, Vincent Bolloré and Bernard Arnault, to name but a few recent and emblematic changes (De Rochegonde and Sénéjoux 2017)[9]. Economic research provides several interesting elements for reflection.

The 2003 article by Djankov *et al.*, which has already been mentioned, launched a major debate that has been of burning relevance ever since. This debate, which now dates back almost 20 years, was recently updated by the report by Cagé and Godechot (Cagé and Godechot 2017), which has the same title as the 2003 seminal article: "Who owns the media?". Both teams come to opposite conclusions. The former shows the significant biases associated with public media and prefers competition between private media, while the latter, concerned with owners invested in sectors other than media, offers donor-funded media far from the search for profitability (Cagé 2016)[10]. In the same vein, Giacomo Corneo (Corneo 2006), a professor at the University of Berlin, published an article in 2006 in which he showed a correlation between media concentration that reduces competition and the increase in information bias, using a game theory model.

Gilat Levy and Ronny Razin, researchers at the London School of Economics and Ines de Barreda (Levy *et al.* 2016), from Oxford University, are interested in the power of media owners in an environment where readers do not identify this power and the resulting information biases.

The authors mention a correlation neglect, in other words a difficulty for players to identify the link that may exist between different media, when they belong to the same owner. Readers consume information from several media as if it were broadcast independently, without any link between them, although there may be a correlation. This correlation is all the more difficult to achieve because in a large number of media groups, information is

---

9 For more information, read in particular De Rochegonde, A., Sénéjoux, R. (2017). *Médias, les nouveaux empires*. First Document, Paris.

10 A new legal structure: the "non-profit media company" is developed in Cagé, J. (2016). *Sauver les médias : Capitalisme, financement participatif et démocratie*. La République des Idées, Paris.

transferred from one to the other after being repackaged in the colors of each media. In the most frequent research, the identification and measurement of media bias was done on a media-by-media basis, independently. A more complete measure of media bias should take into account the correlation between media since an owner can integrate it into his strategy, in order to take advantage of readers' tunnel vision about the correlation capabilities of the owner. The owner's power increases with the number of shares he or she owns. It is therefore probably higher than measurements made in previous research. The authors conclude their article by showing that readers always benefit from the dissolution of a press group, even when all new media owners share the same ideological position.

In a 2006 article, Soontae An, Hyun Jin and Todd Simon of the University of Kansas analyzed the financial performance of U.S. media groups (An *et al.* 2006). The issue raised involves the possible weakening of the informative role of the media in favor of the search for financial performance. The authors distinguish two types of funders. The first type are institutional investors (banks, insurance companies, pension funds, etc.), who are the most present. In 2004, they owned 90% of the press titles of 11 out of 15 of the largest publicly traded media groups. The second ones are investors who run the media. The study of 37 local newspapers shows that media run by managers have higher profitability than media directly run by their owners. The main reason for this is the objectives of owners, who are often more ideological than they are financial, which is generally the opposite for managers. The studies included 12 journals over 13 years.

2.2.5. *Pluralism and competition*

Another area of research focuses on the impact of competition on the quality of media information. In other words, does the fact that there are several media outlets make for more credible media?

In *Media Bias and Reputation*, published in 2006 by Matthiew Gentzkow and Jesse Shapiro (Gentzkow and Shapiro 2006)[11], the two authors show that

---

11 "In this paper, we develop a new model of media bias. We start from a simple assumption: a media firm wants to build a reputation as a provider of accurate information. If the quality of the information a given firm provides is difficult to observe directly, consumer beliefs about quality will be based largely on observations of past reports. Firms will then have an incentive to shape these reports in whatever way will be most likely to improve their

biases are less significant if there are several independent media in competition. Each group of readers with a type of conviction trusts a media outlet, but the number of competing media ensures a plurality of opinions. Indeed, a media outlet's reputation also depends on the quality of the information disseminated in the past. If a media outlet alters information, it takes the risk of having it invalidated by facts and other media. Thus, competition in the supply of information is a way to reduce informational biases.

A few years later, in 2010 (Gentzkow and Shapiro 2010), the two researchers expanded their analysis by publishing a model to measure and separate the different origins of information bias. They conducted an econometric analysis of the words and expressions used by Democrat and Republican elected officials during the 2005 Congress session, using two databases (*Newslibrary database* and *ProQuest Newsstand database*). This indicator makes it possible to classify media from a database by grouping 433 newspapers (or about 74% of newspaper distribution in the USA at the time of the survey). Then, an analysis of the postal codes of newspaper subscribers makes it possible to map the distribution areas and compare the number of subscribers to the results of the electoral votes by area. The bias related to readers' beliefs would explain most of the total bias, while the bias related to owners' ideology would be low. This weakness, in a sample of more than 400 press titles, does not exclude the possibility that a bias may be fully explained by the editorial line wanted by the owner.

In 2018 (Garz *et al.* 2018), Marcel Garz, Gaurav Sood, Daniel Stone and Justin Wallace published a study and used the title of Gentzow and Shapiro's 2010 article to expand on its conclusions. They base their analyses on the U.S. presidential campaigns of 2012 and 2016. Their results are in the same direction, that is, the bias practiced by the media corresponding to the political positions of readers, rather than the ideological choices of the owners. The bias is also reinforced by the development of social networks.

Francesco Drago, researcher at the University of Naples, and Tommaso Nannicini and Francesco Sobbrio, two researchers at Bocconi University in Milan, (Drago *et al.* 2014) are directly interested in the number of press titles and question the link between newspaper competition and the quality

---

reputations and thus increase their future profits by expanding the demand for their products"
(p. 282).

of *political monitoring*. They analyze the daily local press in Italian cities with more than 15,000 inhabitants[12] over the period 1993–2010. The researchers show that the number of press titles is positively correlated with the performance of municipalities measured by various indicators, such as tax collection. In other words, a competitive supply of newspapers also puts ideological biases into competition and improves the overall quality of information. They also analyze an interesting effect of electoral regulation: a mayor who is constrained by a time limit on mandates is less efficient in his last mandate. The study also shows that the local press is more effective on local elected officials than the national press.

In 2013, Andréa Prat and David Stromberg published *The Political Economy of Mass Media* (Prat and Stromberg 2013), the term *political economy* being used here in the sense of economic analysis of public decisions (Magis 2016)[13]. The authors develop a theoretical approach and summarize the previous scientific study. They insist on an informational bias that is not to be neglected, consisting of highlighting information of no political importance in order to divert the attention of voters from essential political decisions. They also show that ideological bias has more influence on unstable voters and when there is little competition between the media, in other words, when the bias promoted by one media outlet is not challenged by other media. They conclude their summary with three statements: 1) media scrutiny increases political accountability; 2) media pluralism and a healthy commercial motive are effective defenses against media capture; and 3) voter information and voting outcomes are affected by the media.

Their conclusion is that the press or media are particular companies, different from others in the sense that competition plays a different role. In addition to the traditional effect on price or quality, competition between media also determines the coverage of public decisions and thus partially explains both the effectiveness of public policies and the electorate's vote.

---

12 The reason for this choice of city size is related to the electoral regulations put in place in 1993. In small municipalities, elections are held in one round and become two rounds when the size exceeds 15,000 inhabitants. Mayor's mandates are limited to two successive terms.

13 As mentioned above, the term *political economy* is often used by other disciplines in a very different sense, as it is a critical approach to the media and generally refers to the Frankfurt school of thought. For a recent presentation, see the article by Christophe Magis, professor and researcher at the University of Paris 8.

The two researchers had conducted a similar study a few years earlier on the development of commercial television in Sweden. They tested voter behavior in two elections in 1988; one before the arrival of commercial television, and one after, in 1991 (Prat and Stromberg 2005)[14]. The result is an increase in the consumption of political information, mainly among those who did not use it during public television. More recently, Sebastian Elligsen and Oystein Hernaes (Elligsen and Hernaes 2015) measured the impact of commercial television on the effectiveness of public policies, but this time in Norway.

Cagdas Agirdas (Agirdas 2015), a professor at Tampa University in Florida, is studying the impact of the sharp decline in the number of newspapers in many U.S. cities. This recent decline is due to the decrease in resources, which is in turn due to the arrival of the Internet. This rapid change in the situation makes it possible to make a comparative analysis of the content of press articles when the number of newspapers was still large and since its decrease. For this purpose, the author studies the archives of 99 press titles over the period 1990–2009. He is particularly interested in the way in which information is reported on the evolution of the unemployment rate. As other authors have shown, there is an ideological bias in all newspapers. Thus, conservative (Democrat) newspapers publish 17.4% (12.8%) additional articles on unemployment when the President is a Democrat (Republican) and when the newspaper has a competitor in the same trading area. In the same area, with a sociology of voters that has not changed, the number of articles in the same context decreases considerably (respectively, 3.5% for articles published in conservative newspapers and 1.1% for Democratic newspapers). This means that the strategy of newspapers is oriented by the search for readership, rather than by an ideological political positioning. When there are several newspapers in the same market, they adopt a strategy of differentiation, and when there is only one newspaper left, the ideological bias decreases in order to have the widest possible readership and to attract former readers of the disappeared newspaper(s).

Fernanda De Leon (De Leon 2016) analyzed 90 U.S. newspapers during the election campaigns for the governor, attorney general and senator elections in 2002 and 2006, that is, 154 campaigns. The study covers seven states (California, Florida, Michigan, Ohio, Oregon, Texas and Wisconsin),

---

14 In 1990, the Swedish law was amended to allow commercial television. Before that date, television was a state monopoly offer.

including 658 counties. The results of the study are that ideological bias can occur when newspapers are in competition: the bias which is chosen then depends on the ideological position of the readers.

2.3. Summary of challenges

Andrea Prat (Prat 2015) summarized the challenges of the media economy in a 2015 article entitled "Media capture and media power". There are four research conclusions on informational bias:

– Informational bias is widespread in the press.

– The origin of informational bias comes from the ways in which media are financed, the cognitive dissonance of readers and the desire of owners and/or governments to influence them.

– According to some authors, informational bias is the result of competition between private media seeking to increase their resources, and for other authors, it is the will of the owners. There is therefore a debate among experts that involves extending the research.

– The study of information biases is naturally based on a long trend of data, and therefore on "historical" media. Research has been undertaken that integrates "new" media and social networks, the data of which are more recent. This is a research area that economists must develop.

The scientific study from one side or the other has been and still is very active on this theme. Indeed, the stakes are high since we are talking here about the foundations of democracy: how should we inform voters properly? Or, in other words, who should own the media? Or do we need a public media policy and if so, which one?

What are the Links between the Press and Politics?

Do governments and politicians influence media?

In an article in the *Handbook of Media Economics*, a reference book published in 2016, Maria Petrova and Ruben Enikolopov (Petrova and Enikolopov 2016) summarize research analyzing the influence of politicians on media. The starting point for the research is the numerous empirical studies that show that media can be *captured* (in other words, under political influence) and that this is a frequent case (the authors cite Freedom House studies that show that 44% of the world's population lives in countries where the press is not free). The capturing phenomena mean that media content can be determined by government preferences rather than public preferences. Content analysis shows that captured or influenced media are different from independent media, sometimes dramatically so. The research then highlights how creative political authorities can get in influencing media: censorship, direct ownership, spending on advertising space or regulating the media sector (regulation, taxation, subsidies, etc.).

Political science was one of the first scientific disciplines to address this issue, using, among other things, the digitalization of press articles to compare the power of politicians. As such, Pamela Ban, Alexander Fouirnaies, Andrew Hall and James Snyder (Ban *et al.* 2018) investigated 50 million articles in 2700 newspapers over a century (1877–1977) and showed that there is a strong correlation between the number of articles regarding politicians and their power.

However, research also shows that there are many mechanisms that prevent the influence of a group or politician.

A recent article in this area is that of Matthew Gentzkow, Nathan Petek, Jesse Shapiro and Michael Sinkinson, who wonder whether the press serves the state. In order to answer this problem, they studied the U.S. press between 1869 and 1928 (Gentzkow *et al.* 2015). The authors count the new newspapers, those that ceased publishing, total circulation, prices, number of pages, etc. of both Democratic and Republican newspapers. There are two main ways to limit governments' influence on media:

1) the legal and constitutional rules that protect press freedom; and

2) according to the authors, *market discipline* and competition;

The authors choose the period 1869–1928 because it is characterized by strong competition between multiple newspapers owned by private investors. In 1928, 470 U.S. cities had at least two newspapers and 25 cities had five or more, all in an environment of strong growth in advertising spending and technological innovation, resulting in lower newspaper prices. In addition, half of the headlines of that time had explicit support for a politician or party, and many of them were created on the initiative of politicians who provided their funding. The influence of politicians on media coverage of political or financial scandals has been the subject of several studies, and the approach taken in this study followed this type of analysis. The study identifies two types of financial links that were very common at the time:

> "…contracts to print government documents […] official forms, notices, laws, […] allocated at inflated prices to newspapers affiliated with the incumbent party. A second form of patronage was the allocation of lucrative government jobs to newspaper editors." (p. 37).

The authors refer to positions as state librarians, postmasters, sergeants, etc. and cite the example of the *Ohio Statesman*, a Democratic newspaper, whose editor was appointed to and paid by that state's senate.

A third financial link is through the direct purchase of newspapers. In Wisconsin in 1852, each parliamentarian received a budget envelope to buy 30 copies of newspapers each day (a significant financial endeavor compared to the print runs of the time). Financial links come from both the federal state and local governments with broader financial envelopes for the federal state. Although it is clear that these financial envelopes are decisive, they are not the only ones to influence the editorial line of a newspaper whose manager must also attract advertisers' revenues. There is therefore a trade-off between political and commercial revenues. The authors mention a watchdog effect, which consists of losing credibility and therefore readership if the newspaper moves too far from its information function. They design a model that integrates two contradictory effects: a party effect and a watchdog effect, the latter of which significantly dominates the former as the advertising market develops, intensifying competition between media. The informational bias is then mainly related to the preferences of the readership.

A further reservation: the influence that a politician can have on the media also depends on how it is perceived. Thus, in 2011, Chun-Fang Chiang and Brian Knight (Chiang and Knight 2011) highlighted the link between the effectiveness of ideological bias, in other words, the evolution of the number of voters for a candidate, and media credibility in the eyes of the reader. They studied the periods preceding the 2000 and 2004 presidential elections in the United States[1]. They base themselves on "the model developed by Calvert (1985), in which he demonstrates that the effectiveness of a recommendation depends on how the recommendation was formulated. If the advertiser biases his message in favor, the effectiveness of his message will be weaker than if he proposed a message against it" (p. 378). The authors show that the effectiveness of ideological bias (in terms of vote evolution) is lower when a politician is supported by a newspaper identified as being on his or her side. Conversely, the impact is even bigger when politicians are supported by a newspaper of a different political persuasion from their own: the effectiveness of bias depends on the source of the bias. This means that voters would filter ideological biases and give them balanced importance according to their source: lower when the source is close to the reader's political position, and higher in the opposite case.

Angela Galvis, James Snyder and B.K. Song (Galvis *et al.* 2016) analyzed the coverage of political scandals between 1870 and 1910. There are 121 scandals in 159 headlines. The method uses an econometric model using keywords and publication frequency. Newspapers tend to highlight scandals involving elected officials of the opposing affiliation, however this emphasis

---

1 The sample size is 116 newspapers in 2000 and 212 in 2004.

is greatly reduced when there is a competition between media of different political affiliation.

Given the acknowledged importance of the press, Christian Bruns and Oliver Himmler (Bruns and Himmler 2016) are interested in the economic model of the press from an original perspective. They question the propensity of individuals to pay for quality information. The press is a good subject for analysis, given that it is paid for by readers who buy or subscribe to it, or sometimes also by donations. However, the difficulty of analysis comes from the fact that an individual can use information by being a "free-rider", in other words, by consuming information paid for by others (e.g. by having access to those newspapers highlighted in stands). If everyone thinks in this manner, the risk would be that no one would want to finance journalism. The authors show that, on the one hand, quality political information is difficult to free-ride given its informative density, and on the other hand, that the demand for information is high because individuals make the connection between information, voting and the monitoring of political decisions. They deduce, through modeling comparing the cost of investigation and political gain, that there is a rational incentive to agree to pay for quality information.

3.1. A diminishing influence

The media seem to have gradually freed themselves from political power over time. This is what research tends to show.

Matthew Gentzow, Edward L. Glaeser and Claudia Goldin (Gentzkow *et al.* 2006) discuss this issue. By using an approach that calls on economic history, which is still called cliometrics (Haupert 2017; Demeulemeester *et al.* 2006)[2], they show how the press has, in their opinion, become more informative over time. To do this, they studied two political scandals in the

---

2 Cliometrics brings together "international quantitative history research structured by economic theory and informed by statistical and econometric methods". This definition is the one adopted by the French Association Française de Cliométrie (French Cliometrics Association) founded in 2001 (www.cliometrie.org). The AFC is the counterpart of the US Cliometric Association, founded in 1983 at the Department of Economics at the University of Wisconsin. Two precursors of this discipline, Douglass North and Robert Fogel, were jointly awarded the Nobel Prize in Economics in 1993. Cliometrics or "new economic history" developed under their impetus in the USA from the 1950s onwards.

United States: the *Crédit Mobilier of America* railroad[3] affair in 1870 and the Teapot Dome bribery scandal in 1920. According to the authors, 89% of newspapers openly claimed affiliation with a political party in the 1870s, whereas 62% of newspapers were identified as independent in 1920. Hence, the title of the article: how did the press become "informative"? The authors use a lexical analysis by measuring the frequency of favorable or unfavorable words to describe an event or politician (such as liar, or dishonest, or impeccable, honorable, etc.). The study covers newspapers in 152 cities. The analysis shows a significant difference in the media coverage of these two scandals.

The Crédit Mobilier scandal involved politicians who received free shares from the bank to cover a process of false invoices, corruption and embezzlement that were related to the construction of the transcontinental railway by the Union Pacific Railway. The Teapot Dome case concerns influence and corruption that is related to the granting of land use rights by bureaucrats and politicians to oil companies on US Navy lands in the state of Wyoming (Teapot Dome is the name of a mountain at the center of these lands).

The rest of the article questions the origin of the decrease in information bias and favors an explanation linked to the development of competition, due to the fall in production costs during that period. The authors state that this had led to an increase in the number of headlines and newspapers in circulation due to lower prices. The informative quality of the press is presented as a consequence of technological developments. The conclusion of this research is that the informative value of the press has improved over time.

More recently, Stephen Ansolabehere, Rebecca Lessem and James Snyder (Ansolabehere *et al.* 2006), all three of them researchers at MIT, have conducted a historical analysis of the U.S. magazine press between 1940 and 2002. They studied two samples: five major papers in five major cities and 92 local newspapers distributed in smaller cities. Their analysis highlights two results: the press adopted a strong Republican bias in the first part of that period in order to evolve towards a Democratic bias in the following years; and the nature of the subjects covered has evolved and newspapers now focus more on elected officials in power.

---

3 Not to be confused with the 1857 financial panic of the French bank of the same name owned by the Peirere brothers.

3.2. The notion of collusion between the media and politicians

In another area of research, Hülya Eraslan and Saltuk Özertürk (Eraslan and Özertürk 2017), two researchers in the Department of Economics at Rice University, are interested in the media bias caused by the actions of a politician seeking re-election. Collusion is at the heart of the analysis. The media needs a close relationship with political authorities in order to obtain information. This proximity search is an incentive for the media to produce positive articles about its sources. However, the positive-oriented temptation can be detrimental to media credibility and therefore have a negative impact on media revenues, as they may see a decrease in their readership and advertising revenues.

The above article develops a game theory model that focuses, on the one hand, on political decisions concerning the media made by ruling politicians and placed in a context of collusion and, on the other hand, on the strategies of the media that decide their positioning (their information bias) in a democracy. There are three possible types of media: honest, corrupt (their objective is to obtain additional revenue through favorable regulations, such as tax regulations or government purchases of advertising space) or strategic (collusion). Before each election, the public receives information from the media without knowing whether it is biased or not. There are two types of politicians, the incumbent and the challenger. The result of the model shows an increase in the probability of being re-elected if the media are corrupt. These results are obtained in a particular context where the media aim to maximize their revenues without political positioning. Further research should be carried out if the media also have an ideological position.

Saltuk Ozertürk (Ozertürk 2018) is interested in bias from the politician's side. He analyzes politicians' behavior towards the media according to whether they are harsh or friendly. However, the way politicians disseminate information in the media can have an influence on the quality of information and on the medium which is chosen by voters to obtain information. Ozertürk studies radio interview strategies. If politicians seek popularity, they select *soft* media and emphasize on them when they want to discuss complex political issues.

Leopoldo Fergusson (Fergusson 2014), professor at Los Andes University in Bogota, focuses on the influence of pressure groups on the editorial line of the media. To do this, he compares the expenses of lobby groups to support a candidate in the U.S. Senate elections (during the 1980 and 2002 period and in three states: Arizona, Colorado and New Mexico) and the frequency of exposure of this candidate in the media. The analysis mainly focuses on television and in the specific North American context of regulating political communication that allows for significant political advertising expenditures in the media during an election campaign. Not surprisingly, the result is that there is a higher candidate exposure rate in correlation with the expenses of lobby groups in a political campaign.

Information bias can also come from the intervention of experts to provide information, as Keith Schnakenberg shows (Schnakenberg 2017). Experts can use their reputation to give credibility to a speech that presents an ideological bias. The author proposes limiting the adverse effects of this type of situation (called manipulative persuasion) by developing competition between experts in order to confront biases.

While in most models, media or press strategies are described using a two-sided model (in other words, describing a complex trade-off between two joint objectives: obtaining revenue from newspaper sales to readers and obtaining revenue from the sale of advertising space to advertisers), Alexandro Castaneda and Cesar Martinelli (Castaneda and Martinelli 2018) propose a three-sided platform in which media strategy also includes support for a politician. For the authors, supporting a politician brings about a possible cost for the media, which could see its resources reduced by the reaction of either readers or advertisers. The vision of the media is then complicated, but promises an interesting future for research on media strategy and the origins of media bias.

Harvard researcher Raphael Ditella and Ignacio Franceschelli (Ditella and Franceschelli 2009) analyze the four main Argentine newspapers between 1998 and 2007. Their study examines the relationship between government spending on advertising space in these four newspapers and media coverage of government corruption. The correlation is strong. An increase in expenditure leads to a decrease in articles denouncing corruption by 28% and 31% of covers (front page).

3.3. Do newspapers run elections?

The impact of the media on global change is an eternal subject of study where all scientific disciplines, including economics, intersect and meet. More prosaically, it is sometimes said that newspapers decide the outcome of an election. Economic research has focused on the role of the media in the performance of a politician.

A classic example is the assessment of Radio Liberty's impact on Russian behavior. A recent study on this subject focuses on the Russian elections in 1991. Javier Garcia-Arenas (Garcia-Arenas 2016) identified the range of radio waves emitted by this radio station located outside Russian territory. He observed voter behavior in these areas and concluded that listeners receiving Radio Liberty were more favorable towards Yeltsin.

Ruben Eniklopov, Maria Petrova and Ekaterina Zhuravskaya (Eniklopov et al. 2018)[4] compared the election results of the 1999 parliamentary elections in Russia between geographical areas with and without access to the only national television channel that was independent of the government. It was accessible to three-quarters of the Russian population. One of the results highlighted is that having access to independent television has an impact on voting. As a result, the vote in favor of the governing party was reduced by 8.9 points.

Further research of this type has been conducted in the United States. Gregory Martin and colleagues (Martin and Yurukiglu 2017) studied the impact of information bias in political information broadcast on cable television channels across the Atlantic and specifically at Fox News, CNN and MSNBC. The author wonders whether the consumer watches a channel simply because it corresponds to their ideas, so the news reinforces the number of voters of a trend or instead, whether watching information with a bias changes the choice of voters and changes the number of voters for a trend. The "Fox News effect" highlighted by Martin is that between 2000 and 2008, not only did the number of viewers increase, but Fox also became more conservative. Martin's results confirm those of Della Vigna, which were established in 2006. Stephano Della Vigna and Eliana La Ferrara (Della Vigna and La Ferrare 2016) offer a summary on the economic and

---

4 Vladimir Putin was elected in 2000 with 52.9% of the votes cast.

social effects of the media, underlining the importance of their role beyond the notion of the fourth power.

In a 2018 article (Song 2018), B.K. Song, a researcher at Hanyang University in South Korea, studies the impact of the introduction of television on the behavior of the press during the presidential elections in the USA between 1944 and 1964. Competition from this new media has changed the ideological bias of the press by moderating it and shifting editorial lines towards more centrist positions.

Augustin Casas and Yarine Fawaz (Casas *et al.* 2016), two researchers at the University of Madrid and the University of Barcelona respectively, and André Trindade, researcher at the Vargas Foundation in Rio, assess the effects of supporting the newspapers of U.S. presidential candidates in the 100 days preceding the 2008 and 2012 elections[5]. These effects are assessed on the basis of daily variations in winning probabilities (obtained from Intrade's probability calculations[6]). The authors distinguish three types of support: support that is consistent with the newspaper's historical editorial line, consistent and surprising support (when the newspaper is not used to supporting a candidate, but the support remains in line with the newspaper's usual political position), or inconsistent support (when the newspaper supports a candidate from another side as was the case for the *Chicago Tribune*, which was usually favorable to the Republicans, but supported Barack Obama). The effects of supports vary according to their nature and the authors show that they are significantly higher when supports are consistent, and that they have virtually no impact when they are inconsistent, even when they generate a surprise effect. The underlying idea is that readers of the press give credibility to support, based on the history of previous positions. The choice of support from a newspaper must therefore be consistent if it wishes to both maintain its revenues by satisfying its readership and also effectively supporting a candidate.

On the contrary, Oliver Latham (Latham 2015) is interested in the attitude of newspapers towards the English government, and focuses on a possible change in this attitude in line with the evolution of polls. The starting point for the analysis is based on the assumption that newspapers behave differently depending on whether the government is popular or not.

---

5 As a reminder, in 2008, it was an Obama election against McCain and in 2012, Obama against Romney.
6 Intrade is a company based in Ireland and created in 2001. Its purpose is "market prediction" for products or elections. See: www.intrade.com.

The agenda is partly guided by the polls and by an attitude that the author calls "back the winner", as soon as the polls show a surge of opposition in a pre-electoral period. Latham first seeks to verify that media behavior is linked to the evolution of polls. The author then wonders about the origin of this link: it could be either on the side of voters whose newspaper would follow preferences (give more articles that are unfavorable to the government when it becomes unpopular), or on the side of the ideals of the owner and their relations (ideological and/or financial) with the government. (The media would then tend to limit information that is unfavorable to the government when the latter is popular, in order to contribute to what is left.)

In order to assess the attitude of the press, Latham uses the Puglisi method, in other words, he identifies financial problems related to elected officials and checks whether press coverage of the same type of event varies according to government polls. He concludes that the link between declining popularity and negative press coverage is verified. The tests also show that the cause of this positioning is on the demand side (adapting to reader demand), rather than collusion between the newspaper and the government.

All this work is part of a broader economic research environment that is focused on communication, trust and persuasion in a market (Gentzkow and Kamenika 2017).

3.4. The importance of press freedom

Laws on freedom of expression allow the role of monitoring public actions to take place. They are therefore intended to allow politicians and bureaucracy to be monitored in order to make their decisions and operations more effective.

Following in the footsteps of Aymo Brunetti and Béatrice Weder, in their 2003 article "A free press is bad news for corruption", Sambit Bhattacharrya, a researcher in the Department of Economics at the University of Sussex and Roland Holder, a researcher at the University of St. Gallen in Switzerland, question the synergy or substitution between democracy and press freedom (Bhattacharrya and Holder 2015). In other words, is press freedom sufficient or should it be combined with political and/or economic freedom?

To do this, the authors designed a two-period game theory model. There are two types of politicians: those who act for the common good and those who seek to increase their incomes. In the first period of the game, politicians determine the level of corruption. The level of corruption is identified by voters through press reports. In the second period of the game, they must vote and choose either the corrupt politician or the one who is not. The model was tested in 129 countries over the period 1980–2007. The press freedom indicator is that of Freedom House, and the corruption index is that of the PRS (Political Risk Service). The political institutions of each country were then analyzed, which made it possible to determine a democratization index. The result of the test is that the two freedoms are complementary.

Krishna Vadlamannati, a researcher at the Norwegian University of Science and Arusha Cooray, from the University of Nottingham in Malaysia, suggested analyzing the impact of laws based on an econometric test (Vadlamannati and Cooray 2016). The two researchers developed a reflection that is linked to a very dynamic trend in economics: the economic analysis of law (Law & Economics).

Initially developed in the United States upon the initiative of two judges, Guido Calabresi (Calabresi 1970) and Richard Posner (Posner 1972)[7], and logically incorporated into a law derived from the Common Law, the economic analysis of the law extends outside the English-speaking world.

This discipline uses economic reasoning to understand the appearance of legal rules and analyze their relevance, as defined by Yannick Gabuthy (Gabuthy 2013; Barraud 2016) in a special issue of the journal *Economie et Prévisions*. "The economic analysis of the law has both a positive and a normative aspect. The first has two objectives. Firstly, it is a question of studying the way in which individual and collective behavior reacts to the incentives provided by the rules of law. Secondly, the approach consists in using economic theory as an analytical tool to explain the emergence of these rules" (p. 3).

A remarkable summary of the work in economic analysis of the law is offered in the Encyclopedia of Law and Economics, edited by Boudewijn Bouckaert and Gerrit De Gedest, professors at Ghent University (Bouckaert and De Geest 2000)[8].

Box 3.1. *Economic analysis of the law*

---

7 Judge Posner is also a professor at the University of Chicago.
8 Also consult the article at the *Stanford Encyclopedia of Philosophy* and written by Lewis A. Kornhauser, professor at New York University School of Law: https://plato.stanford.edu/entries/legal-econanalysis/.

For this purpose, they selected a panel of 132 countries over the period 1990–2011. This period was chosen because, according to the authors, most of the laws in favor of freedom of expression were enacted there. The tests performed by Vadlamannati and Cooray are based on the *Law and Order Index of Societal Infrastructures and Development* (SID[9]). This index measures law and order based on 10 factors. The corruption index is the one established by Transparency International. The model tests the correlation between freedom of expression and corruption.

The conclusions of the study are twofold: laws are effective, but this effectiveness takes time. Laws on freedom of the press belong to the long term; such laws are effective if they are accompanied by other measures such as democracy (political competition) and press freedom (competition and media pluralism), which means that the freedom to inform depends on established economic and political freedoms.

Armando Pires (Pires 2016) is interested in the essential problem of plurality of information, and by way of introduction, mentions Article 11 of the Charter of Fundamental Rights of the European Union (freedom and pluralism of the media must be respected) and the First Amendment of the U.S. Constitution. The author studies a model with two different environments. In the first case, there are two private media outlets, whereas in the second, a privately-owned media company coexists with public media (in the sense of being government-owned and funded). In the case of a private duopoly, the media outlets are presumed to seek the best profitability. In the case of a mixed duopoly, the private company targets profitability, while the public media is presumed to target social welfare (via the quality of information disseminated). Pires studies the case of news (which should be understood in the sense of current events). He shows that well-being and plurality are not necessarily superior in the case of a mixed duopoly than for a duopoly with only private companies. Indeed, contrary to commonly accepted ideas, the results are more complex because they also depend on the political preferences of readers and the size of the advertising market. In other words, the solution that is often mentioned to ensure media pluralism by financing public media does not seem to be guaranteed. Pires is currently pursuing further research in order to study the evolution of results with offers of information on the Internet, where readers interested in politics have more clear-cut positions and become more loyal to them over time.

9 See the site: http://www.clinecenter.illinois.edu/research/sid/.

Scott Gehlbach, a researcher at the University of Madison and Konstantin Sonin, from the Department of Economics at Moscow University (Gehlbach and Sonin 2014), are interested in the different ways in which governments control the media, in addition to the causes of the evolution of press freedom. Control is important when the government is autocratic because it wants public support, and one way to do so is to limit the sources of information and opposition. Another motivation for control is the size of the advertising market. The authors show that while the latter is important, it is favorable to the development of pluralism. Occupying part of the market with public media can then be seen as a way to limit pluralism.

3.5. Differences between local and national press

In 2010, James Snyder and David Stromberg (Snyder and Stromberg 2010) used a *geographical approach* and analyzed the impact of the press by identifying geographical areas that elect a senator corresponding to a newspaper's circulation area. To do this, they studied 161 U.S. headlines[10] and 385 electoral districts from 1991 to 2002. They measured the number of articles referring to the senator, representing the geographical area. The aim was therefore to test the correlation between the area, newspaper and senator in an econometric way. Press coverage was strong in some areas and less so in others, given the less significant presence of a media in the area observed. The geographical areas best covered were those where the elected representative was best identified (10% of additional voters knew the name of their elected representative) and their positions.

3.5.1. *The local press is more influential*

The areas with the highest coverage are also those where the number of voters in elections is highest. In these areas, senators defend local interests more openly than the positions of their political party. The concrete manifestation of this political attitude is that in areas that are well covered, federal funds are allocated more heavily as a result of elected officials'

---

10 142 headlines are analyzed via the NewsLibrary.com database, eight via the legal database LexisNexis and 11 from their own website.

interventions[11]. This is related to the fact that when there is a convergence between the media's broadcasting area and that of the elected official, the numbers of articles describing their actions are more numerous (the authors show an increase of 50%). At the beginning of the 20th Century, a very large number of cities had their own local newspapers. With the decrease in the number of headlines checked over the past 50 years, the weight of the local press has decreased. Nevertheless, the role it plays in shaping economic policy remains crucial. Indeed, in the USA, few readers read a national newspaper. In 2010, the print run of the three main newspapers (*New York Times*, *USA Today* and *Wall Street Journal*) was 6 million for a total circulation of all titles of 50 million, or 12%. The opposite is generally true in other countries where the national press occupies a large area, compared to the local press.

3.5.2. *The Internet confirms this influence*

The arrival of the Internet has little influence on these results. In 2010, 1300 local newspapers had a website, but readers do not necessarily want to seek political information on the Internet. In his 1957 book, Anthony Downs (Downs 1957) highlighted a weakness in political information: individuals have difficulty identifying the costs and benefits of a policy for themselves, particularly in the case of economic policy. This difficulty is mainly explained by the complexity of the processes of collecting public resources, and by the complexity of public budgets, which makes it very difficult for non-specialists to understand them. The consequence is a lack of interest in political information. For Downs, this is a fundamental trend that he predicted would intensify as decision-making becomes more complex.

3.5.3. *The case of Japan*

Similar studies have been conducted in other contexts, such as one regarding the press in Japan (Yazaki 2017), which has an important characteristic: there are impressive circulation figures for the daily written press. In the world ranking of newspapers by circulation, established by the

---

11 The difference is significant since the amounts transferred are on average $2,700 per head, compared to $2,000 (calculations are based on figures provided by the Consolidated Federal Funds Report).

World Association of Newspapers (WAN[12]), there are four Japanese daily newspapers in the five largest newspapers in the world (the fifth one, which occupies fourth place, is an Indian newspaper). For example, *Yomiuri Shimbun* has a print run of 9 million, while the smallest, the *Nihon Keizai*, has a print run of nearly 3 million. The only French daily newspaper among the top 50 is *Ouest-France*, which ranks 47th.

Yukihiro Yazaki, a researcher at Tokyo Metropolitan University, shows that the increase in the circulation of local newspapers is concurrent with a decrease in public spending, in the form of rents or benefits that are allocated to pressure groups. The author also analyzes the cross effects between the national and local press and their complementary influence on public policy decisions. The study covers the years 1998–2010 and 105 newspapers, mixing national and regional press. The model used is based on the geographical principles of the Snyder and Stromberg model, to which the author refers. Here too, the study identifies geographical areas that highlight a "congruence" between an elected official and a local newspaper. The results also cover the comparative influence between the national and local press. There is a time shift between the themes highlighted by the national press and the local press, which means that it is the national press that sets the tone of the media agenda. Nevertheless, the author nuances his results, since the study did not include other media, and in particular the Web, in the analysis.

---

12 See http://www.wan-ifra.org. By comparison, *Le Figaro* and *Le Monde* print about 300,000 copies a day. http://www.acpm.fr/Chiffres/Diffusion/La-Presse-Payante/Presse-Quotidienne-Nationale.

4

Does the Press Need Advertisers?

Press companies choose very different economic models, ranging from free to full subscription. But whatever economic model is chosen, the purpose of the press is to be one of the key players in the production of ideas. Business models and the production of ideas are closely linked: this is what makes the newspaper business a business that requires special attention.

The press sector has been in crisis for several years. The crisis in the print media is not new, but it persists. The entire sector, which was about 1% of French GDP in the 1970s and 1980s, has fallen below 0.5% since 2010.

In total, the turnover of the French written press, which was €7.5 billion in 2015, is down by more than 3% in its eighth consecutive decline, according to Senator Michel Laugier's press report[1], based on data from the DGMIC (*Direction générale des médias et des industries culturelles*). In 2015, sales fell again, but advertising fell even further.

Indeed, advertising investments in the press are having difficulty breaking out of the downward spiral. Although net media advertising revenues recovered for the second consecutive year in 2017 (+1.2% to €13.7 billion),

---

1 Opinion presented by Michel Laugier, Senator on behalf of the *Commission de la culture, de l'éducation et de la communication* (Committee of culture, education and communication) on the draft finance bill for 2018, adopted by the French National Assembly. November 23, 2017.

the press continues to suffer a decline, according to the annual advertising market barometer conducted by Irep, France Pub and Kantar Media (2018).

Investments in the press fell by 7.4% in 2017 to €2.1 billion. A slightly stronger decline than that recorded in 2016 (–6.7%) or 2015 (–5.9%).

Most press families are at half-mast. Investments in national newspapers fell by more than 8%, while the regional press held up slightly better (–4.6%). Magazines suffered the largest drop (–11.4%) in their advertising revenues. "The press, more than any other historical media, is suffering from the shift from advertising to the Internet". Michel Laugier pointed out in his report at the end of 2017, highlighting that the press has seen its advertising turnover fall by more than 50% in 10 years.

All the analyses over a long period of time are, in this respect, quite appalling. In the space of two decades, GAFA have destroyed the historical media, and particularly the press. According to a report published in the summer of 2018 by *BearingPoint* for the Ministry of Culture and the Audiovisual Council (Dahan *et al.* 2018)[2], between 2000 and 2017, revenues from historical media (television, press, radio, billboard, cinema) in France fell by 43% to €6.7 billion. At the same time, the share of Internet advertising revenues – mainly Google and Facebook – rose from almost 0% to 35%, to €3.6 billion.

The press was the most affected. Since 2000, net advertising revenues on print have fallen by 71% to €1.5 billion, and Zenith estimates predict a further 22% decline by 2020. Over the same period, press distribution also plummeted.

However, it is difficult for the press to ignore advertising. Even though the proportion of advertising has decreased and varies according to the type of publication, it still represents a little more than 30% of the turnover of the "publisher" press in 2015. Specifically, 28% for the national press for general and political information and 46% for the technical and professional press in 2015 (Ministère de la culture et de la communication 2015).

---

2 See also Alcaraz (2018b).

4.1. Advertising-free newspapers?

In order to avoid dependence on advertising, some media have chosen to be without advertisement. The inclination towards *no ads* has flourished. *Le 1*, a French newspaper launched in the spring of 2014 by Eric Fottorino, former director of the newspaper *Le Monde*, was built on an advertising-free economic model:

> "*Le 1* is not dependent on any financial or advertising group. In order to guarantee you reliable information, far from any pressure, we have chosen to be independent and advertising-free" (https://le1hebdo.fr).

In the online press, several media have chosen an advertising-free model. This is the case of one of the pioneers called *MediaPart*, who embarked on an economic model in 2008 that was relatively original at the time – the paid subscription:

> "Financing through advertising means giving advertisers an increasingly intrusive place that displeases readers. It prohibits a strong editorial identity and, in the process, the creation of a loyal and invested readership. It does not allow the development of strong journalistic skills and the production of reference information. The so-called "free" sites on the Internet are obviously not so. However, a newspaper whose funding entirely depends on advertising revenues cannot claim, economically, to remain permanently independent. Current advertising revenues on the Internet are primarily calculated for millions of visitors, thus for content that attracts a general public audience that is not compatible with the requirements of a quality and reference press" (MediaPart 2008).

Explicite, the medium created by iTélé alumni (renamed *CNews*), also chose a subscription-based, advertising-free model:

"Our first choice and first bet was to believe in the virtues of subscription, rather than rely on an economic model based on com, advertising and uncertain distribution on Facebook and Twitter. To think that we only wanted to be accountable to subscribers and that many of you would join" (Ravanello 2016).

According to media sociologist Jean-Marie Charon:

"This reflects the expectations of a number of readers who do not want to receive advertisements. However, not having advertising also means having an audience that is willing to pay more for their newspaper. It is the press of culturally rich people and bourgeois bohemians, but also teachers etc., and all those who want to have an impact on society" (Alcaraz 2018a).

The trend, however, is not just a recent one. The century-old newspaper *Le Canard enchaîné* also chose the advertising-free route, and successfully so, seeing as the newspaper makes a profit.

4.2. Pressure from advertisers and readers

Some examples of pressure from advertisers on newspapers have been widely reported in the media.

4.2.1. *When advertisers apply the pressure*

Let us take the example of the *Daily Telegraph* in Britain, in 2015. Editor-in-chief Peter Oborne left the newspaper with a bang, pointing his finger at management, saying that it had given in to the pressure of advertising in the *SwissLeaks* affair. Specifically, he accused the newspaper's management of deceiving readers on the subject of revelations about tax evasion orchestrated by HSBC Bank. He said that executives removed articles on the case and limited coverage of the scandal, in order to avoid risking offending one of its main advertisers, HSBC, which was widely covered by other newspapers.

In an open letter published on the *OpenDemocracy* website, Peter Oborne details the case at length (Oborne 2015). The bank reportedly cut advertising budgets following the publication of articles on offshore accounts. Oborne also called for an independent investigation into HSBC's possible influence on the Telegraph's editorial line in recent years. For its part, the Telegraph denied "these staggering and groundless attacks", via a spokesman interviewed by the BBC. "The clear distinction between advertising and our editorial treatment has always been fundamental to our newspaper".

Another major British newspaper, *The Guardian*, rebounded on the case, saying HSBC had put its advertising account "on hold".

In France, several cases have also been revealed. In the summer of 2018, the editor of *Le Monde*, Luc Bronner, spoke about the pressure his newspaper faced at the International Journalism Festival in Couthures-sur-Garonne. When asked by a member of the public about the subject, he replied:

> "Sometimes we go through difficult times. For example, when we work on Panama or the Paradise Papers, and we say that a fairly powerful company in France called LVMH – at least, important people in this company in terms of shareholding – has limited practices, we are immediately punished because there is the temptation for this company to cut advertisers' budgets. We take responsibility and we manage to make it known. That's why they come back after. And we won: we did our information work, they applied some form of pressure and in the end, they came back" (de Rochegonde 2018).

Le Canard Enchaîné had mentioned a significant loss of advertising revenue in *Le Monde* a few months earlier, following the revelations of the newspaper about Bernard Arnault – the CEO of LVMH – regarding the so-called "Paradise papers" case. However, the French luxury giant denied having cut its advertising budgets in *Le Monde*, indicating that it was considering its media investments.

In January, many editorial offices and journalists' collectives signed a platform to denounce the methods of Vincent Bolloré and his group, who were accused of putting pressure on the media investigating the businessman's African activities. The Bolloré group and its commercial partner, the Luxembourg holding company Socfin, have thus launched some 20 defamation proceedings against the media, journalists and independent organizations over the past decade.

4.2.2. *When readers put pressure on advertising*

Advertising blockers (adblockers) are increasingly being used by online information readers. Out of a desire for reading comfort or irritation with advertising that is considered intrusive, readers download software that, once installed on a computer or mobile phone, blocks a large part of online advertising. According to the Adblocks barometer conducted by IPSOS Connect for the IAB in France, 36% of French users had installed this type of tool on their machines at the end of 2016, 20% higher than in January 2016 (Gilbert 2016). The study shows that although the whole population is involved, young people use advertising blockers more significantly: 55% of 16–24 year-olds and 45% of 25–34 year-olds.

The rejection of online advertising, if legitimate, is a problem for sites that live partially or totally from advertising. Freeing oneself from advertising by an apparently harmless act weakens the media, who see a decrease in their revenues. More and more newspapers are trying to circumvent the phenomenon by encouraging Internet users to watch advertising. Some sites are not visible if you have an adblockers. For example, TF1 cut off access to Internet users who were using advertising blockers during the 2014 World Cup.

Some media also take creative initiatives by offering the choice between watching or not watching spots. For example, in 2016, the Swiss newspaper *Le Temps* launched an article-based payment solution after the reader reaches the paywall (the free limit ranging from one to five articles). The idea is to give the reader a choice: either he/she watches an advertising video to access the article or buys it.

Newspapers also offer digital subscriptions that make it possible to eliminate all advertising, just like what exists on other platforms in music or video. In 2016, the *New York Times* announced the launch of such an offer. More recently, *Les Echos* has set up a premium *digital first* offer, with exclusive preview information, conferences and debates with journalists and editorial management, etc. as well as the "comfort of browsing without advertising".

Research has studied the effect of adblockers. Benjamin Shiller, Joel Waldfogel and Johnny Ryan (Shiller *et al.* 2018) show that the impact of this software is substantial, given that an additional 1% of Internet users using an adblockers generates a traffic reduction of 0.67%, and a 1.5% reduction in overall resources. Adblockers are therefore a considerable problem given the economic model of many sites that are highly dependent on advertising revenues, as Laurent Benzoni, a professor of economics at Paris 2, and Sara Clignet point out (Benzoni and Clignet 2017). The latter also remind us that in 2015, for the first time in Europe, total online advertising revenues (€36.4 billion) exceeded television advertising revenues (€33.3 billion).

4.3. Can media say everything?

The impact of advertising revenues on press content is a recurring topic. According to its analysis, economic research does not provide a clear answer, but it does give several indications.

4.3.1. *Seducing advertisers*

First of all, there is a whole trend showing that advertising leads to homogenization. From the work of Jean Gabszewicz, Didier Laussel and Nathalie Sonnac (Gabszewicz *et al.* 2001; Gabszewicz *et al.* 2002), we have seen that optimizing advertiser revenues can lead the media to seek consensus, that is, to adopt a particular form of bias that consists of having a neutral position. Neutrality is seen here in a negative way, in the sense that it is the opposite of the plurality of opinions and it does not contribute to the debate of ideas.

Following a similar approach, Matthew Ellman and Fabricio Germano, researchers at the University of *Pompeu Fabra* in Barcelona, show that if the advertising market is very active and represents an important source of income for the press, then this leads to a reduction in the ideological bias that is linked to an increase in competition to broaden readership (Ellman and Germano 2009).

As we have seen in the previous chapters, ideological bias can have two origins. It can be on the demand side, in other words, on the side of market strategies of media companies. The bias is thusly caused by the desire to attract a readership and/or advertisers. It may be on the supply side. The ideological bias then results from the will of journalists and/or owners. The identification of the causes of bias has resulted in numerous publications. Opinions are divided between the demand and supply sides. There are also divergent opinions among those who support a demand bias. Scientific discussions are supported. This intensity is consistent with the importance of the subject which, depending on the way it is perceived, may lead to the proposal of radically different methods of regulating the media sector.

Two movements propose different conclusions. The first trend forecasts *faded* information that is intended to please everyone in order to increase the readership by not angering anyone, thus increasing advertising revenues based on the greatest number. An approach that promotes the volume of readership would then explain a decline in information. The second trend takes the opposite position. Readership would generate higher revenues when segmented, each segment corresponding to a readership with specific characteristics that can be valued by the advertiser.

Box 4.1. *The ideological bias of the media*

However, broadening the readership involves capturing its attention in a world where the reader's or Internet user's attention is highly solicited and becomes a rare commodity.

Simone Galperti and Isabel Trevino, researchers at the University of San Diego, are developing a theoretical model in which the reader's attention plays a pivotal role (Galperti and Trevino 2017). The authors develop a model in which producers compete for the attention of individuals. The result of the model is that competition for attention leads to a homogenization of information, even when consumers are seeking heterogeneity.

Yi Xiang, a professor at the University of Hong Kong, and Miklos Savary, the University of Insead, Fontainebleau, analyze the informational bias by taking the experience of readers into account (Xiang and Savary 2007). The latter have been consuming information from a variety of sources for a long time. They have thus acquired a bias filtering ability. They are seeking multiple biases, in other words, competition between biases, in order to compare them and build their opinion. These readers thus have a preference for multiple and competitive biases rather than a single bias, even if it is neutral.

The Attention Economy, developed since the early 2000s (Davenport 2002; Falkinger 2007), identifies attention as a rare commodity in a world where there is abundant information. This is the paradox in which we live. Attention is limited, which implies developing an *attention-seeking arms race* through marketing that can lead to overproduction of advertising, sometimes triggering rejection (such as Naomi Klein's *No Logo*) or a collapse of *deep attention*. Deep attention is a concept highlighted by Nicholas Carr in a bestseller entitled *The Shallows: What the Internet is Doing to Our Brains* (Carr 2010). He differentiates between the deep attention that corresponds to that of reading a book (concentrated, in-depth attention) and the hyper attention required when we are multi-screening (fragmented, discontinuous reading).

Box 4.2. *The Attention Economy*

On the contrary, in an article published in 2012 (Petrova 2012), Maria Petrova shows that ideological bias even persists in a context where media are looking for important sources of income through advertising. Indeed, if the audience can be finely segmented, and if the audience segments give significant importance to an ideological bias, the search for advertising revenue can lead the media to adopt an ideological bias in order to capture as many readers as possible in a market segment. The idea here is to contrast *niche markets*, whose size may vary with all or most of the market. The effect of advertising on content is therefore not systematic and can vary.

The impact of advertising market segmentation is particularly well analyzed by Ester Gal-Or, Tansev Giliani and Tuba Pinar Yildirim in an article that was also published in 2012 (Gal-Or *et al.* 2012). Here, reader profiles are at the heart of the model as advertisers are looking for a readership that is potentially interested in their products or message.

The authors demonstrate that advertising can serve as a polarizing or moderating force, depending on the degree of heterogeneity of advertisers that are seeking to attract readers with different political preferences.

Advertising can therefore have two opposite effects. If a newspaper's strategy is to target the widest possible readership, then it must display minimal bias. If the advertiser chooses to invest in a single newspaper, then the newspapers are in strong competition with each other to win the advertising market. They then seek to differentiate themselves. One way to differentiate is to display an ideological bias.

Alexander Dyck, Natalya Volchkova and Luigi Zingales do a fairly close study of the Russian press (Dyck *et al.* 2008) between 1999 and 2002. Likewise, Marco Gambarro and Riccardo Puglisi look into the Italian press in 2015 (Gambaro and Puglisi 2015). They measure the impact of an increase in space purchases by a company on the number of articles dedicated to it. The relationship is a positive one and the figures are enlightening: an increase in expenditure of €75,000 generates eight additional articles for one month. The study is conducted on six newspapers (*Corriere della Sera, Repubblica, Stampa, Resto del Carlino, Mattino di Padova, Tirreno*) and 13 companies (Campari, Edison, ENEL, ENI, FIAT, Finmeccanica, Geox, Indesit, Luxottica, Mediolanum, Telecom Italia, Tiscali and Tod's). The choice of six newspapers includes three national newspapers and three local newspapers. As for companies, they are chosen because they have significant advertising expenses in the media (a minimum of €200,000). The period studied is 2006–2007. Here again, the correlation between space purchase and press coverage is verified.

For their part, Vincent Bignon and Antonio Miscio studied the case of France at the very beginning of the 20th Century (Bignon and Miscio 2009). They focus on the Panama Canal scandal. They highlight the expenses of the Panama Canal Company in the media: 13 million francs between 1880 and 1888. The authors identify these amounts as one of the causes of the lack of press vigilance in the Canal case. They did the same with another case: that of the banker Rochette, who also owned three financial newspapers. He was accused of spreading false information in his newspapers and was sentenced to three years in prison.

Another question in economic research concerns the impact of competition on content. In an article published in 2014, Matthew Gentzow and Jesse Shapiro, researchers at the University of Chicago, and Michael Sinkinson, a researcher at Wharton – the University of Pennsylvania – raised the issue of diversity and competition (Gentzkow *et al.* 2014). Does competition lead to a weakening of diversity? They propose an original approach, since it consists of analyzing the content of the U.S. daily press in 1924. The reason for this is that during this period, the number of newspapers present in each city was high, reflecting sustained competition between newspapers. In addition, the newspapers of the time either displayed a political affiliation or official support for a politician. Moreover, television was not yet present, which made it possible to analyze competition limited to the press. The authors design a game theory model with variables such as the number of newspapers, their editorial line, selling prices per issue and advertising space prices. The result of a complex statistical test using databases on all variables shows that newspapers choose clearly differentiated editorial lines in a situation of strong competition. The authors therefore suggest a strong link between diversity and competition.

4.3.2. Can media oppose an advertiser?

Can a car magazine criticize a car brand that is its main advertiser? A recurring question for many press observers is whether a medium can say anything, even though it means angering its advertisers.

Gregory Miller, a Harvard researcher, studies the arbitration in media between reporting fraud (mainly exposing insider trading) and finding advertisers in the financial sector (Miller 2006). Being an effective medium for describing the functioning of financial markets and their possible excesses is seen as a way to improve the credibility of the newspaper and therefore its readership. The medium then anticipates an increase in single-issue sales or subscriptions from readers who are seduced by the quality of the information released. The question asked in the article regards the possible reaction of the advertisers implicated in the information released, and who could reduce their purchases of advertising space. The author examines the articles on 263 companies identified by the SEC (Securities and Exchange Commission), the U.S. stock exchange regulator, in the national press (*Wall Street Journal*, *Business Week*) and in the local press

(*LA Times*, *Miami Review*). More so than the amount of advertising revenue, the quality of information is related to the diversification of advertisers.

Andrea Blasco, researcher at Harvard, Paolo Pin, researcher at Bocconi University in Milan, and Francesco Sobbrio, professor in the Department of Economics at the Free University of Rome (LUISS), study what happens when an advertiser finances advertising in a newspaper with information defending the qualities of its product, or denouncing the defects of its competitors' products as a counterpart (Blasco *et al.* 2016). From their model, they deduce that competition in the product market does not necessarily prevent the appearance of a commercial bias in the media. The article shows that the commercial bias is not automatic and is linked with the quality of the advertiser's product.

If the product is in a weak position compared to the competition, then the pressure from the advertiser will be high and vice versa. On the one hand, if advertisers have quality products, they will cooperate to eliminate negative information about them. On the other hand, if competition is between firms with quality products, as opposed to firms with poorer products, then the firm with quality products has no interest in collaborating to reduce negative information, quite the contrary. In the first case, it is in the interest of firms to finance the media in order to eliminate negative information, and not so in the second case. Let us reproduce here the example given by the three researchers.

"Imagine a magazine specializing in computer products. The magazine offers readers articles in which it assesses the quality of computers. Let's imagine two companies. The first one sells computers of poor quality. If the magazine is not primarily concerned about its reputation, it may agree to exchange its silence or a less critical article for purchases of advertising space. However, the firm that sells good quality products sees competition intensify because of items that are favorable to its competitor. It may therefore decide in turn to influence the media by raising the price of advertising space" (p. 252).

The authors conclude that even in the absence of pluralism (in their example, there is only one newspaper) or the media's desire to have a good reputation, the information may ultimately be of good quality as a result of an increased advertising expenditure by competing companies. The quality of information and the reputation of the media are then consequences of competition between advertisers. However, this result is not always verified. In order to explain this, the authors take a second example:

> "Gasoline-powered cars cause pollution problems, regardless of the brand or model. This is a general problem. But more information will be available on the deficiencies of a brand or model of car than on the general problem of pollution caused by traffic. Automobile companies have an interest in minimizing articles on pollution that can impact the sales of the entire economic sector, even if it means accepting unfavorable comparative articles between brands or models" (p. 259).

As another example, the authors also take the case of the pharmaceutical industry as a whole and the criticism of certain medicines. The nature of commercial bias depends on how product quality is correlated between companies. In the case of tobacco industries, the products are almost identical and it took a long time for information on the dangers of tobacco to increase. In the case of computer manufacturers, product quality is not correlated between firms because competition is strong and there is a wide variety of products, so the information on the worrying use of rare earths in batteries was quickly brought to light.

It can therefore be seen here that research on the consequences of partial or total funding of the press through advertising must be continued.

Subsequent articles focus on analyses based on the newspaper content. In 2006, Jonathan Reuter and Eric Zitzewitz analyzed a specific bias: that of financial information (Reuter and Zitzewitz 2006). They question the possible link between advertising that is financed by investment fund managing firms and reporting on these same firms in newspapers that have benefited from their advertising investments. They identify a positive link for financial newspapers specializing in personal wealth management (*Smart Money*, *Money*, *Kiplinger's Personal Finance*). However, the link is not convincing for major newspapers such as the *New York Times* or the *Wall Street Journal*. The authors explain this difference by the weight of advertisers, which are more concentrated in the first case and more numerous in the second, and by the amount of advertising spending. The study examined the articles published between 1996 and 2002 in five newspapers, which were selected because they received the highest amounts of advertising revenue from investment funds[3]. These publications received 45.3% of the portfolio managers' advertising expenditures between 1996 and 2002. For the *Wall Street Journal*, advertisers who manage funds represent 3.8% of advertising revenue, while for *Kiplinger's*, they represent 28.2%. In other words, the more diverse the advertisers in a medium, the less sensitive it is to pressure.

4.3.3. *The impact of taxation*

There are few studies on tax measures for the press. When they are set up, they either provide financial assistance to the press when it encounters financial difficulties or give it the means to counterbalance the fluctuations of advertising revenues. Hans Kind and two other researchers from the University of Tübingen note that many countries grant tax measures that are favorable to the press (Kind *et al.* 2013). One of the most frequent is the VAT rate reduction, as in the case of France (the press benefits from a VAT rate called "super light", or 2.1%[4]). This measure has three objectives, as defined by the European Commission: to lower the price of newspapers in order to improve their distribution and therefore the profitability of press companies; to allow greater investment; and to encourage more differentiation between newspapers, thus improving pluralism. The three researchers suggest verifying the validity of this virtuous chain of events. They develop a two-sided model to take the other press market into account, in other words, the advertisers' market and the sale of advertising space. The VAT rate reduction should make newspapers financially secure and allow them not to compete for additional resources through advertisers. This should allow the press to focus its efforts on the reader and invest in qualitative journalism.

The authors review the study in order to show that research on two-sided markets does not incorporate reflection on taxation to this day, and that the

---

3 *Wall Street Journal* ($48.5 million), *Money* ($22.1 million), *Mutual Funds* ($14 million), *New York Times* ($14 million), *Kiplinger's Personal Finance* ($12.2 million) and *SmartMoney* ($8.7 million), (p. 7).

4 The special rate of 2.1% (Art. 281 quater *et seq.* of the CGI) is reserved for medicinal products that are refundable by the social security system, sales of live animals for slaughter and sausage to non-taxable persons, television license fees, certain shows and press publications registered with the *Commission paritaire des publications et agences de presse* (Joint Publications and Press Agencies Committee). Source: https://www.economie.gouv.fr/cedef/taux-tva-france-et-union-europeenne.

study on direct taxation has not focused on two-sided markets. They conclude that this is a counterproductive measure depending on the size of the advertising market. If the advertising market includes many advertising space buyers, then the press offers a slightly different profile to have the largest number of readers in order to have the largest number of advertisers (the authors cite the English tabloids as an example). According to the authors, it is therefore not taxation that ensures pluralism, but the strategy of press groups in view of the size of the advertising market.

5

Is the Printed Newspaper Gamble Crazy?

The arrival of the Internet, along with the possibility of digitalizing information and putting it online, puts forward three questions to economists who study the press:

– How can the historical economic model migrate?

– How can innovation be managed?

– Does the online press produce a more or less significant informational bias than the paper press?

The arrival of digital technology 20 years ago was both hopeful and a great concern. It was hopeful because the press crisis had begun long before. There was a hope to regain lost readers and especially young people. The average age of the press readership was high, very high for the regional daily press. It was also a huge concern because it raised many issues, the two main ones being: how journalists work in this new context, and how the press builds its new business model.

There were 20 years of trial and error, hesitation and sometimes backtracking. And 20 years of financial difficulties because evolving and taking risks is particularly complex, when things are initially going wrong and press companies are not capitalizing well. There were not enough financial reserves to afford the luxury of experimenting, just like in a laboratory (they are emerging as *La Provence Innovation*, launched in January 2018 by the local daily newspaper of the same name[1]) in order to make the right choice. Furthermore, there were not enough financial resources to take the risks inherent in the future of companies in an ever-changing world.

5.1. Is it the end of printed papers in the United States?

Many "Cassandras" have predicted the end of printed papers in recent years. For example, at the beginning of this decade, the Center for the Digital Future at the University of Southern California (USC) Annenberg – a school of communication and journalism – predicted that the main paper newspapers in the United States would end within 5 years[2]. It must be said that this highly discussed prediction at the time proved to be false.

However, the traditional "paper" press is not at its best. As Professor Jeffrey Cole of the Center for the Digital Future observes in a recent post, taking stock of this forecast of "paper death": print is declining and newspapers have disappeared.

In the United States, the figures speak for themselves. According to an analysis by the Pew Research Center[3] published in mid-2017 and based on the figures from the News Media Alliance (NMA), the distribution of U.S. newspapers is at its lowest level since 1945. And in 2016 alone, the "distribution" of paper editions during the week fell by 10%.

Even though digital subscriptions jumped, which particularly benefited from the U.S. presidential election (the *New York Times* or the *Wall Street Journal*, for example, benefited strongly), overall, the industry decreased: the press fell by 8%, taking print and digital (on weekdays) into account. In other words, the 28th year in the red.

---

1 See http://laprovence-innovation.com.

2 Center for the Digital Future, Five years later: the prediction on the end of printed newspapers, Cole, J., March 7, 2018. Available online: http://www.digitalcenter.org/columns/prediction-printed-newspapers/.

3 Pew Research Center, Newspapers Fact Sheet, published on June 2, 2017. See also: Despite subscription surges for largest U.S. newspapers, circulation and revenue fall for industry overall, Barthel, M., June 1, 2017. Available online: http://www.journalism.org/fact-sheet/newspapers/ et http://www.pewresearch.org/fact-tank/2017/06/01/circulation-and-revenue-fall-for-newspaper-industry/.

5.1.1. *Preparing for a change of era?*

Some press owners are beginning to prepare for a paperless future. For example, in February 2018 in an interview with CNBC[4], the CEO of the *New York Times* indicated that the paper press could disappear in the United States within 10 years. All while noting that he hoped to see the paper format survive as long as possible, Mark Thompson acknowledged that from a financial point of view, the paper model was no longer sustainable in the long term.

Similarly, in Europe, Gaël Hürlimann, the editor-in-chief of digital content for the Swiss newspaper *Le Temps*, believed in early 2018 that the newspaper would disappear as we know it, to the benefit of the whole digital world in three years' time. "Bringing the news makes no sense anymore", he explained in an interview with the INA, recalling that distribution was becoming increasingly complicated[5].

In France, some press owners are also as bold as to talk about a paperless future. "If we can distribute information of such high quality without paper tomorrow, ultimately for newspaper companies, it's not bad", stated Alain Weill, the head of *SFR Médias* (now CEO of SFR), as part of the Digiworld Future (organized by IDATE) in June 2017. The owner of *L'Express*, *Libération* and *SFR Presse* added:

> "the traditional press is heading into a wall. There is not a single paper newspaper that is growing. In the past, I controlled the daily newspaper *La Tribune* and I was very surprised to see the economic and industrial model of the press. Sixty percent of paper newspapers were not sold! This model is doomed"[6].

---

4 CNBC.com, New York Times CEO: Print journalism has maybe another 10 years, Ell, K., 12/02/2018. Available online: https://www.cnbc.com/2018/02/12/print-journalism-may-last-another-10-years-new-york-times-ceo.html.

5 INA Global, *La presse vue en 2018* by Gaël Hürlimann, comments collected by Xavier Eutrope, X., January 1, 2018. Available online: https://www.inaglobal.fr/presse/article/la-presse-en-2018-vue-par-gael-huerlimann-10048.

6 Les Echos.fr, *Le patron de "L'Express" et de "Libération" aimerait se passer du papier*, Schmitt, F., June 6, 2017. Available online: www.lesechos.fr/06/06/2017/lesechos.fr/030368923171_le-patron-de-l-express-et-de-liberation--aimerait-se-passer-du-papier.htm#72m kG5ff76Ut9zE2.99.

Several newspapers in trouble had already gone digital. The mythical *France Soir*, which was created in 1944, stopped printed publishing in favor of digital publishing in 2011, with significant job losses. In 2012, *La Tribune*, which was in trouble, published its last paper issue.

More recently, in Canada, the newspaper *La Presse* has taken the step of becoming 100% digital. After testing the weekday paper stop in 2016, the newspaper decided to stop the Saturday edition in 2018. "The vast majority of readers quickly changed their habits in order to adopt La Presse+ (its application for tablets and mobile phones), first during the week, but also on Saturdays. In 2016 alone, the enthusiasm for La Presse+ resulted in an impressive 18.7% increase in its audience", as stated by Pierre-Elliott Levasseur, president of the newspaper, in June 2017[7].

However, the gamble did not pay off, despite an "undeniable success" with the public (with nearly 2 million unique readers per week on tablets, web and mobile platforms). The tablet edition, which was reinforced after the discontinuation of the paper edition during the week and then the weekend edition, was intended to generate enough income to ensure the newspaper's profitability. However, the model was not sustainable: the newspaper suffered from the decline in advertising revenues, against a backdrop of fierce competition.

In May 2018, the Power Corporation announced the sale of the over 100-year-old French-language daily newspaper in Quebec to a non-profit organization. Rather than changing their completely free-of-charge strategy, the newspaper's managers wanted to appeal for donations and government assistance. "We have no intention of returning to a paid model", said Pierre-Elliott Levasseur in the AFP report[8]. Studies have shown, according to him, that 100,000 subscribers at best would be willing to pay $5 a month and that's too little to support one newsroom among some of the largest in Canada. "It would be devastating on the business model", he added, wanting to take inspiration from the example of *The Guardian*, the British daily newspaper, which has expanded its audience while appealing for donations.

---

7 Lapresse.ca, "*La Presse* deviendra 100 % numérique à partir de 2018" Pierre-Elliott Levasseur, June 1, 2017. Available online: http://www.lapresse.ca/debats/mot-de-lediteur/201706/01/01-5103410-la-presse-deviendra-100-numerique-a-partir-de-2018.php.
8 AFP. "Du papier au tout numérique, La Presse lance un appel aux dons au Québec", published May 8, 2018.

5.1.2. *Digital reading exceeds paper reading*

Audience analysis also reflects changes in behavior, to the benefit of digital technology.

Digital reading has thus become a standard practice, as evidenced by various analyses and surveys. Now, according to the ACPM's One Global 2017 study, three quarters of French people (76%) read at least one press brand in digital format (computer, mobile, tablet).

Similarly, digital readings (54%) now far exceed paper readings (46%). In the digital world, the mobile phone has established its dominant position: 24% of readings are done on mobile phones, in front of the computer (20%) and the tablet (10%).

Another indicator is that media site traffic has been rising for several years. In 2017, an 11% increase in visits to press sites and applications was recorded (after a 7% increase in 2016), according to data from the ACPM-OJD. Within it, visits to mobile and application sites jumped by more than 28% in 2017[9].

Above all, contrary to what has been feared for many years, it seems that there has been no cannibalization between printed issues and the Web. On the contrary, newspapers that have invested in the Web are more resilient, as observed by experts from the ACPM-OJD[10]. Another reassuring conclusion is that 43% of readers only read one press brand's print (exclusively). However, this figure is down (2 points compared to the last round[11]).

With the constant belief that digital technology seems to be the future, most media have therefore sought to develop their digital versions and, above all, to monetize them, particularly via subscription.

The example of the *New York Times* is worth noting. According to CNBC, it is the first news organization to have crossed the threshold of 1 million digital subscribers.

---

9 Press releases: ACPM-OJD on the distribution of the French press, April 12, 2018 and One Global 2018 V1.

10 Les Echos, "Première hausse de diffusion en dix ans pour les quotidiens nationaux", Marina Alcaraz, April 13, 2018.

11 Comparison of One Global 2018 V1 and 2017 V4.

In March 2018, the U.S. newspaper had 2.8 million online subscribers (+139,000 new subscribers in the first quarter).

The media has set itself ambitious objectives. According to Mark Thompson, CEO of the newspaper, who was interviewed by *Le Monde* in 2017, the target of 10 million digital subscribers is within reach:

"In the long run, reaching 10 million or even more subscribers is credible. It took us much less time to reach our second million subscribers than the first one[12]".

The daily newspaper was one of the first major newspapers to implement a policy that was firmly focused on the Internet, making its site profitable from the very beginning of the decade. Quite quickly, the number of digital subscribers exceeded the number of print subscribers. The newspaper has implemented several techniques to acquire new subscribers and especially to retain them: sending e-mails with article proposals, ergonomics of the site dedicated to new subscribers, as well as invitations to events dedicated to subscribers among other events, etc. The newspaper has also launched promotional campaigns, focusing on fans of its best sellers, crosswords and recipes[13]. It has also innovated a great deal by hiring data scientists, for example.

The famous newspaper also invested in its editorial content, notably for the cover of the Trump administration, allowing it to win several Pulitzer Prizes. The *New York Times* has thus become increasingly prominent in the United States, whether in politics or in the Weinstein case.

Another interesting example, although totally different, is *The Guardian*. In the summer of 2018, the British newspaper announced that its digital revenues had exceeded its paper revenues for the first time, thanks to the voluntary financial contributions made by its readers.

---

12 Le Monde.fr, The "New York Times" can reach 10 million digital subscribers, interview with Mark Thompson, comments collected by Piquard, A., April 10, 2017. Available online: http://www.lemonde.fr/economie/article/2017/04/10/les-medias-doivent-preciser-ce-qu-ils-attendent-des-reseaux-sociaux_5108639_3234.html#eZXto8HoTvfVvaDw.99.
13 Read also: l'adn.eu, *Le New York Times génère 60% de ses revenus grâce à l'abonnement en ligne*, Bertaux, M., February 12, 2018. Available online: http://www.ladn.eu/media-mutants/case-study-media/le-new-york-times-genere-60-de-ses-revenus-grace-a-labonnement-en-ligne/.

Digital revenues (including advertising and reader contributions) increased by 15% year-on-year, while paper revenues declined by 10%. David Pemsel, CEO of GMG (Guardian Media Group, the company that publishes the press title), said that by choosing to rely on the generosity of its online readers rather than adopting a paid model, *The Guardian* had created "a third way to pay for quality journalism", as reported by AFP[14]. For the record, the British press title had chosen the model of a free site, with donations from its readers. Anyone can become a member and obtain a number of benefits in exchange for "contributions". It should be recalled that at the beginning of 2018, while in financial difficulty, GMG decided to convert *The Guardian* to the tabloid format in order to save money, in parallel with a recovery plan initiated earlier (cost reductions, job cuts, etc.). David Pemsel, CEO of *The Guardian*, said that the group's financial structure allows it to keep a paper edition "as long as our readers are attached to it".

In France too, digital press is becoming the leading source of distribution for national daily newspapers. For example, *Le Monde* passed a symbolic milestone in 2017: digital subscriptions have become its main source of paid distribution, ahead of paper subscriptions and newsstand sales[15].

5.1.3. Difficult print launches

It must be said that not all traditional print launches have been successful. For example, in France in 2018, there were two important paper magazines: the weekly *Ebdo* magazine launched by the founders of the magazine *XXI*, and *Vraiment*.

Ebdo, launched with great fanfare on January 12, 2018, did not last three months. The media promised to take a step back from the flow of information, while remaining accessible, as presented by Patrick de Saint Exupery and Laurent Beccaria, the founders of the magazine *XXI*. Sold at a newsstand price of €3.50, it was ad-free but did not attract enough

---

14 AFP.com, *Les revenus numériques du Guardian dépassent ceux du papier*, published on July 24, 2018. Available online: https://www.afp.com/fr/infos/2260/les-revenus-numeriques-du-guardian-depassent-ceux-du-papier-doc-17w4t32.
15 LesEchos.fr, *Le digital va devenir le premier canal de diffusion des médias*, Basile Dekonink, March 12, 2018.

subscribers, so Rollins Publications, the company that published the magazine, declared itself bankrupt in March.

Similarly, *Vraiment*, which presented itself as a *new generation* general news weekly magazine that wanted to develop in-depth subjects, far from the hot news, launched in March 2018, and suspended its publication in May. "Unfortunately, the sales trend and available resources do not allow the possibility of selling a balance of 40,000 copies within 18 months", said *Polaris News*, the publishing company.

In an article by INA Global[16], media specialist Jean-Marie Charon asks himself this essential question: can we still launch a paper magazine in France? Recalling the successful launches of *Le 1* or even *Society* in recent years, the sociologist looks back at the factors for the success of a "print" or web launch. Among them, the media are generally "non-substitutable" and easily recognizable, with clear biases in terms of how information is processed (e.g. in-depth multi-part files for *Le 1*) or in terms of form (e.g. *Le 1*, viewed as a "new press experience", is interesting in this respect). Their economic model is based on the fee-based model. Another distinctive factor is the idea of "making a community", that is, the idea of a reading contract with the public, accompanied by activities of this community (e.g. *Mediapart* has increased the number of meetings with its readers). They have been able to find niche readership (with a rather high level of education, diversified cultural practices and a high consumption of information, a commitment or at least a strong motivation "towards the life of the city and the ideas that run through it", etc.).

Ebdo and *Vraiment* had brought together several of these key success factors, but Jean-Marie Charon points out that the two press titles probably did not distinguish themselves sufficiently. In addition, the targeted consumers are very demanding. "This means that the bar for entering the market is set much higher in terms of innovation, whether it be regarding the novelty or highly distinctive nature of the editorial formula. This implies a strong capacity for adaptation and the ability to bounce back very quickly in the event of an insufficient response from the public", he stated. The editor

---

16 Inaglobal.fr, *Peut-on encore vraiment lancer un hebdo papier en France?*, Charon, JM., published on June 11, 2018. Available online: https://www.inaglobal.fr/presse/article/peut-encore-vraiment-lancer-un-hebdo-papier-en-france-10213.

of *Vraiment* made a similar observation[17]: "We have nothing to be ashamed of", said Jules Lavie shortly after the announcement of the press title's end. "Looking back, our main mistake was being on a generalist concept. We wanted to make a newspaper that we wanted to read. Given the competitive world, it would have been better to create media that covers a particular target or areas of interest, which could be summarized in one sentence".

Finally, it is necessary to question the self-standing bias of these two new publications, according to Jean-Marie Charon. "The justification for print must be absolutely indisputable in terms of rendering quality, aesthetics, pleasure of touch, desire to preserve, etc.". Marketing, "brought back to its place of detailed knowledge about the public and its practices", would undoubtedly have made it possible to service each offer in relation to the target audience, and in particular, to assess how there could be any redundancies when compared to previous launches. He could also perhaps have questioned the timing and the risk of not observing how audiences, in addition to the distribution network (newspaper sellers), first responded to the *Ebdo* offer, before releasing *Vraiment*.

5.2. Among pure players: the free model is crumbling

Several newspaper creations have gone straight for the Internet in recent years: the pure players. However, several media based on free models, financed through advertising and especially through brand content, have suffered.

For example, in the autumn of 2017, the U.S.-based *Buzzfeed* announced a decline of about 8% in its workforce, or about 100 people, mainly in the United States and in sales functions. The group also warned that it would not achieve its objectives that year. The media aimed for a turnover of $350 million, but specified that it would be below 15 to 20%, although still growing. In the spring of 2018, *Buzzfeed* indicated that it was considering closing the French site.

---

17 LesEchos.fr, Vraiment *s'arrête après un peu moins de deux mois*, Alcaraz, M., published May 9, 2018.

Another pure player, *Vice Media*, warned that it was not going to reach its revenue target in 2017 either[18].

The free pure players exclusively finance their activity by selling advertising space. However, the offer of spaces for sale is very high, given the numerous amounts of sites or blogs feeding on this market. A high offer means very low prices per click or per performance. In addition, advertising expenses is strongly correlated with the economic situation, and is often one of the first variables of adjustment for companies financing advertising. Finally, the advertising market is also a playground where not all players are the same size: thus, GAFAM[19] are omnipresent in the online advertising market. Advertising budgets are increasingly shifting to Google and Facebook.

In France, these two companies represented approximately 78% of the digital advertising market – excluding comparators, affiliations and e-mails – in 2017, compared to 76% in 2016. They alone capture 92% of digital growth, according to the e-pub observatory of the SRI (Syndicat des régies Internet) and the UDECAM (Union des entreprises de conseil et achat media), produced by PwC[20], which we will discuss in detail later.

The major problem with the transition from print to the Web, or a mixed solution, has been the disappointed expectation of advertising revenue. Thus, in the early days of the arrival of the Web, many press titles thought that online advertising revenues would compensate for the loss of print resources or even allow them to change their business model from a paid one to a free one. But the online advertising market did not compensate for the decrease in print revenues.

Some studies, such as that of Shidar Shrihari and Sriram Srinasaraghavan (Shrihari and Srinasaraghavan 2015), have shown that the decrease in the latter is mainly due to structural reasons (the press crisis, the decrease in

18 Les Echos.fr "Buzzfeed va supprimer 100 postes et se réorganiser", Nicolas Rauline, November 29, 2017. Available online: https://www.lesechos.fr/tech-medias/medias/03095499937 4-buzzfeed-va-supprimer-100-postes-et-se-reorganiser-2134350.php#bY1clIcj3pvKKWVx.99.
19 GAFAM = Google (which has since become Alphabet), Apple, Facebook, Amazon, Microsoft.
20 19th edition of the SRI e-pub Observatory, produced by PwC, in partnership with UDECAM, published on January 25, 2018.

readership), rather than to the overtaking of print revenues by web revenues. Thus, by a study made on 50 U.S. press titles between 2005 and 2011, the two authors show that when online advertising brings in an additional $1 to a press title, the latter loses on average $22 in print advertising revenue. Thus, 17% of this decrease is due to the shift in advertising investments from print to the Web, the balance (83%) being due to the decrease in readership, which is independent of the arrival of the Web.

Hence the evolution of the business model chosen by the *Wall Street Journal*, which was one of the first to choose the option of the paid Web. Rather than targeting rare and complex advertising revenues, the newspaper has preferred to invest in building readership loyalty, as Alfonso Vara-Miguel and Carolina Díaz-Espina point out (Vara-Miguel and Díaz-Espina 2014).

The realization of an impossible advertising gold mine has led many press titles to question their first attempt based on a free online press model and to replace it with paywall or subscription solutions, even though, as Lesley Chiou and Catherine Tucker (Chiou and Tucker 2013), researchers at the MIT School of Management, show, the change of model forces them to face a difficult financial period. This financial difficulty could be because site traffic falls considerably, possibly to a temporary loss of over half.

Revenues based on online advertising are all the more problematic given that the often free and easy-to-install software on your computer makes it possible to block it (see Chapter 4).

5.3. The online press mainly chooses the paid model

The era of free Internet seems to have run its course. More and more media have adopted paid models. According to a study by the Reuters Institute for the Study of Journalism in 2017[21], of 171 publications in six European countries (Finland, France, Germany, Italy, Poland and the United Kingdom), 66% of daily newspapers have a paid model and 71% have weekly magazines.

---

21 See http://www.digitalnewsreport.org/publications/2017/pay-models-european-news/#france and   https://www.inaglobal.fr/presse/lu-sur-le-web/la-presse-en-ligne-europeenne-se-convertit-au-modele-payant.

In France, 95% of newspapers and magazines have a paid model. The most common model is the *freemium* (partly free and partly paid, with higher added value), followed by the *metered paywall* (where readers have access to a number of articles that vary according to the commercial policy of the press titles and must subscribe to read beyond the "wall").

The principle of online subscription has become a standard practice. The time of massive piracy in the field of music or cinema seems to be moving away. Web users are seduced by reasonable prices and quality streaming services. While subscription sites such as Spotify or Netflix are developing, the willingness to pay for the press is also increasing, at least in the United States. According to the 2017 report of the Reuters Institute for the Study of Journalism (Newman *et al.* 2017), 16% of Americans say they pay for online information (subscriptions and other types of payments), almost twice as many as in 2016 (9%).

The trend is particularly noticeable among young people. The proportion of 18 to 24-year-olds paying for online information increased from 4% in 2016 to 18% in 2017. Similarly, those on the left were more likely to pay for information. In the United States, again, one of the main reasons is the desire to finance journalism.

In the rest of the countries studied (about 30), the main concern is to be able to access information on mobiles and tablets (30%) and the desire to have access to several sources (29%). Strangely enough, access to your favorite newspaper does not top the list of reasons for payment.

Another fact of this study is that respondents are more willing to pay for video (e.g. Netflix), music or mobile applications than for the press. Hence the steps taken by many press players to multiply media, images, videos and sound.

In practice, in France, among pure players, several online newspapers have adopted a paid model from the start. This is the case of *Mediapart*, which celebrated its 10th anniversary in 2018, or even more recently *Les jours*, which launched in 2016 by a handful of former *Libération* members, both on paid models.

For *Mediapart*, the gamble was a success. The site, which had about 10,000 subscribers at its inception in 2008, now has more than 140,000 (as of March 2018). The site has been profitable for three years. The media, whose business model is based on readers' subscriptions, posted revenues of €13.7 million (+20%) in 2017.

In the United States, the example of the pure player *Axios* is interesting. This new media, created in early 2017 by former Politico alumni, has started as a free service and on social networks. However, it announced that it wanted to develop on a paid model with a high subscription ($10,000 per annual subscription!). It was particularly known for the scoop on Donald Trump's decision to withdraw from the Paris climate agreement.

5.4. Managing the model change

The Internet's surge in the media has caused an earthquake in the economic model of newspapers, as shown by research on the impact of both the number of newspapers and employment.

Korean researcher Daegon Cho, Mickael Smith, a professor at Carnegie Mellon University in Pittsburgh, and Alejandro Zentner, a professor at the University of Texas at Dallas, are studying the "survival rate of the print media" following the arrival of the Internet (Cho *et al.* 2016). They are analyzing the situation in 90 countries from 2000 to 2009. The databases contain information on Internet penetration, daily local and national circulation of printed newspapers, and the number of local and national newspapers. The results show that the increase in Internet penetration explains a great deal about the decrease in newspaper circulation and the number of newspaper titles.

The impact of the Internet is steeper for the local press than for the national press. The reason seems to be a greater dependence of local newspapers on classified ads, which were a major source of revenue. Classified ads have migrated quickly to the Web on the initiative of sites that are often created by entrepreneurs from the free press, who have found a way to boost their activities. Another interesting result is that the disappearance of newspapers obviously reduces the overall circulation of the paper press, and that surviving paper newspapers do not benefit from it: in other words, the lost market is for all newspapers, both those that disappeared and the survivors.

Similarly, statistics from the Pew Research Center show a decline in the number of press titles in the United States between 2000 and 2009, from 1600 press titles to less than 1400, in other words, about 200 fewer press titles. The decrease in circulation goes from 63 million copies to 45 million copies; almost 20 million fewer copies. The database for the 90 countries is the WAN (Word Association of Newspapers[22]) database.

In 2016, three other researchers, Luis Andrès, Alejandro and Joaquin Zentner (Andrès *et al.* 2016), reached the same conclusions, this time studying OECD countries more precisely. Their study, which was produced as part of the World Bank's Sustainable Development Department, reluctantly shows the decrease in the circulation of printed newspapers, but welcomes this decrease through the prism of the environment. Indeed, the authors list the products used in the printing industry, mainly "bleached" paper, as well as the chemicals that enable this result, such as chlorine or hydrogen peroxide or various forms of dioxins, a set of products that are highly toxic to the environment and humans.

5.4.1. *Absorbing the negative effects of the Web on print*

An important consequence of the partial or total transition from print to the Web has been a decrease in the number of journalists in editorial offices. Clémence Aubert-Tarby, research professor at the Paris School of Economics, Octavio Escobar, associate professor at ESG Management School, and Thierry Rayna, researcher at Polytechnique (Aubert-Tarby *et al.* 2018), are interested in the impact of digitalization on employment in the French press. They note that between 2003 and 2012, 16,200 journalists' jobs were eliminated in the daily press and 38,000 in the magazine press in the United States, while online employment only accounts for 10% of that destruction, illustrating a strongly negative balance of the switchover to digital press (5,400 jobs). Concerning the French press, they analyze professional data for 2011 and 2012. To do this, they use two separate databases: the database of the CCIPJ (Commission de la Carte d'Identité des Journalistes Professionnels[23]), an organization that issues a professional press card to journalists and whose data serve as raw material for the Observatoire des Métiers de la Presse[24]; the OJD database, which includes

22 See http://www.wan-ifra.org.
23 See http://www.ccijp.net.
24 See http://www.ccijp.net.

print and web editions of a large number of press titles in France (481 press titles). By crossing these two databases, it is therefore possible to know how many journalists are employed by a newspaper and how this figure has changed. Journalists working in the press represent about 70% of journalists.

The results of the study are particularly interesting. Overall, the transition to digitalization has destroyed jobs. The net balance between creation and destruction is negative. However, the destruction was greater in small structures and less so in large structures that quickly and massively switched to digitalization, in which the creation of new jobs was the most dynamic. The people recruited are generally young and on fixed-term contracts, while those dismissed are generally older and on permanent contracts. Fixed-term contracts are more frequent in small structures, while permanent contracts remain common in large newspapers. Salaries also change according to the degree of digitalization (10% of digitalization leads to a 1% increase in remuneration). The pay difference persists among employees with a 5% gender difference in favor of men.

Other recent data on media employment come from the Pew Research Center in 2018, recalling that the media have had to significantly "cut" their staff in recent years. Between 2008 and 2017, the number of employees in various media (including television, etc.) fell by 23%, according to the Pew Research Center[25]. Of these, it is the press that has suffered the most with a 45% drop in employees from 71,000 to 39,000 people.

Although editorial offices of the digital media created jobs (+79%), this represented a total of 6,000 additional jobs. This was not enough to compensate for the decline in the paper media.

5.4.2. *The copy/paste temptation*

Benjamin Ho and Peng Liu (Ho and Liu 2015), researchers at Cornell, are doing original research by looking at the speed at which information appears and disappears on the Web. Ho and Liu are building their study on a database that is compiled by three U.S.-based magazines (*Times, Newsweek, US News & World Report*), during the period of January 2011 to August 2009. These three magazines were chosen because they have the three

25 Pew Research Center, Newsroom employment dropped nearly a quarter in less than 10 years, with greatest decline at newspapers, by Grieco, A., published on July 30, 2018.

largest market shares in the newspaper segment occupied by the magazine press. The researchers select about 20 keywords reflecting the most popular themes during this period. The three magazines offer 1655 articles or surveys on these topics. Newspaper circulation is measured using statistics provided by the ABC (Audit Bureau Circulations). The study highlights two joint phenomena: on the one hand, individuals are more interested in the information that other individuals are interested in (there is therefore a popular demand for information), and, on the other hand, individuals are getting increasingly tired of the information they receive.

The consequence is therefore for competing media to produce popular information and renew it frequently, in a market where attention is scarce and where they wish to attract a wide readership. This leads to a trend towards mimetic information and a low investment in the search for originality, unless one has a powerful press brand whose power depends on the originality of the positioning.

According to the case made by three researchers, namely Julia Cagé, a professor of economics at Sciences Po Paris, Nicolas Hervé, a research engineer at Ina, and Marie-Luce Viaud, a researcher at Ina, in a book published in 2017 entitled *L'information à tout prix* (INA Editions) (Cagé *et al.* 2017), almost two-thirds of the information published in France (64%) on the Internet is copied/pasted. In order to achieve this result, the three specialists worked on 2.5 million documents, from 86 sources in France (newspaper sites, TV channels, pure players, news agencies, etc.) over the year of 2013, using algorithms and focusing on hot news.

Why was there such a standardization of information? The authors see several reasons for this, including the decline in the number of journalists: the size of news media editorial offices in France has decreased by an average of 1% per year since 2013, which corresponds to a 1.2% decrease in the original information produced each year.

Moreover, and this is perhaps the most striking point, original articles are not rewarded in the short term: on a day-to-day basis, the link between the production of exclusive information and the increase in a site's audience is too weak to be monetized. Even so, in the long term, authors are more optimistic at the aggregate: level, the production of original media content is strongly correlated with the average audience of its site. On average, increasing the production of original information for an article each day in 2013 would increase the number of unique visitors by 14,000, which is far from negligible. The production of original information has an effect on reputation, which affects audiences.

Another interesting conclusion is that it takes on average a little less than three hours for one media to take over another's information, two hours when the information comes from AFP (Agence France Presse, an international news agency). However, half of the events (the news, by and large) spread in less than 25 minutes, and a quarter in only 230 seconds! Let us be reminded that before the Internet, a scoop lasted 24 hours, the lifetime of a paper newspaper.

Since there is a trend for some media outlets to mimic, an important question is whether the Web conveys ideological biases, and, if so, are these biases more pronounced on the Web than on print?

Matthew Gentzkow and Jess Shapiro (Gentzkow and Shapiro 2015) are developing a model similar to those they developed for the print press and then for the Web (Gentzkow and Shapiro 2011). The model confronts information producers (who are in a two-sided market, from which they derive two forms of income: direct sales and audience-related advertising on the site) and Internet users (who choose to consult a site according to the quality of the information and the ideological bias that corresponds to their opinions). They use a ComScore Data Metrix[26] database to define 119 national policy topics, based on which they measure both the distribution and ideology of Internet users, all over a one-year period (2009) with a panel of 1200 people. The results are that individuals mainly choose the sites they visit according to their editorial line and cross-behaviors (visiting a press site on the other side) are uncommon. On the other hand, it is common to increase the number of visits to sites with the same ideology. The authors conclude that there is no more ideological polarization of online press sites than there is for print media. Polarization is a process by which groups or public opinion radicalize towards extreme ideological currents, to the detriment of centrist positions.

---

26 "Media Metrix data come from comScore's panel of over one million U.S.-resident Internet users. Panelists install software on their computers to permit monitoring of their browsing behavior, and comScore uses a passive method to distinguish multiple users of the same machine" (Gentzkow and Shapiro 2015, p. 6).

5.5. The press in start-up mode

Til Vos and Jane Singer (Vos and Singer 2016) are interested in how press managers and journalists speak for themselves during the period of 2000–2014. They show a major change.

As recent developments have led to considerable decreases in the number of journalists in editorial offices, the latter have converted, where possible, to other structures, often to communication services of companies or local authorities, or have even become self-employed (the authors cite a 2014 article that coined the term *newspreneur*, a contraction of newspaper and entrepreneur). These changes have profoundly altered the way journalists perceive themselves, as Robert Picard (Picard 2015) reports in a major study for the Reuters Institute. The change is that the historical separation between journalism and commercial functions within a newspaper, seen as essential and guaranteeing the quality of journalists' work, is no longer seen in the same way. The subject is highly sensitive and generates discussions within the profession about the *fall of the wall*, as Mark Coddington (Coddington 2015) puts it, between the two functions of a newspaper: informing and finding financial resources.

Many researchers, including Robert Picard and Lowe (2016), Achtenhagen (2016), Küng (2015), Doguel (2014), Bruns (2014) and Augey *et al.* (2013), to name but a few, wonder why change management is particularly difficult in the media field, and highlight the need for further research in this area.

5.5.1. *Is the future in code?*

Lucy Küng is conducting a study of *The Guardian*, the *New York Times*, *Quartz*, *Buzzfeed* and *Vice Media*. She emphasizes a diagnosis that is often made in management teams: the future of information is code (Lischka 2016), coupled with the profound dismay caused by this observation (Küng 2017). The subject is a major one and has given rise to a scientific journal entirely dedicated to it: *The Journal of Media Innovations* created in 2014 at the initiative of Charles Ess, a researcher at the University of Oslo. The most recent publications focus on the press "in start-up mode" in order to experiment with new solutions, just as in Christoph Sommer's article (Sommer 2018).

Sommer perfectly summarizes the issues:

"By reviewing the scientific study, it can be concluded that the market orientations for media are different than for other markets, given the particular nature of media that address two markets together. Study on entrepreneurship and startups in the media field is rare [...] and the two-sided market aspect and information networking have not been sufficiently studied and taken into account" (p. 39).

Sommer, a researcher at the University of Zurich, is studying four start-ups: ADA in Brazil, a content creation and curation start-up, GO BALLER, INFORMERLY and UPSTRT, three U.S. companies, the first two are specialized in content aggregation and the third in curation. The four start-ups have different business models that are based either on advertising or on subscription marketing. The main result of the study is that the approach of these young companies is based, above all, on the *user experience*, which is their main concern: to facilitate the consultation of information by the public and the freshness of the information provided. In order to achieve this, the proposal is to make greater use of artificial intelligence. Investment and research expenditure in this area is a priority.

An international conference dedicated to media innovation was held for the sixth time in 2017 in Tallinn by Robin Mansell, a professor at the London School of Economics, and Stuart Cunningham, a professor at the University of Queensland in Australia[27]. The seventh conference is being organized by Professor De Zuniga from the Media Innovation Lab of the University of Vienna, and has as its theme "media innovation and social transformation". The University of Oslo also organizes the International Symposium on Media Innovations (ISMI) every year[28].

This confirms a sustained interest in research in the field of innovation, illustrated by a magazine and an international conference, among other things.

---

27 See http://medit.tlu.ee/events/ismi-2017.
28 http://www.hf.uio.no/imk/english/research/center/mediainnovations/events/ismi2018.htm.

In a remarkable article, Joel Waldfogel (Waldfogel 2017) evokes a digital golden age. He describes the apocalypse that was and still is the digitalization of music for record labels (Major companies that controll the entire production and value chain). Financially exhausted by piracy, they are in a bad position. But alongside the weakening of these old organizations, a more agile world is developing in which new players are multiplying, stimulated by the tremendous drop in production and distribution costs made possible by the arrival of digital technology. This is coupled with an awareness among audiences that free music (and piracy) has a cost that can go as far as the disappearance of a sector, and that leads individuals to take out subscriptions on new music platforms such as Deezer or Spotify.

Waldfogel mentions music, cinema, books, television and so on, but not the press. The difference mainly lies in the high cost of producing quality information, which remains a near-traditional practice, linked to individuals who question, research and write, even though robots occupy part of the journalistic field (as we will see in the last chapter). This is not a digital golden age for the press, but certainly a new way of producing and distributing. Becoming rich by producing music has been and remains an opportunity. Revenues have changed: they now mainly come from live shows or streaming subscriptions. Becoming rich by producing information was not the case yesterday, it will probably still not be the case tomorrow, but on the other hand, digitalization allows information to always exist and to obtain sufficient funding in order to ensure a different sustainability.

5.5.2. *The hope of finding new resources*

Caught in the turmoil of declining advertising revenues, the media have sought to diversify their revenues and rely on other revenues.

In a white paper on the press, published by Ipsos and Weborama, François Mariet (Mariet 2017), a media specialist and a professor at Paris Dauphine University, gives an overview of the opportunities and challenges facing the press today. One way is to better exploit data that is seen as an "inexhaustible and recyclable resource". The author suggests some ways to better use data and make it so that it can be sustainably monetized.

For him, the press must be considered as "a data set. In particular lexical data that can be analyzed by artificial intelligence tools". In the long term, "visual recognition will also make it possible to take data from semiological analyses of images into account". This will allow for finer targeting. The job of the press is to mobilize all its data in order to monetize them immediately or indirectly.

In a paper published in 2017 by a team of researchers from different countries, John O'Sullivan, Leopoldina Fortunati, Sakare Taipale and Kevin Barnhurst (O'Sullivan *et al.* 2017) discuss press innovations. Even though some believe that the print press is dead, researchers, on the contrary, take examples where newspapers on the Web have gone backwards, such as *Newsweek*, which made its comeback in 2014 after disappearing for a year.

They recall the investment of several personalities in the press, such as Warren Buffett – considered a financial guru – in regional newspapers or Jeff Bezos (CEO of Amazon) in the *Washington Post*. Researchers highlight newspaper initiatives to improve the coexistence of print press and digital press, such as QR Codes in paper articles in *La Republica* (Italy) or the *Wall Street Journal* that provide access to videos or complementary elements on the media site, or even the implementation of "augmented newspapers". For example, *Entertainment Weekly* launched video ads integrated into the newspaper in 2009. Another innovation is the use of robots – as we will see in Chapter 8 – or the use of drones for reporting.

In similar terms of innovation, two Danish journalists undertook a long investigation in search of the world's best innovation ideas. After a year of research in some 50 editorial offices in nine countries, Per Westergaard, editor-in-chief and director of several regional and national press titles, and Søren Schultz Jørgensen, a journalist for several Danish media, collected dozens of ideas in a book, the main conclusions of which were published in Nieman Lab and in an interview with Méta-Média[29].

The two journalists start from a basic assumption: the media crisis is structural and not just linked to economic models to be reviewed or technological challenges to be overcome. As the general public buys fewer

29 NiemanLab, 54 newsrooms, nine countries, and nine core ideas: Here's what two researchers found in a yearlong quest for journalism innovation, by Per Westergaard and Søren Schultz Jørgensen, July 11, 2018 and Méta-Média, *Enquête: 9 pistes explorées par les médias pour innover*, Alexandre Yeh, July 23, 2018.

newspapers or spends less time listening to radio and television, how can we reconnect journalism to citizens and restore its position? They mention nine leads. Among which, the two authors widely develop the media/journalism link: they advocate a "club" strategy, by involving communities in the life of the media (as *Mediapart* did, in addition to the *New York Times*) or by organizing conferences and festivals (such as *Le Monde*). More and more editorial offices are seeking to get closer to citizens, both through direct exchanges and meetings, in order to gather their opinions. The survey cites, for example, the German *Braunschweiger Zeitung*, which covers questions sent by its readers. In the same spirit, some media seek to go beyond distance obligations (towards companies, interest groups, etc.) by involving civil society in their work, in a process of co-creation. Some media could move from an observer status to an activist status, supporting causes, such as *The Guardian*, which has openly committed itself against Brexit.

Ultimately, the survey urges the media to make full use of journalists' skills by deploying training sessions, for example in the form of paid MOOCs[30] or diploma courses such as the FAZ Executive School MBA[31], launched in 2012 and scheduled to close in 2014. While this major attempt may have failed in its initially broad ambition, thinking about valuing skills in terms of transferring knowledge in a form to be defined remains an important subject to consider.

These examples remind us that the media are increasingly focusing on diversification. The press has thus tried to infiltrate into other professions: organization of conferences, trade fairs, training, publication of books or sporting events in the regional press, etc., using their brands as a basis.

One of the most common developments has been the one towards video. More and more media have developed video on their sites and social networks (as we will see in Chapter 6). Some have even gone further by moving closer to television or video-on-demand subscription platforms (SVOD). This is the case, for example, for *The New Yorker* magazine, which was featured in a series on Amazon Prime in 2016, or the *New York Times*, which launched a documentary series called *The Weekly* in 2018.

---

30 Like the MOOCs on the Rue89 site of the L'Obs (MOOC = Massive Open Online Course).
31 FAZ = Frankfurter Allgemeine Zeitung.

Lastly, many media have launched themselves into related professions, mainly related to trade and e-commerce, such as *Le Figaro*, a newspaper that successively acquired *Maisons du voyage* and the pure player *Marco Vasco*, which specialize in tailor-made travel. Several press titles have set up market places in recent years (e-commerce sites where products are offered in the world of articles). For example, *l'Equipe* had set up a market place around sport, which, according to the latest information, has since stopped. The Marie Claire group has also launched a market place that offers its readers the opportunity to buy cosmetic products selected from flagship brands discussed in the newspaper. Additionally, some pure players have made it their specialty and the driving force behind their revenues, such as the *MylittleParis* boxes and the e-commerce sites of the Aufeminin group (acquired by TF1).

However, diversification does not necessarily guarantee success. Condé Nast (publisher of *Vogue*), who embarked on the e-commerce adventure in 2016 with a major project, threw in the towel after a few months.

5.6. Understanding the algorithmic agenda

The media agenda function is one of the most essential functions performed by the media (McCombs and Shaw 1972). An important question is whether the agenda changes when changing technical support and when the information is offered on the Internet instead of on paper.

Evaggelia Pitoura and Panayiotis Tsaparas (Pitoura and Tsaparas 2017) are interested in the specific bias that occurs when information is online. They put forward a method to measure this bias, the essential importance of which they point out with the development of search engines and social networks. Online information providers (OIP) use algorithms to provide us with a list of selected information. This information is of any nature, be it commercial or political, according to the keywords used in the request. As we are increasingly becoming informed about the Internet, the way in which this list is drawn up is of considerable importance because it gives us the *opportunity to think* and build our opinions. POIs are frequently suspected of inducing informational bias or even participating in an era of post-truth.

Among researchers specializing in machine learning, a bias can creep into the design of an algorithm during its construction: discrimination can be introduced in the way personalized advertising is directed towards an Internet user. This type of discrimination comes in two forms: according to personal criteria (such as gender, race, income level, geographical area, etc.) or by differences in the prices of products highlighted by advertising. The research focuses not only on the bias induced by customer relationship management that is related to e-commerce and online advertising, but also on the delivery of content through platforms.

The personalization and filtering of information by algorithms places individuals in an echo chamber and in an information bubble, because algorithms generally build their filter on the preferences of individuals that have been identified from their browsing or the preferences of their friends on social networks. The idea of consuming more information on the Internet than on the paper press amplifies a phenomenon that is already present with the historical press. An individual chooses a paper journal according to its editorial line.

The phenomenon of cognitive dissonance explains the choice of a newspaper that we consider to be more credible than others, because it resonates with our beliefs and convictions. With the predominance of information consulted on the Internet, the phenomenon of cognitive dissonance would be amplified for two reasons:

– the volume of information received is increasing (in particular with the intensification of information consultation on smartphones, in which we are multiplying applications that continuously push information);

– the frequency of exposure to information is very high given that the information is produced continuously and can also be consulted continuously.

Here, Pitoura and Tsaparas distinguish two types of bias: user bias and content bias. The first bias exists if the discriminating criterion can be a source of value, in other words, if there is an increase in clicks on an advertising banner and an increase in purchases. One of the materializations of this bias is the ranking of search results in a search engine. We have all tested a search using the same keywords, but using different search engines. As they use different algorithms, the lists of results are significantly different. The modeling of the bias measurement is as follows. R_1 and R_2 are two lists provided by the search engine to two different Internet users using the same words for the search. The difficulty of the analysis is based on the need to establish an unbiased reference list. The authors suggest further research for which they propose a human-in-the-loop approach[32], a reference list established by a group of individuals replacing processors. The two researchers conclude that their article requires a strong need for research on this delicate topic.

The subject is all the more complex as algorithms are the *wealth* of companies that filter information. Indeed, the success of search engines that compete with each other is linked to the performance of the answers they provide us: speed, relevance (in our eyes) and sometimes other criteria intervene, such as the security of personal data (which is the argument put forward by the Qwant search engine). However, the performance of search engines is based on their proprietary algorithm. Access to the source codes of search engine algorithms is therefore limited, if not impossible.

Matthew Weber and Allie Kosterich (Weber and Kosterich 2018), researchers at Rutger's University, are specifically interested in application algorithms that filter the information we receive on our mobile phone. To do this, they visit the open source codes of 59 applications. The authors quote

---

32 Source: https://www.figure-eight.com/human-in-the-loop-machine-learning/.
Human-in-the-loop (HITL) is a branch of artificial intelligence that leverages both human and machine intelligence to create machine learning models. In a traditional *human-in-the-loop approach*, people are involved in a virtuous circle where they train, tune and test a particular algorithm. Generally, it works like this:
First, humans label data. This gives a model high quality (and high quantities of) training data. A machine learning algorithm learns to make decisions from this data.
Next, humans tune the model. This can happen in several different ways, but commonly, humans will score data to account for overfitting, to teach a classifier about edge cases, or new categories in the model's purview.
Finally, people can test and validate a model by scoring its outputs, especially in places where an algorithm is unconfident about a judgment or overly confident about an incorrect decision.
Now, it is important to note that each of these actions comprises a continuous feedback loop. *Human-in-the-loop* machine learning means taking each of these training, tuning and testing tasks and feeding them back into the algorithm so that it gets smarter, more confident and more accurate. This approach – especially feeding the data back into a classifier – is sometimes referred to as active learning.

Martin Baron, Executive Director of the *Washington Post*, who makes the following comment:

> "Journalism must be reinvented; the historical economic model is disintegrated... a symbiotic relationship between engineers and journalists is essential for innovation".

The article highlights the *role of the algorithm's editorial judgment* instead of that of the editor in the selection of topics, and therefore puts the algorithm forward as the one playing an editorial role. The subject is a major one given the use of mobile phones. At the same time, we spend more and more time there and consume more and more of our media. Recent studies have focused on the differences in concerns between developers and journalists. The authors conclude that the algorithms underlying the applications are motivated by technical challenges, rather than journalistic concerns. The method consists of *auditing the code*, knowing that 58% of the applications are written in Python, 31% in Java and the rest in C++. The code audit shows that 43% of applications first look for their information on social networks (Twitter, Facebook, Reddit). Additional information comes from the media (*New York Times*, *Huffington Post*) and Google News. A piece of the application code of the English newspaper *The Guardian*[33] shows that it is sustained by the *Voice of America News*[34] service.

We have just seen that economists are interested in the functioning of search engines that provide us with lists of information sources when we make keyword searches. The list is the result of an algorithm chosen by the platform. When we look at current events, sport and politics, the agenda is no longer just the one put forward by the media. The agenda, the prioritization of information, can be the result of a computer program that chooses the relevance of the proposed information. If historical media sometimes have informational biases that are related to economic pressures or the beliefs of journalists or owners, what about algorithms? Do they provide us with what we are asking for or the information that will allow us

---

33 The excerpt from the code is reproduced in the article on page 10.
```
<outline category="en_US" text="VOA News"
htmlUrl="http://www.voanews.com/api/epiqq"
xmlUrl="http://www.voanews.com/api/epiqq" />
```
34 For *Voice of America News*, see https://www.voanews.com.

to make informed decisions? It must be remembered that search engines are free of charge. They are remunerated by selling advertising space or by auctioning the keywords we use. In the first case, it involves selling a banner, a pop-up and any other form of advertising display positioned on our screen when we use the Internet. In the second case, it involves selling a position at the top of the proposed list in response to a keyword.

The digitalization of information leads to profound changes. One of the most important is related to the development of social networks, as we will see in the next chapter.

Are There Dangerous Links between Media and Social Networks?

Je t'aime, moi non plus… "I love you, me neither" – this could reflect the love/hate relationship between the media and social networks.

6.1 The indispensable social networks

Social networks have become essential for information. According to the Digital News Report 2017 (Newman *et al.* 2017) study published by the Reuters Institute Study for Journalism, 51% of U.S. residents use social networks to access information, 5 points more than the previous year and almost twice as many as in 2013. However, this does not mean that they are totally neglecting other media: only 2% solely use social networks.

Among young people, the trend is even bigger. Across all countries, one third of 18–24 year olds report that social networks are now their primary source of information. In this age group of *millennials*, social networks (33%) are ahead of television (24%) as the primary source of information. The phenomenon tends to be generational given that, conversely, among those over 55 years of age, the percentage is only 7%.

It is striking to note that only 5% of 18–24 year olds indicate that the press is their primary source of information (compared to 11% of those over 55).

The Reuters study also looked at algorithms and shows that readers are primarily faced with selections made by robots (whether in social networks or search engines, etc.) rather than by a human (e-mail, mobile notification, etc.): 54% of respondents said they had accessed information the previous week mainly via an algorithm (54%) rather than from a publisher (44%). This is even more true for those under 35 years of age (64% via algorithms).

As a result, readers are increasingly exposed to sources that they did not necessarily want at the basic level. In total, 36% of respondents who use social networks indicated that they read information from media that they did not usually use.

However, the 2017 study remarks that access via social networks is declining in several countries. For example, in France, 38% of respondents used social networks as a source of information, down 2 points over a year. The authors of the report suggest several possible explanations: it could be due to a saturation of the market, or a change in Facebook's algorithm giving priority to friends, but it could also be the fact that Internet users are abandoning social networks in favor of messaging applications.

This trend is confirmed by the latest Reuters Institute study (Newman *et al.* 2018) published in 2018: the use of social networks to access information has declined in several countries. In the United States, the percentage of people using Facebook as a source of information dropped 9 points in one year (to 39%). The authors of the study of 74,000 people in 37 countries point out that this is probably a consequence of the sharp increase in the use of social networks at the time of Donald Trump's election. But it is not that alone, given that in the United Kingdom and other countries, the downward trend can also be observed. This is despite the fact that Facebook's use for its other purposes has remained relatively stable since 2015. The authors point out that most of the study was conducted before the change in Facebook's algorithm at the beginning of the year, which has since led to a decline in information content.

One of the reasons for the decline of Mark Zuckerberg's network is the rise of messaging companies such as WhatsApp, particularly in specific countries. For example, in Malaysia, 54% of respondents use WhatsApp to get information and comment on current events (up 3 points), while in Brazil, the percentage is 48%. WhatsApp and Instagram are growing strongly in Latin America and Asia.

Snapchat is a free application created in 2011 that is growing more and more in the United States and Europe. It is particularly popular among young people. The authors particularly point out that when commenting on current events, respondents prefer messaging services that have a higher regard for privacy, but nevertheless continue to use large networks (such as Facebook) to search for information.

6.1.1. *Strategies to take advantage of social networks*

Most media have developed strategies to make the best use of social networks. Most of them post content on Facebook, Twitter, etc. in order to make themselves known. Some people buy advertising on Facebook to promote articles.

Many newspapers also use social networking tools such as *Instant Articles*, a "new" way to access articles without leaving Facebook, allowing for optimized reading and faster loading of articles or AMP (Google). These tools generate audiences that are far from neutral for the press.

Many media have gone one step further, and have chosen social networks as their only channel of distribution. For example, this is the case of *MinuteBuzz* in France: the media for young people, recently acquired by TF1, closed its site in 2016 and has since completely moved to social networks, in order to better adapt to the practices of its readers. This media, which indicates that it reaches 12 million people a day, 80% of them being "millennials"[1], posts several videos a day, mainly on Facebook.

Other media companies have also completely moved to social networks. Emmanuel Chain's French production company, *Elephant*, also launched *Monkey* in November 2017, which is 100% social and video, and which deciphers a current topic in three minutes every day. The objective is to seduce young people attracted by the image and summarized information.

More recently, in April 2018, Prisma Media[2] launched *Simone*, new French media that is exclusively video and digital. *Simone* initially planned to post one to five videos a day on major social networks, including Facebook, as well as on *Femme actuelle*'s website, so as to give it visibility. This is the first launch dedicated to the social networks of the Prisma Group's women's division, with the aim of attracting a younger readership. At

---

1 LesEchos.fr, TF1 brought 20% more revenue to *MinuteBuzz*, Madelaine, N., April 25, 2018.
2 LesEchos.fr, Prisma launches new 100% video media, Alcaraz, M., April 22, 2018.

about the same time, *Le Figaro* also launched *Mad*, with short fashion-oriented videos for 25–35 year olds on social networks and *Madame Figaro*'s website.

As for historical media, such as the French regional daily press, Nathalie Pignard-Cheynel and Brigitte Sebbagh (Pignard-Cheynel and Sebbagh 2012) developed an analysis of 58 regional press titles in 2012 and highlight a low production of journalism that is specifically dedicated to social networks, as well as a modest interactivity between regional press titles and their readers.

6.1.2. *Media at the mercy of networks*

However, social networks are far from being a gold mine for the media in many regards. This is firstly because the media are at the mercy of algorithm changes.

In January 2018, Facebook announced a change of algorithm giving priority to family and friends, thus reducing the share of media. Mark Zuckerberg then estimated that sharing of news should increase from 5% to 4% on Facebook pages. The result: the traffic brought to publishers by Facebook has decreased worldwide since the beginning of January, according to Chartbeat figures that were published in mid-February 2018 and taken over by Digiday[3]. Google is thus in front of Facebook. The media have suffered. For example, at the end of February in the United States, *LittleThings*, a lifestyle specialist (cooking, beauty advice, etc.), announced that it would be closing its doors and laying off 100 employees because of the sharp drop in its traffic.

The media were forced to seek a solution by diversifying their focal points in order to reduce their "Facebook dependency". They have all implemented strategies ranging from explaining how to keep appearing on their readers' feeds to setting up groups based on affinities and interests. Many of them favored articles or photos that encouraged interaction, "likes", etc., with readers, in order to be given more prominence.

As for Google and, more generally, GAFA, they are trying to show their support and multiply initiatives in favor of the media. For example, in 2013, Google launched a fund for digital press innovation in France. With a budget

---

3 Digiday, "As promised, Facebook traffic to news publishers declines again, post news-feed change", Moses, L., February 19, 2018.

of €60 million over three years, it was intended to promote the "long-term development" of the online press providing political and general information in France. This fund was replaced by another Europe-level fund at the end of 2015, as part of the €150 million Digital News Initiative. Then, in March 2018, Google launched a new program for publishers around the world, this time investing $300 million over three years. This program includes several focuses, including work on algorithms, and also subscription solutions ("subscribe with Google") for the media. The user can thus directly subscribe to newspapers – initially, mainly the English-speaking press – and Google charges a commission.

6.1.3. *The media brand is fading away behind the social network brand*

One of the criticisms made to social networks by the media is that they cut the link with the reader. And indeed, the media brand often disappears.

In a study conducted by Media Insight Project (involving the American Press Institute and The AP-NORC Center) in the United States, 1500 Internet users were interviewed[4] in order to understand how these people placed their trust in sources of information on social networks. The verdict is irrevocable: the person who shares information has more influence than the source itself, as we will also see in the next chapter on "fake news". Similarly, they remember the person who shared the article more than the source itself.

Another conclusion that can also be found in the Reuters Study of Journalism[5] study of British respondents: about two-thirds of respondents recalled the path by which they found information (Google, Facebook, etc.), but less than half recalled the original source of the information itself when it

---

4 Media Insight Project (2017). 'Who Shared It?': How Americans Decide What News to Trust on Social Media. Published on March 20, 2017. The study was conducted between November 9 and December 6, 2016 via online interviews with 1489 Americans. Available at: https://www.americanpressinstitute.org/publications/reports/survey-research/trust-social-media/.
5 Newman, N. and Kalogeropoulos, P. (2017). I saw the News on Facebook – Brand Attribution from Distributed Environments. The study was conducted in March and April 2017. Available at: http://www.digitalnewsreport.org/publications/2017/i-saw-news-facebook-brand-attribution-distributed-environments/ [Accessed May 1, 2018].

came from a search engine (37%) or social networks (47%). People who have already been in touch with a media brand remember it better.

6.1.4. *The problem of revenue sharing between media and social networks*

The other major criticism that the media is making of social networks is about revenue sharing. The media produce information, and social networks distribute it. What distribution key should be adopted in order to share the advertising revenues that are essential to both?

The French digital advertising market is growing more and more, but this increase is mainly in favor of GAFA. Investments increased by 12% in 2017, compared with 8% in 2016, according to the SRI (*Syndicat des régies Internet*, Union of Internet agencies) and Udecam (*Union des entreprises de conseil et achat media*, Union of consulting and media buying companies) e-pub observatory, conducted by PwC. This is the strongest growth in four years. The e-pub has thus reached the symbolic milestone of €4 billion (€4.094 billion, more precisely), affirming its leading media position. The digital market had surpassed television in 2016 and remains well ahead in 2017.

In this context, Google and Facebook represent approximately 78% of the market – excluding comparators, affiliations and emails – compared to 76% in 2016. They alone capture 92% of digital growth. In the background, other traditional media (press, television, radio) therefore share the rest. The trend was the same in the first half of 2018, according to data from the e-pub observatory, published in the summer of 2018. The Google and Facebook platforms account for the bulk (79%) of digital investments, 93% of them being on mobile.

In an attempt to fight the Internet giants, the media have tried to put initiatives in place. This is the case, for example, of *Alliance Gravity*, which was created in 2017. This group, dedicated to optimizing the sale of online advertising space, included more than 25 publishers of press and e-commerce sites (including *Prisma, Lagardère Active, Fnac Darty, SFR, M6, Les Echos, L'Equipe, SoLocal* or more recently the *NRJ Group, Mondadori 3W Régie*, publishing director of the *Cdiscount.com* site, etc.) at the end of 2017. With the guiding idea that unity is strength, the members of the alliance pool their data to rely on the (automated) programmatic advertising market, which is largely dominated by GAFA. With nearly 50% daily coverage of the Internet user population (17.8 million individuals) at the end of 2017, *Alliance Gravity* was the third most powerful offer on the market behind Google and Facebook. It targeted 15% of the (automated) programmatic advertising market by 2021 in France, representing approximately €200 million in revenue.

Le Monde and *Le Figaro* also decided to join forces, announcing in the summer of 2017 that they would market their most sought-after (premium) digital advertising spaces (videos and banners) as part of an alliance called Skyline.

Apple:

Sales (financial year 2017): $229.2 billion

Market capitalization (end of July 2018): approximately 922 billion. At the beginning of August 2018, the group even crossed the very symbolic threshold of $1 trillion of capitalization! Apple alone thus weighs as much as the 10 largest stocks in the CAC 40 index and as much as Mexico's GDP, according to *Les Echos* in August 2018. The share has increased by a factor of 48 since March 2000.

Amazon:

Sales: $177.9 billion

Capitalization: approximately 867 billion

Google – Alphabet:

Sales: $110.9 billion

Capitalization: approximately 850 billion

Facebook:

Sales: $40.6 billion

Capitalization: approximately 500 billion

That is a cumulative income of almost $560 billion. These GAFA figures show their cumulative income is higher than Denmark's GDP in 2016.

Cumulative capitalization (end of July): more than $3.1 trillion.

Box 6.1. *Understanding the supremacy of GAFA*

6.2. The social network eco-system

Economists are interested in social networks because they are the places where effects that are well known to economists are manifested: externalities. In other words, interactions between individuals generate effects associated with individual choices that can return to affect the individual, either positively (positive externalities – I plant flowers on my balcony that other individuals look at) or negatively (negative externalities – I barbecue on that same balcony and the wind blows the smoke into my neighbor's house). As Matthew Jackson, professor in Stanford's Department of Economics, Brian Rogers and Yves Zenou (Jackson *et al.* 2016; Jackson 2014) point out, social networks systematically produce externalities. This implies that the economist must take an interest in:

– the way in which social networks are built. Individuals do not necessarily realize the societal impact of their behaviors in social networks, nor the opportunity cost (mainly in time) involved in maintaining their social networks (negative externalities);

– the way in which social networks can become facilitators in education, in the fight against crime or in the implementation of new technology (positive externalities).

Aldabert Mayer (Mayer 2009), the Washington College Economics Chair, shows that economic analysis is particularly useful in four areas where social networks are substantial: the labor market, the financial market, international trade and economic development.

6.2.1. *The influence of social networks*

While the general influence of the media (and particularly the Internet) on the effectiveness of public policies and corruption has been studied extensively – demonstrating a positive relationship between media distribution, press freedom and public performance, as shown by Rajeev Goel, Michael Nelson and Michael Naretta (Goel *et al.* 2012), among others – similar analyses have been conducted specifically on social networks.

Do media-powered social networks (e.g. journalists' social networks) play a comparable and complementary role in historical media with regard to monitoring public policies?

Chandar Kumar Jla and Sidipa Sarangi (Jla and Sarangi 2017), both economists and researchers in Syracuse – New York State – and Berlin, ask this question in a study of 150 countries. The study is based on the CCI (Control of Corruption Index), established by the World Bank, and the ICRG (International Country Risk Guide), established by the private group PRS (which measures country risks). The penetration rate of social networks is calculated from several sources, such as QUINTLY[6] for Facebook. The results are that the link is clearly positive and that the effects are even stronger when other media (and in particular the press) are not free. In other words, social networks have a beneficial effect on country risk and the reduction of corruption.

Ruben Enikolopov, Maria Petrova and Konstantin Sonin (Eniklopov *et al.* 2018), who have already conducted studies on the link between historical media and the reduction of corruption, expand the analysis to social networks with a methodology that is similar to the one used by Jla and Sarangi. The three researchers mainly focus on non-democratic countries, in which press freedom is restricted and focus on Russia. The question asked concerns the quality of the information relayed in social networks.

Since the cost of entry is very low (nothing could be easier than opening a Facebook or Twitter account), governments can easily deploy propaganda messages on it. The link between the development of social networks and the effectiveness of public policies may not be systematic. In order to address this sensitive issue, the authors act in three stages. They conduct an impact study of the messages broadcast on social networks and concerning the corruption of government-owned company executives. The authors then analyze the effects to see if they are short-term effects or if the development of social networks leads to a sustainable change in leaders' behaviors. Lastly, the authors look more closely at the comments made on social networks by Alexei Navalny, the host of a very popular blog in Russia before he became an important political figure. The Russian version of @navalny, created in October 2009, was followed by 2.22 million readers in 2017.

Despite significant waves of privatization since the 1990s, many companies are still state-owned and represent more than 50% of GDP. Social networks are being developed in Russia, with the authors predicting an

---

6 See the site: https://www.quintly.com. The QUINTLY company markets statistics on social media usage (*analytics methods*).

average use of more than 10 hours per month in 2012. In the same year, Russia had 60 million active Internet users out of a total population of 144 million, or about 40%. One of the most popular social networks is *Livejournal*[7]. This is a site created in the United States that hosts 45% of blogs run by Russians. Russian social networks enjoy relative freedom of expression. The study was conducted from January 2008 to August 2011. The main results are that the influence of social networks on corruption is real, despite the presence of messages infiltrated by the government, and that the influence is all the stronger as the message sender does so in the name of the fight against corruption (there is a strong link between Navalny's posts and the stock market listing of companies whose corrupt attitude he criticizes).

Seok-Jin Eom, Hanchan Hwang and Jun Houng Kim (Eom *et al.* 2018), three researchers at Seoul University in South Korea, ask a similar question: does social media improve government response? The authors note that there is little research on whether the use of social media by local elected officials (mayors) leads to a more responsive national public administration. To do this, the authors conduct a study on the interactions between the Mayor of Seoul, the local government and citizens via Twitter. The research results show that the Mayor of Seoul plays the most important role. The study was carried out over one year (November 2015 to September 2016). It covers a selection of different hashtags such as *#SeoulCity*. The mayor's role as a hub in the Twitter network helps to improve the government's responsiveness by overcoming the disconnection between citizens and local government, in addition to the asymmetry of information between the mayor, civil servants and citizens.

We are increasingly consuming information from the recommendations of our close and distant friends, on social networks that we visit more and more frequently on the applications on our smartphones. And when we do not use social networks, we have a strong inclination to *google* everything that happens within reach of our desire for information, whether during a dinner with friends or at work. Mario Gambaro (Gambaro 2014) also notes that the world of social networks is particularly sensitive to the distribution

---

7 See the site: https://www.livejournal.com. "LiveJournal is a unique place where people share their life stories, give advice and exchange ideas. Join the community and share your stories".

of images and videos, and that their use is and will be strongly developed by the media as a source of virality, and therefore of audience and advertising revenue.

6.2.2. *The way in which we inform ourselves is not unbiased*

In a 2018 article (Kennedy and Prat 2018), Patrick Kennedy and Andrea Prat ask themselves "how do people get informed?". Their article echoes recent U.S. political events. Many observers have questioned the role played by social networks used by U.S. residents, or possibly powered by other countries, concerning the election of President Trump. Facebook was largely pointed out. In particular, in the summer of 2017, the U.S.-based firm acknowledged that fake accounts had purchased advertising on its platform during the campaign in order to promote messages that were "likely to divide the population". "Our investigation suggests that these accounts and the pages linked to them were operating from Russia", Facebook's security director said at the time.

We know what the market share of television channels is, but surveys are necessary in order to know which of the channels an individual may watch in order to obtain political information. The question is even more critical when it comes to knowing whether an individual is informed by the multiplicity of websites or by the recommendations of their social networks. The data used by Kennedy and Prat are those of the Reuters Institute for Study of Journalism in 2015, which we have detailed earlier in this chapter. This is a survey conducted in 18 countries (including France) on 31,000 people (approximately 2,000 people per country). The survey was conducted online and therefore carries risks of underestimating the results for countries that are still poorly equipped (e.g. the equipment rate in Turkey is 56%, compared to 96% in Denmark). In each country, a focus was placed on the 15 most significant media groups.

The results show that in all countries combined, 80% of individuals first get information on political issues from television, 40% also get information from newspapers and 25% get information from the Internet (social sites or networks). Internet sources are also more commonly used when they come from media. On average, each individual gets information from five different sources, even in countries with a very wide range of political information.

Additional research was conducted by Reuters in six countries, which asked participants about their political affiliation.

There is another interesting result. In all the countries observed, the concentration of information sources is significant. In every country, at least one media press attracts 14% of people's attention. Another significant result is that the consumption of political information depends on many criteria. Thus, graduates over the age of 65, CSP+, consume twice as much political information as young people over 25, CSP-, who do not have a diploma. There is therefore an inequality of access to political information. Based on the GINI coefficient used to measure income inequality, the authors construct a GINI coefficient for political information. The coefficient shows a high inequality in the United States that is much higher than that observed in Western European countries. In the last part of their article, Djankov and Prat ask themselves whether public media are able to reduce this inequality. The answer given by the two researchers is a negative one, since individuals who use public media are generally older, richer and more educated than those who consume little political information (young people with low incomes and low degrees) and who also consume private media as a priority.

In 2017, Xiaoli Luo (Luo 2017), from the University of Shenzhen, was one of the first to integrate social networks as an additional player in game theory modeling, in order to analyze information bias. Luo introduces two categories of individuals: *partisans* who have a strong presence on social networks and *non-partisans* who learn about social networks, but are not active producers of information. Taking social networks into account led him to define what he calls a collective bias, the extent of which depends on the proportion of *partisan* individuals.

That being said, Qin, from the University of Hong Kong, David Stromberg and Yanhui Wu, researchers at the University of South California, wonder why Chinese political authorities give a certain degree of freedom by allowing the use of social networks (Qin *et al.* 2017). They analyzed the content of 13 billion posts on the Sina Weibo platform between 2009 and 2013. Weibo was opened in 2009: it is a platform whose characteristics are similar to a mix between Twitter and Facebook. They were surprised to find many posts challenging official information or denouncing acts of corruption. Weibo is a very popular platform, given that 50% of Chinese people have access to the Internet and 20% of Chinese people use Weibo. Given the number of visitors to this network, the posts can therefore be significant in terms of influence.

Current technologies make it possible to identify the content of a post as well as its sender and readers. Knowing who reads what, who is commenting on who on a social network, is easy. It would therefore be easy for the Chinese authorities to take action against the critics. The authors give two reasons to explain the relative freedom of expression on Chinese social networks. The first is that it allows the authorities to identify dissidents or disgruntled people, to control them and to monitor the possible evolution of the protest in order to decide when to act against it. An apparently free social network is actually a surveillance network. The second is linked to the desire of the central government to be better informed about the behavior of local governments, which have many responsibilities. Observing the content of posts allows the central government to be informed of local corruption or local government deficiencies. Here again, the social network becomes a tool for political monitoring. Monitoring is twofold: by the Party on individuals and by the Party on the Party. In turn, the government directly uses social networks as a propaganda tool by posting information on them. By identifying keywords, the authors identified approximately 600,000 accounts that were directly managed by the government under different pseudonyms. These accounts generate about 4% of the published posts. This article shows that it is not necessarily in a government's interest to ban social networks. The social networks can be used to their advantage as a tool for control and propaganda.

Recently too, in 2017, Kirill Pogorelski, a researcher at the University of Warwick, and Matthew Shum, a researcher at CalTech, (Pogorelski and Shum 2017) published a working paper in which they analyzed the consequences of new ways of getting information. Pew Research Center surveys conducted in the United States in 2015 show that 61% of U.S. residents between the ages of 18 and 33 are using Facebook, compared to 39% of baby boomers. The characteristic of social networks is the way in which information is circulated, which is more likely to be accessed by the account holder if it is recommended (liked) by a network member who has been accepted as a friend. Individuals are thus in their own filter bubble (Pariser 2011)[8], *surrounded by invisible self-propaganda, and indoctrinated by their own opinions.* Studies show that individuals who indicate their political preference on their profile generally have a network of friends with similar profiles. The authors conducted an experimental economics test with students from Warwick Business School in June, July and August 2016, in two or three groups of 10. Each test lasted between 50 and 80 minutes. A total of 450 students participated. The initial media bias is accentuated by the information circuit within social networks. The authors conclude that the quality of initial information is essential in order to avoid the problematic effects of the information bubble that each individual creates for themselves on their social networks. David Siegel (Siegel 3013) also mentioned the risk of amplifying the *status quo* (in other words, the immobility of positions or beliefs), due to the fact that individuals select their preferences when accessing media.

6.2.3. *The influence of social networks on decisions*

In a recent article, Levi Boxell and Matthew Shapiro, professors at Stanford, along with Jesse Shapiro (Boxell *et al.* 2017), a professor at Brown University, look at the influence of information viewed on the Internet with regard to individuals' political choices and voting. To do this, they combine various measures in order to establish an index of political polarization. The result highlighted by the three researchers is that the intensification of polarization in recent years is stronger for a demographic group that is less likely to use the Internet and social networks. Thus, polarization is stronger among the elderly than among young people who are aged 18–39. In 2012, only 20% of people over 75 years old used the Internet and social networks, compared to 80% of those who were aged 18–35. This result contradicts the

---

8 The *filter bubble* expression is due to Eli Pariser in his 2011 book.

There are two types of filters: filters that individuals voluntarily choose using the personalization options provided by social networks, and filters set up by social networks using an algorithm that is based on information collected on individual choices from our behaviors on the networks.

For a description of these two types of filters, see the study conducted by four female Master's students at the University of Amsterdam in 2017.

https://mastersofmedia.hum.uva.nl/blog/2017/10/25/face-the-bubble-revealing-how-facebook-selects-users-news-stories.

echo chamber hypothesis that makes the Internet an essential source of polarization. The method used by the three researchers is based on nine polarization measures, established by political science researchers. The three authors identify polarization through responses to questionnaires.

There is a great deal of research on this topic in political science, as well as scientific publications on the notion and causes of polarization (Farrell 2012). In 1960, 5% of Democrats or Republicans said that they were "embarrassed by the fact that their son or daughter married someone with beliefs pertaining to the opposite party to their own". This figure has risen sharply as the answer to the same question was shared by 50% of Republicans and 30% of Democrats in 2010. Polarization is significant for both the youthful and elderly populations (+0.38 index points for those over 75 years of age and +0.05 points for those who are younger), with a higher degree of polarization for the elderly. It is also possible that the polarization of young people is due to social networks, while it is due to other factors for older people. The study was conducted from 1996, when the first surveys on Internet use were conducted, to 2012. The database for elections is ANES (American National Election Studies), which is commonly used in this type of study because it contains many variables describing the profile of voters (including the percentage of voters with access to the Internet). The Pew Research Center database has also been used since 2005, when the institute began investigating the use of social networks.

Pablo Barbera (Barbera 2015; Barbera and Rivero 2015)[9], a researcher at New York University, is interested in Twitter users and their political choices. He also questions the *echo chamber* hypothesis. He points out that an individual present on social networks is well-connected, because of the very functioning of the network and the intertwining of recommendations between Internet users with information from outside of the chamber, in other words, information that the Internet user would not have found had they not gone through the complex paths of information on the Internet. Social networks would therefore be factors of political depolarization. Barbera built a model that allowed him to test this hypothesis on several thousand voters in three countries: Germany, Spain and the United States. The author highlights the

---

9 The authors make a similar analysis of the parliamentary elections in Spain.

importance of weak ties, in the sense of Granovetter (Granovetter 2000)[10], in relation to the strong community ties of beliefs that most of us have with our friends or followers on social networks.

His findings oppose those of Michael Conover, Bruno Goncalves, Alessandro Flammini and Filippo Menczer (Conover *et al.* 2012) at Northeastern University in Boston, who studied 18,000 Twitter users during the mid-term elections of the U.S. Congress over an 18-week period from September 2010 to January 2011, during which 6747 Republican users and 10,741 Democratic users produced 1.39 and 2.4 million tweets respectively. Here, the researchers' findings point towards the use of social networks to accelerate the circulation of one-party information within a group of followers. The identification of political preferences is based on the hashtags used and subscriptions to politicians' threads[11]. The authors find that Twitter users are increasing political publications and viewing a greater number of posts with political content. This political activity is more intense among Republican Internet users, who more systematically broadcast the tweets received and distribute them to a larger number of people.

Mario Haim, Andreas Graefe and Hans-Bernd Brosius (Haim *et al.* 2017) also relativize the filter bubble hypothesis that makes individuals "blind" by hyper-selecting the information filtered by the platforms. They study how *Google News* works and do not see a polarization of information according to individuals. In the face of these contradictory results, research on this important subject is very intense and must continue.

Che-Yuan Liang and Mattias Nordin (Liang and Nordin 2012), researchers at Uppsala University, show that there is a limited influence of technological developments on political attitudes, since they show that there has been little

---

10 In this book, which develops his 1973 founding article, the author clarifies the concepts of links. His contribution is to have demonstrated the *strength of weak ties* and the importance of *embedding individual relationships*. An individual belongs to a group (strong link), and also has links with individuals belonging to other groups (weak links). This link of a second nature allows a circulation of new information. Thus, Granovetter showed the essential role of personal networks in job searching (in his 1973 article, he showed that 50% of the individuals in his sample had found a job through their network).

11 A similar approach is made from the information posted by Internet users on the Facebook network. Bond, R. and Messing, S. (2014). "Quantifying Social Media's Political Space: Estimating Ideology from Publicly Revealed Preferences on Facebook". *American Political Science Review*, 109 (1), 62–78.

change after the transition from Internet to broadband. The study covered Sweden from 2002 to 2007, while Nicholas Davis, from the University of Louisiana, and Johanna Dunaway, from TAMU University (Texas), (Davis and Dunaway 2016) highlight a mixed relationship between the Internet and political positions. Their study shows that the impact is stronger on individuals who already had a strong political commitment before the development of social networks.

The Pew Research Center has classified Twitter conversations into five categories[12]:

– polarized or thematic conversations (communities are boxed in on a theme);

– tightened conversations (around a hashtag with few exchanges with other conversations);

– brand conversations (conversations dedicated to a brand or a political party);

– circulation conversations (usually around a current topic and from an information source, such as media or a journalist);

– support conversations (a conversation whose meaning has been reversed to the original source of information, either to support or, on the contrary, to denounce a defective product, for example).

Box 6.2. *Twitter conversations*

6.3. Social networks are transforming the information business

The development of social networks has important consequences for the profession of journalists. They are strongly present in different ways.

6.3.1. *Journalists in networks*

Journalist directly feed into the network (e.g. by following the threads of politicians) or write directly (by editing their own news feed – many journalists are present on Twitter, for example) or indirectly via the media

---

12 "Mapping Twitter topic networks: From polarized crowds to community clusters". http://www.pewinternet.org/files/2014/02/PIP_Mapping-Twitter-networks_022014.pdf.

that employs them, which are often present on social networks[13]. An example of this is the journalist David Fahrenthold of the *Washington Post*, who won the Pulitzer Prize[14] for national reporting for "a model of transparent journalism", after asking his Twitter subscribers to help track Donald Trump's donations to charities.

Social networks are also a place of expression for amateur journalism, also known as *citizen journalism*. Journalists in some media have experimented, as Frank Rebillard (Rebillard 2011) reports, with "regulated participatory journalism consisting of co-production between non-professionals and professionals", without the experimentation leading to a more developed mode of article production.

There are many journalists' books that reflect the questions of a profession facing profound changes (Antheaume 2016; De Biaf 2015; Degand and Grevisse 2012; Malka 2016). Researchers are also very present and question ongoing developments (Alloing and Pierre 2017; Burger *et al.* 2017; Jeanne-Perrier 2018; Mercier and Pignard-Cheynel 2018). As Mike Friedrichsen and Wolfgang Mühl-Benninghaus, editors of the *Handbook of Social Media Management*, point out:

> "social networks are on the agenda of all media and journalists" (Friedrichsen and Mühl-Benninghaus 2017).

We could also add "of all researchers".

Na Yeon Lee and Yonghwan Kim, researchers at Sungshin University in Seoul, and Yoonmo Sang, of Howard University in Washington, D.C., examine the factors that influence patterns of use of Twitter by journalists (Lee *et al.* 2017). The study covers 163 journalists working in the

---

13 Let us quote a Parisian example and one from the south of France. The national daily newspaper *Les Echos* has a variety of different Twitter accounts, the main one being *@lesechos* with 1.15 million subscribers (May 2018), as well as: *@LesEchosWeekend*, *@LesEchosTechMedias*, *@LesEchosExecutive*, *@LeCercledesEchos* and *@LesEchosStart*. A large number of *Les Echos* journalists have their own Twitter feed. The media is also present on several other social networks, including Facebook.
The regional daily newspaper *La Provence* has about 500,000 followers on its Facebook site. https://fr-fr.facebook.com/laprovence and is present on Twitter (210,000 followers).
14 See also: https://www.huffingtonpost.fr/2017/04/10/les-prix-pulitzer-recompensent-trois-journaux-que-trump-ne-peut_a_22034413/.

national press. Journalists use Twitter for several reasons: their own promotion, providing continuous information, interacting with their readers and seeking information.

Many media outlets have recognized the potential of social media as a journalistic tool and have used social media marketing to attract online audiences. Sounman Hong (Hong 2012), a Harvard professor, proposes a study whose objective is to measure the impact of a media presence on a social network. The study focuses on the presence of media on Twitter. Online traffic is measured by the number of unique visitors, based on monthly data from 337 U.S. daily newspapers (with a website) between January 2007 and December 2010. The data comes from COMSCORE and COMPETE. The year 2007 is important because Twitter was launched in July 2006. The results show that the adoption of social media by newspapers is positively associated with an increase in their online readership, and that this association increases the size of newspapers' social media networks (here, the number of followers on Twitter).

In a 2015 paper (Zeller and Hermida 2015), Frauze Zeller and Alfred Hermida study the impact of social networks on journalistic practices, through interviews with nine professionals in Canada (online media executives and journalists). Although this sample is small, as the authors of the article themselves agree, it provides some insight. One of the ideas that emerged was that everyone can create information, but the journalist has an "auditor" role and is viewed as someone who can confirm a credible source of information. One of the journalists interviewed highlighted the risk that a journalist might only give his opinion on his personal Twitter account, for example. Lastly, the authors point out that concerns about the impact of immediacy on the quality of information are relatively absent in the interviewees' talks. "The increased speed of information due to social networks is therefore assessed as a positive development" that could allow journalists to be more responsive.

6.3.2. The role of social network algorithms

As we saw in a previous chapter, algorithms have an important influence.

Michael Devito (Devito 2017) is particularly interested in the case of the Facebook news feed. The functioning of Facebook's news feed is partially described on the social network site[15]:

> "Posts that you see in News Feed are meant to keep you connected to the people, places and things that you care about, starting with your friends and family. Posts that you see first are influenced by your connections and activity on Facebook. The number of comments, likes and reactions a post receives and what kind of story it is (example: photo, video, status update) can also make it more likely to appear higher up in your News Feed. Posts that you might see first include:
>
> – a friend or family member commenting on or liking another friend's photo or status update,
>
> – a person reacting to a post from a publisher that a friend has shared,
>
> – multiple people replying to each other's comments on a video they watched or an article they read in News Feed".

Unable to directly access the code of the news feed algorithm, Devito overcomes this difficulty. He analyzes the content of Facebook's patents, brand press releases and Securities and Exchange Commission reports in order to identify a set of algorithmic values that determine the selection of information on the Facebook news feed. The author's hypothesis is that "algorithms necessarily have embedded values during their design by their encoder" (p. 5).

The notion of "embedded values" is developed by Tarleton Gillespie, who details the algorithm's promise of *objectivity* (Gillespie 2014), often announced when these new technologies emerge. The hypothesis of an algorithm with less ideological bias due to its algorithmic nature has often been put forward as a challenge to better understand how people construct algorithms.

The study of the indirect sources of information retained by Devito during the 2006–2014 period highlights nine criteria that seem essential regarding the way in which Facebook operates: relationships with

---

15 See https://www.facebook.com/help/327131014036297/.

friends, interests explicitly expressed by users, prior commitments of users, implicitly expressed user preferences, age, platform priorities, the relationship page, negatively expressed preferences and content quality. However, the essential criterion retained by the content provider, the most important criterion, which largely dominates all the others, is "friends' preferences". This result raises concerns for an individual who mainly consumes information via Facebook, with the possibility of locking himself or herself in an echo chamber caused by the polarization of the information received. The author talks about a personalization of news from the algorithm (algorithmically driven personalization of news) and emphasizes that this trend is not only specific to Facebook, but also to other social networks operating on similar logic.

In an article published in the same year, Michael Devito, Darren Gergle and Jeremy Bimboltz (Devito *et al.* 2017), three researchers at Northwestern University, studied the social network Twitter. They analyzed 102,827 tweets from #RIPTwitter. Announcements of changes in Twitter's operating mode multiplied in 2016: from rumors announcing the end of the 140-character limit to the announcement of the arrival of a new algorithm. Since then, users, annoyed by these rumors and worried about possible changes, have taken the initiative to create a hashtag of dissatisfaction: #RIPTwitter. By analyzing the content of the tweets, the authors highlight a strong resistance to change, which can be explained by the mystery surrounding the algorithms used. With little or no information about the content of algorithms, users rely on their use of them to build trust. It is their use of it, in addition to the satisfactions or disappointments that they experience, that serves to build their judgment, trust or mistrust. Testing its use takes time, so algorithm changes are badly perceived because they challenge the *status quo* and involve restarting the essential period of testing that individuals implicitly carry out.

Tetyana Lokot and Nicholas Diakopoulos (Lokot and Diakopoulos 2015) also focus on the robots used by the social network Twitter, after noticing that the robots are also used by Facebook, Reddit and Wikipedia. They interact with users and produce content in different ways. The authors specify that 8.5% of Twitter accounts and 7% of Facebook accounts were automated (by a robot) in 2014.

Lisa George, a professor of Economics at CUNY – City University of New York, and Christiaan Hogendorn (George and Hogendorn 2013), an economist at Wesleyan University in Middletown, Connecticut, are interested in *Google News* in 2010, because it was then (June 30, 2010) that Google modified its interface to add automatic user geolocation. The researchers then ask themselves whether the design change in the algorithm has an influence on the viewing of media sites. By analyzing the visits of 43,087 users from the ComScore Web Behavior database, the authors show that the modification of the algorithm led to an increase in the number of visits to local press sites (in other words, corresponding to geolocation). However, the increase was small (4 to 6%).

6.3.3. *The impact of social network development on the quality of information*

Alexandre De Corniere and Miklos Sarvary (De Corniere and Sarvary 2018) highlight another key issue. The two economists – the first is a researcher at the Toulouse School of Economics and the second is a professor at Columbia Business School – are examining the consequences of platform development (synonymous with social networking) on competition between media and, consequently, on the quality of information. In order to do this, they build a model in which the platform is in a monopoly. There are two types of content: what the authors call *news*, produced by journalists on media sites, and information produced by UGC (user-generated content[16]). Individuals are heterogeneous, that is, they prefer one form of information or another. The platform uses an algorithm (newsfeed) that it formats to mix the two types of information and chooses the proportion of news presented to the platform's users. If the news appears on the platform, then the advertising revenue from this exhibition is shared between it and the media. The main purpose of a platform is to distribute UGC content, for which it does not have to share revenues, between its members.

As more and more of us use social networks and our time is consumed, just as our attention is, the strategy of media is to position themselves on platforms rather than wait for readers to voluntarily connect to their website. The development of social networks increases indirect access to news and weakens the use of direct connections to press sites.

---

16 User-generated content consists of content presented by users (texts, images, videos, music, etc.).

A strategy of the press or media could have been to become platforms in order to remain in control of their readership. However, experience shows that their delay in imagining the changes resulting from the digitalization of information, as well as their delay in acquiring technical skills or believing in certain economic models, now prevent them from being credible platforms. We could also imagine that platforms, shaded by their dominant position, forget the care to be taken around the user, such as respect for privacy and personal data. Slip-ups such as those Facebook (caught up in the Cambridge Analytica case) have been accused of could highlight the reputation, quality and reliability of historical media.

The model developed by Alexandre De Corniere and Miklos Sarvary shows that the platform's interest is initially to offer its users a significant proportion of news from the media. The reason for this is that in this way, the platform hopes to attract a larger number of users who would have been tempted to directly visit press sites. The question then is: what is the effect on the quality of information? On the one hand, the media have greater access to an audience, which makes competition between them softer, given the much larger size of their market. But, on the other hand, the media also want to keep their readership on the website, because they are not obliged to share their advertising revenues, hence an incentive to offer high-quality information reserved for their subscribers alone, for example.

The conclusion of the model is that there are two types of media. Those whose identities are less established and who are then forced to share their resources with the platform, which represents a significant risk to their ability to invest in the quality of information, and those with a strong brand and who can at least partially withdraw from the platforms' news feed and keep their loyal readers on their own site. However, if those with a strong brand compete with other strong-branded media, they find themselves acting on two competitive fronts: revenue-sharing with platforms and direct competition with other media. The authors conclude that social networks are "bad news for the media" (p. 20).

To conclude, let us move on to research and questions about the overall influence of software use in the writing of articles and choosing topics.

David Drake (Drake 2017), journalist and researcher at the London School of Economics, points out that in 2017, Google generated 50% of all online advertising revenue in the United States, while Facebook generated

13%. This concentration of advertising revenues in the hands of Internet giants has strong implications for the media world. One way to attract a large audience to sites is to provide a news feed, which is what all Google-type platforms do. The algorithm used to build the news feed has a personalization bias, given that it is based on individuals' preferences or keyword search history. However, journalists also do research on the Internet and also use social networks as a source of information. Journalists may also be looking for visibility for themselves or for the media for which they work: there is therefore also a temptation to be present on the news feed, which can lead the media or journalist to set up the editorial content to be selected by the algorithm:

> "Audience measurement tools are offered by platforms that highlight trending topics that, in turn, immediately highlight the preferences of Internet users on a continuous basis" (Drake 2017, p. 32).

One of the consequences of monitoring public opinion through audience measurement tools, such as Google Analytics or Chartbeat[17], is that it could lead to a diversification strategy among journalists, who would then be encouraged to cover topics that they may not have chosen in order to stay relevant on a topic that other media would cover. However, following the statistics proposed by the platforms can also be counterproductive.

Indeed, Twitter users, for example, are not representative of all readers because the active users of this social network are essentially young, urban and educated. However, these real-time audience-tracking and topic-selection decision-support software are increasingly being used by the mainstream media, as Frederica Cherubini and Rasmus Nielsen point out in a report written in 2016 for the Reuters Institute for Journalism (Cherubini and Nielsen 2016). The readership temptation is inseparable from the press since it lives on a two-sided market. The possibility of an online offer and permanent monitoring carries a risk of amplifying the phenomenon of information impoverishment, ultimately only targeting the consumer readership of social networks.

---

17 Chartbeat is a paid solution to track the popularity of a publication on the Internet. The company's promise is: *the story of your content. A content intelligence platform that energizes your business, centralizes data around your distributed audience, tells you how content engages readers, and helps grow your audience. A window into your readers. See how your audience connects with your content in real time.* See the site: https://chartbeat.com.

Will Fake News Kill Information?

In recent years, the term *fake news* has become part of common vocabulary. With the development of the Internet and social networks, misinformation has drowned the public, who are finding it increasingly difficult to distinguish between what is true and what is false.

Fake news was even crowned word of the year by the famous Collins dictionary in early 2018. The fake news saying began to develop in the 1990s on U.S. television in order to describe "false news, generally exaggerated, disguised as real information", before exploding in 2015, and even Donald Trump helped popularize it. When questioned by U.S. television in the fall of 2017 on this subject, the President seriously assured that the word "fake was one of the best [*he*] invented" in his life. "Maybe other people used it in the past, but I never noticed it [...]" (Salmon 2017). Since 2016, Collins notes that the use of the term fake news has increased by 365%!

Fake news, taken in its most general sense, covers very different things: on the one hand, there is shared misinformation, where the reader is not aware that it is basically a hoax. Such an example is the satirical *Gorafi* column, taken up by an Algerian newspaper. *El Hayat* was indeed tricked, by repeating misinformation on the front page of the newspaper from this parodic site, according to which Marine Le Pen wanted to surround France with a wall paid for by Algeria.

There is also the misinformation intended to propagate political ideas or generate revenue: the idea here is to publish highly reworked content, which ensures a large audience and advertising revenue.

As Arnaud Mercier[1], a professor of Information Communication at the *Institut Français de presse, Université Paris 2 Panthéon-Assas* (French Press Institute, University of Paris 2 Panthéon-Assas), points out: "It is better to avoid talking about 'fake news' – an old and common concept, legally recognized in the unwavering French press law of 1881 – but rather we should talk about falsified information, of forged information". Fake news is designed to look like journalistic information.

Fake news has all the more impact because the public likes to believe in conspiracy theories. According to a study by Ifop for the Jean Jaurès Foundation and the Conspiracy Watch observatory, published in early 2018 and relayed by Francetvinfo[2], 79% believe in at least one conspiracy theory, 61% believe in at least two theories, 47% in at least three theories, 34% in at least four theories and 13% in at least seven theories. The researchers tested several "conspiracy theories" that are more or less widespread in French society.

The majority (54%) of those surveyed believe that "the CIA was involved in the assassination of President John F. Kennedy". An estimated 32% of them believe that the "AIDS virus was created in a laboratory and tested on the African population before spreading throughout the world".

Adhering to five or more conspiracy theories, the majority of convinced conspirators represent 25% of French people (6% adhering to five theories, 6% to six theories and 13% to seven or more theories).

Another interesting conclusion is that young people are much more open to conspiracy theories. People below 35 years of age are almost twice as likely to agree with at least seven conspiracy theories as those above 35 (21% versus 11%).

---

1 Mercier, A. (2018). Fake news : tous une part de responsabilité !, *The conversation*. Available at: https://theconversation.com/fake-news-tous-une-part-de-responsabilite-95774.
2 Reichstadt, R. (2018). Le conspirationnisme dans l'opinion publique française. Fondation Jean Jaurès. Available at: https://jean-jaures.org/nos-productions/le-conspirationnisme-dans-l-opinion-publique-francaise.

Although this study raised some criticism and questions about its methodology, it did remind us of the penetration of conspiracy in society.

7.1. From media and network initiatives to a law

Although "misinformation" is old, social networks have amplified the phenomenon so much that fake news may have led to tragedies. Recently, in India, assaults and lynchings have been reported following information of a network of child traffickers spread through the WhatsApp messaging system.

Most social networks have implemented initiatives to try to fight against fake news. Having been much criticized, they had to redeem themselves and try to prove that they were not being inactive, if only to avoid scaring away advertisers, who regularly criticize social networks. For example, according to an article in the *Washington Post*[3] in July, more than 70 million Twitter accounts that were suspected of spreading fake news were suspended in 2 months.

Google has also set up initiatives. The *CrossCheck* project set up by Google in 2017 allows Internet users to report suspicious content seen on the Internet, social networks and so on, or to ask questions via a dedicated platform, so that *CrossCheck* partners can conduct the survey and directly respond to requests on the platform.

As for Facebook, it launched a tool in April 2018 to provide users with context information about the articles that are present on their news feed. In the form of a button dubbed "About this article", the tool relays other posts from solid sources on the topic covered, as well as the latest publications of the media concerned. It provides a link to the publisher's Wikipedia page. A few months ago, Facebook had decided to block advertising from sites that broadcast fake news. "Fake news hurts everyone. It makes the world less well-informed and it undermines trust", Facebook stated at the time. In order to recognize this misinformation, the social network specifies that these pages must be considered false by "a third party, having verified it" (Cazares 2017).

---

3 Timberg C., Dwoskin E. (2018). Twitter is sweeping out fake accounts like never before, putting user growth at risk. The Washington Post. Available at: https://www.washingtonpost. com/technology/2018/07/06/twitter-is-sweeping-out-fake-accounts-like-never-before-putting-user-growth-risk/?noredirect=on&utm_term=.afc1560b7751.

According to the Duke University Reporters' Lab, cited by the AFP (*Agence France Press*, a major French press agency), there are 149 fact-checking initiatives in 53 countries recorded in the summer of 2018.

Faced with the resurgence of fake news, the media themselves are tempted to develop verification tools. This is the case with the *Decodex* of the newspaper *Le Monde*, launched in February 2017, to give just one example in the written press. Its objective is to provide as many people as possible with simple tools to assess the accuracy of the information, as explained on the *Le Monde* site, by proposing a program to indicate whether the site is reliable. In 2017, the *Décodeurs* team of *LeMonde.fr* had referenced a little more than 600 information sites, not taking their political or ideological orientation into account, but above all, their journalistic reliability: do they publish verified information? Do they give their sources? Can we identify the authors?

More recently, in the spring of 2018, public audiovisual groups joined forces to create a *fact-checking* platform. On the *Franceinfo* website, "Vrai ou fake" ("real or fake") includes initiatives to decipher information and verify the facts of various public service media.

An interesting fact – and an indicative one – in the Philippines[4], the world's largest user of social networks: training camps have been created in order to teach people how to track down fake news, provided by ABS-CBN, the main television network in the country.

Let us return to France, where the government has also declared war on fake news. While Emmanuel Macron was targeted during his campaign by attacks and rumors, the President called for an anti-fake news law. In the summer of 2018, a law was being prepared to combat misinformation, particularly during elections. The proposed laws on "information manipulation" passed a first legislative step. The texts were adopted by the French National Assembly in July 2018, but by the summer of 2018, it had not completed the legislative process, as the draft laws (organic and regular) were highly controversial. The Senate rejected the texts as a whole.

---

4 AFP (June 29, 2018) looked at training camps in the Philippines to track down fake news (http://www.france24.com/fr/20180629-philippines-camps-dentrainement-demonter-fausses-nouvelles).

In the summer version of the text, one of the key provisions provides that 3 months before elections, when misinformation "likely to alter the sincerity of the vote" is deliberately, artificially or automatically distributed on a massive scale through an online communication service, the judge hearing the case may be asked to stop its distribution.

The definition of misinformation has been debated at length by the members of the parliament. In early June, the draftsman of the text proposed a new wording: "any allegation or imputation of an inaccurate or misleading fact". The idea of the text is to make the platforms responsible for distribution, according to its initiators.

These laws also aim to increase transparency on the part of platforms (Facebook, Twitter, Google, etc.). Those exceeding a certain volume of connections must have a legal representative in France. They must provide the identity of the sponsors and the amount of remuneration received for the promotion of information content related to debates of general interest.

7.2. Fake news and post truth

As Arnaud Mercier points out[5], the notion of fake news is linked to another notion; that of post-truth, Oxford Dictionary's sacred word of the year. The dictionary defines it as an adjective referring to circumstances in which objective facts have less influence in shaping public opinion than appeals to emotion and personal opinions.

In a lengthy analysis in *The Guardian*[6], Katharine Viner, the Editor-in-Chief of the newspaper, looks back at the Brexit campaign and the role of the media, wondering whether truth still matters: in an era of post-truth politics, a peremptory lie can become king. In particular, she explains that when a fact begins to look like what you think would be true, it is very difficult to distinguish between facts that are true and "facts" that are not.

---

5 Mercier, A. (2018). Fake news : tous une part de responsabilité ! *The conversation*. Available at: https://theconversation.com/fake-news-tous-une-part-de-responsabilite-95774.
6 Viner, K. (2016). How technology disrupted the truth. *The Guardian*. Available at: https://www.theguardian.com/media/2016/jul/12/how-technology-disrupted-the-truth. See also: Vinogradoff, L. (2016). Les médias dans l'ère de la politique post-vérité. *Le monde*. Available at: https://www.lemonde.fr/big-browser/article/2016/07/12/les-medias-dans-l-ere-de-la-politique-post-verite_4968559_4832693.html.

She recalls in particular what Arron Banks, supporter of the Leave campaign, who greatly financed the campaign too, confided in *The Guardian* about the U.S. victory. "In politics, a campaign is won more by emotion: facts don't work".

With social networks, false truths circulate extremely quickly. And everyone has their share of responsibility in this resurgence of fake news, reminds Arnaud Mercier. In particular, he quotes those politicians who believed that in order to be elected:

> "it was just a matter of making bigger and more sophisticated lies, merchants of doubt, communicators and lobbyists ready to twist the facts, to deny the achievements of science in order to defend the interests of their industrial clients (cigarettes etc.), social scientists, foreign powers etc.".

But journalists and the media too:

> "who do their work badly, who, through clumsiness, urgent and reckless treatment, poor scooping, insufficient checks, publish erroneous information, and thus erode the credibility of the entire profession by contributing to misinformation. Including by poorly digesting scientific publications, via a risky popularization",

or social networks such as Facebook:

> "who have never spontaneously fought against fake news, but allowed a political economy of fake news to take root, from which *the* firm benefits".

Arnaud Mercier concludes:

> "I, me, you, we are responsible, we who have given in at one time or another to the temptation to *like* or *share* dubious content because you never know, it may be true, because if it's not true, it's still funny, because we clicked on the share button on the sole basis of the title [...], because under the shock of the news (attacks, for example) we are confused, we lose critical reflexes and give in to the temptation of that which is spectacular or emotional".

7.2.1. *Misinformation circulates very quickly*

Misinformation circulates extremely quickly. More precisely, six times faster than real information.

This observation was made by three MIT researchers, Soroush Vosoughi, Deb Roy and Sinan Aral (Vosoughi *et al.* 2018), who analyzed the tweets of 3 million people over the 2006–2017 period, using the *TWEETVISTA* (Prashanth *et al.* 2017)[7] conversation exploration software. They divided the tweets into 126,000 stories or rumors. These stories themselves have been divided into two categories: stories with false content and those with real content. To differentiate between true and false, the authors used content analyses from six independent fact-checking organizations.

As highlighted in the 2016 report of the "Reuters Institute for the Study of Journalism", verifying information and uncovering misinformation has been a fast-growing activity since its inception in the United States in 2000. In 2016, *Reuters* had 113 independent organizations in 50 countries, 90% of which were born after 2010 (Cherubini and Graves 2016). All that remains is to measure the time needed for information put on Twitter to be broadcast to 1,500 people. The comparison of broadcast times shows that misinformation circulates faster and that there is an even stronger difference for policy conversations for which the broadcast speed is highest.

Another interesting result of the study by the three Boston researchers is that traffic depends on Internet users rather than information distribution robots. Distribution and its acceleration are here from a human source, not mechanical. The tendency to distribute misinformation could, according to the study, come from the novelty of this information and its ability to surprise readers more than real information. Moreover, misinformation is often information with negative or worrying content, similar to the studies we have already encountered on content, particularly negative content. The authors also show that robots spread true and false information at the same speed. They are not endowed with emotions and are therefore not sensitive to the content or appeal of the novelty.

---

7 The Market being highly demanded, there are many solutions for conversation exploration, such as *BigFish*, marketed by *Weborama* and used by Ipsos, among others.

Camille Alloing and Nicolas Vanderbiest (Alloing and Vanderbiest 2018) are interested in how a false rumor spreads on Twitter. They are studying the distribution of misinformation and rumors following the Nice attack of July 14, 2016. The rumor is that there was a hostage situation at the Hotel Negresco. The starting point is an error in analysis, based on testimonies collected by the *LCI* information channel. The study is based on 23,323 tweets divided into three categories: original messages, those that are re-tweeted and those sent in response to a message. For French accounts, 56% of them do not produce or relay information, as users are essentially "consumers" of tweets.

Nevertheless, Twitter is built on a design that is particularly adapted to the distribution of a rumor because the messages are very short (the famous 140-character limit) and easy to relay. Alloing and Vanderbiest refer to a study by Muneo Kaigo, a researcher at the University of Tsukuba in Japan, regarding the speed of information dissemination during disasters, such as an earthquake in Japan. By applying a similar logic, the authors show that the Nice rumor spread between 9:21 pm and 10:33 pm, at which point it was denied (Ministry of the Interior's Twitter account). The rumor spread very fast. This speed was nourished by each person's emotion, which gave way to a wide ripple of unfounded information.

7.2.2. Fake news and social networks

This is a broad subject because, as we saw in the previous chapter, the use of social networks to get information has become more prominent. To summarize the issues in a few words, let us refer to an article published in INA Global in 2017[8], in which media sociologist Jean-Marie Charon recalls the link between fake news and social networks, which are being increasingly used for information:

"How would this transformation regarding the means of obtaining information have anything to do with the position taken by fake news or alternative facts? First, it operates a form of flattening. All sources of information are at the same level:

8 Charon, J.M. (2017). Pour combattre la past-vérité, les médias condamnés à innover. InaGlobal. Available at: https://www.inaglobal.fr/presse/article/pour-combattre-la-post-verite-les-medias-condamnes-innover-9656.

media, institutions, companies, influencers, parties, etc. One media is one source among others just as the trend shows that information could be one opinion among others, as suggested by the reference to alternative facts".

Second, according to him, social networks "bring an additional effect to this flattening of sources, by somehow reversing credibility factors", recalling that on networks, readers tend to trust the person who shares information more than the source itself.

The research focused on the influence of recommendation with regard to the credibility of a media or article. In a study from 2017[9], "The Media Insight Project" (a collaboration between the American Press Institute and the Associated Press-NORC Center for the Public Affairs Research) shows that the person who shares information has more impact than the media itself.

In order to achieve this result, the authors of the study created a Facebook post about an article on diabetes and presented it to a sample of 1,489 U.S. residents in late 2016. Part of the test samples knew that the article came from the AP (*Associated Press*), and the other part thought that it came from a fictional site. The analysis was based on the sharing of people considered trustworthy after studying the respondents, ranging from presenter Oprah Winfrey to personalities recognized as medical experts.

First observation: as expected, those who saw the article through the recommendation of a trusted person rated it more positively on different criteria (such as accuracy, diversity of points of view, pleasure of reading, etc.), and were more inclined to share it again or to follow the person who shared the article.

Second observation: even though other declarative surveys show that individuals have little confidence in social networks, this experience shows

9 The Media Insight Project (2017). Who shared it: How Americans decide what news to trust on social media. *American Press Institute*. Available at: https://www.americanpressinstitute. org/publications/reports/survey-research/trust-social-media/. See also a blog from the editorial staff: Vinogradoff, L. (2017). On networks, there is more trust in the person sharing than in the source of the information. *Le Monde Big Browser*. Available at: https://www.lemonde.fr/ big-browser/article/2017/03/24/sur-les-reseaux-on-fait-davantage-confiance-a-la-personne-qui-partage-qu-a-la-source-de-l-information_5100532_4832693.html.

things from a different perspective. Thus, the study concludes that a person perceives information from a reliable person, even from unknown media (in this case, *DailyNewsReview.com*, created from scratch), better than information from a credible source which is shared by a person who is not trusted by the respondent. For example, 52% believe that the information was well-reported/trustworthy in the first case (trusted person, unknown source), compared to 29% in the second.

In the first case, the respondent will also be more likely to share information in turn or to follow the person who shared the article on the networks. In other words, the trust placed in shared information on social networks depends more on the person who shares it than on the source of the information itself. The "Media Insight Project" concludes that it is important for the media to create communities, stressing that readers are also brand ambassadors.

In 2017, another study by Myojung Chung (Chung 2017), a researcher at the School of Communication and Information at Nanyang Technological University in Singapore, analyzed the role of social network indicators (the number of recommendations, sharing, etc.) in the perception of online information. The question asked is: is media credibility more important than recommendations?

The study involves a sample in the United States, based on articles on a bacterium in hamburgers. First, the recommendations have an influence: respondents consider the information to be of better quality. The presence of recommendation indicators has more influence for a source that is not considered very credible. Finally, the brand of the media, as well as personal interest, plays a role in the subject.

David Westerman, Patric Spence and Brandon Van Der Heide, researchers at West Virginia University, Western Michigan University and Ohio University, respectively, analyze the credibility of information relayed on Twitter. They show that the credibility felt by individuals mainly depends on the number of re-tweets in a world where information providers are not necessarily known or identified (Westerman *et al.* 2012). Another source of credibility is the number of followers.

Here, media economics meets contemporary advances in economic theory. Robert Shiller, an economist renowned for his work on speculative behavior and financial bubbles, winner of the 2013 Nobel Prize in Economics, was the first to take an explicit interest in the way information is reported. He published a very remarkable and innovative paper called Narrative Economics (Shiller 2017), in which he explained that the way things are said is essential as it contributes to the virality of information and influences economic results. Shiller also proposes reversing the relationship between narrative and economics, by using the tools of the economist to understand the narrative, in other words, by carrying out quantitative and econometric analyses. He welcomes "an unusual collaboration with the literature department of his university" (p. 970). He then uses a mathematical model (the Kermack–McKendrick SIR[10] model) developed to assess and explain epidemics in order to analyze what he calls "narrative epidemics of economic theories", particularly during economic crises such as the one in 2008.

Box 7.1. *The narrative economy*

7.3. Why fake news?

Nir Kshetri, from the University of North Carolina, and Jefrey Voas (Kshetri and Voas 2017) define misinformation in two ways: bad information and disinformation. In the first case, the information is erroneous, while disinformation induces intent. The authors classify fake news in this second category. There is a lot of fake news and it is very present on social networks because it does not require anything particular, only a connection and access to one or more social networks.

Kshetri and Voas propose an economic model that analyzes the value of fake news. An individual engages in the distribution of fake news if the benefits they receive from it seem to have a value greater than the disadvantages to them. The benefits are possibly financial (in this case, one can be close to fraud), psychological in nature weighted by the probability of convincing, while the costs consist of direct costs, the probability of being arrested and convicted (depending on the nature of misinformation and

---

10 SIR = susceptible, infective and recovered. The method consists of dividing the population into three categories: susceptible, infected and recovered, and then it discerns the number of people in each category in order to determine whether an epidemic is occurring and where it is progressing.

the regulations in force in the country of the person who supplied the misinformation).

Research shows that most fake news is motivated by financial objectives. On the consumer side of fake news, the authors refer to several tests carried out by researchers at the University of Stanford on young people attending secondary school, showing that the latter are not very vigilant about the information received and are therefore easily duped.

The speed of continuous information distribution means that the media are often taken into the circle of fake news distribution. Sometimes relayed with misinformation, the media lose their credibility, which they regain thanks to a proactive strategy of seeking fakes and revealing fakes. For example, 60 media have created the "Trust Project" in the United States, which aims to raise journalists' awareness of new ethical and deontological rules that are adapted to the speed of information distribution and the risk of fake news. Since a majority of fake news originates from social networks, the latter now have a responsibility to secure the distribution of information. The problem is current with recent reflections on Facebook's behavior.

7.3.1. *The impact of fake news and rumors*

A hot topic in the news is the impact of fake news, which has been the subject of studies by economists. Hunt Allcott, an associate professor of Economics at New York University, and Matthew Shapiro, a professor of Economics at Stanford, are both interested in a major phenomenon: the explosion of fake news and rumors during the 2016 U.S. presidential election. Allcott and Gentzkow (2017) start from the worrying observation that an individual broadcasting information on social networks, in some cases, when the information becomes highly viral, can reach as many individuals as a CNN program, Fox News or an issue of the *New York Times* when there is no third-party filtering or checking of the information. The two economists approach this problem by describing fake news as biased within a game theory model where individuals' decisions are partly based on misinformation, thus generating sub-optimal or even negative decisions (not buying a product because you think it is bad, not buying a company stock because you think it is in crisis, etc.). The model is then used over the period of the U.S. presidential elections, where the authors identify 156 widely relayed conversations, of which 115 are pro-Trump fake news and 41 are pro-Clinton fake news.

Thus, the authors' first comment is to highlight the asymmetry in the volumes of misinformation. This fake news has been widely distributed. It was shared approximately 760 million times in the month before the election, representing an average of three fake news exposures per adult U.S. resident within voting age. For this sustained exposure to fake news to have influenced voters, they must have believed it. The two researchers conduct post-election tests by proposing to consult a site built for the test to a panel of individuals. This site contains 50% of misinformation composed of misinformation distributed during the campaign and new misinformation invented for the test, which has never been disseminated; 15% of the panel believe false pre-election information, and 14% believe false placebo information. This figure means that the misinformation distributed the month before the elections had an influence on voter turnout.

This fascinating article studies the history of big fake news beliefs, such as that gas chambers did not exist (2% of the population), Lyndon Johnson commissioned Kennedy's assassination in 1963 (17% of the population) and Barack Obama was not born in the U.S.A. (13% of the population), using the results of studies conducted by the American Enterprise Institute. From this information, the authors try to see if the trend towards fake news is increasing or not. They conclude that it should be because, on the one hand, we are subject to much more intense exposure to information of all kinds, given that it is easy to produce and distribute (since there are no technical or financial barriers to entry) and, on the other hand, we are trusting our media less and less.

Ming Jia, Hongfei Ruan and Zhe Zhang (Jia *et al.* 2016), researchers at Xi'an Jiaotong University, focus on the influence of the media on the stock prices of listed companies in China. They are mainly interested in the spread of rumors and biased information. Since 2007, the CSRC (China Securities Regulatory Commission) has required companies listed on the Shanghai and Shenzhen stock exchanges to publish financial information, in response to rumors about them. The authors' study covers the 2007–2012 period. By studying the financial press, they highlight a cumulative phenomenon: an initial negative information about a firm that comes from a credible source leads to a similar intensification of information. Therefore, the only way to stop the phenomenon is for the company to intervene by disseminating convincing technical counter-arguments. The reason for the spread of the rumor is, according to the authors, due to the desire to broaden the readership that is supposed to be more attracted by negative information, leading to a more attractive narrative. Here, the authors repeat the conclusions of Harvard professor Steven Pinker (Pinker 2005)[11], a cognitive psychologist, on the bias of negativity. We could have a negative bias, in other words, an appetite for negative information because it is subconsciously more important. Indeed, we have developed the habit of prioritizing information according to whether it is important or not, in terms of survival. However, negative information awakens our vigilance and can trigger survival reflexes in us. We would therefore naturally be more attentive to negative information, hence the aphorism often stated: "good news is no news".

7.3.2. *Fact checking versus fake news*

Oscar Barrera and Ekaterina Zhuravskaya, researchers at the Paris School of Economics, along with Sergei Guriev and Emeric Henry (Barrera *et al.* 2017), researchers at Science Po Paris, question the fact checking capacity to counter fake news. As their field of analysis, they take the French presidential elections of 2017. They studied a panel of 2,480 French people of voting age, residing in five French regions where the far right has high electoral scores.

The participants were divided into subgroups that are subject to different information consultation, depending on the group. Some only read misinformation, while others read both fake and invalid news. The results of the study show that the most influential information was fake news. The authors put forward a hypothesis in order to explain this result: fake news in politics is often embedded in a complex narrative that triggers strong emotion, and it is this emotion that is often the basis of the vote. Fact checking type of information is generally descriptive and cold. Truth versus emotion: the authors believe that emotion wins.

Emotions are also central to the research of Vian Bakir and Andrew McStay (Bakir and McStay 2018). The two researchers are also interested in the 2016 U.S. presidential election, during which a significant number of fake news was broadcast and produced in Veles, a small town in Macedonia, by paid students without any particular ideological or political motivation. As with the French analysis, fake news' success is explained by its content,

---

11 See https://stevenpinker.com

which is better remembered and more attractive. Bakir and McStay are concerned about the possible development of fake news because it could quickly be produced by advanced robots whose algorithm could give them empathy. If robots produce emotion, there would be no limit to fake news, hence the authors' suggestion that negotiations with software manufacturers should be held in order to reflect on the development of automatic empathy.

7.3.3. *Bad news*

Another theme, which is somewhat related, is what we could call *bad news*, which highlights the public's appetite for negative news.

In a 2015 article, Matthias Heinz and Johann Swinnen (Heinz and Swinnen 2015) were among the first researchers to look at bad news in the German press. They report the frequency (20 times more than good news) and the negative influence of individuals' decision-making in economics and politics.

They analyzed 7,700 articles over 8 years (December 2000 to September 2008) and compared media coverage announcing job creation with that of job destruction in one of the main German daily newspapers: *Die Welt*. The 7,700 articles are divided into 666 articles corresponding to 112 companies creating jobs (an average of 6 articles per company) and 7,065 articles corresponding to 498 companies that have made redundancies (an average of 14 articles per company). During the 10 years studied, the German unemployment rate fell by 2%. The econometric analysis of the data from the press articles therefore shows: (1) more firms laying off rather than recruiting, which is not consistent with the decreasing unemployment rate during the period, and (2) more than twice as many articles on a company laying off as on a company that is recruiting.

This article follows the study by Guido Freibel and Matthias Heinz (Freibel and Heinz 2014), published in 2014, on the handling of foreign companies in the German press. For this purpose, the authors carry out an econometric analysis based on 5,394 articles in the daily newspaper *Die Welt* between December 2000 and September 2008. The tests reveal a negative bias towards foreign firms, illustrating economic xenophobia towards foreign investors, which could result in them being reluctant to invest in Germany. The authors then verify that this result is generalized to the German press and not only for *Die Welt*. They conducted a randomized study of articles in six other newspapers (*Handelsblatt* and *Financial Times Deutschland* (FTD), the *Frankfurter Allgemeine Zeitung* (FAZ), *Süddeutsche Zeitung* (SZ), *Frankfurter Rundschau* (FR) and *Die Tageszeitung* (TAZ)). This comparative analysis confirms the existence of an unfavorable bias against foreign companies, regardless of the press title.

In the same year, Jill McCluskey, Johan Swinnen and Thijs Vandemoortele (McCluskey *et al.* 2015) wrote an article on the economics of bad news. According to the authors, the frequency of bad news is explained by readers' demand. There are two types of articles in a newspaper. Readers want to read "good news" because it gives them information that is useful to improve their well-being, while there is a demand for "bad news" because it is useful to them, as it leads them to review their choices and correct welfare losses. An economic model that assumes that readers have a risk aversion (a hypothesis often advanced and often tested in economic models, which means that individuals prefer situations in which they can act in order to reduce the uncertainty that is associated with choices they have to make) leads to media publishing more bad news.

7.3.4. *Fake news and economic expectations*

The role of information in the political and economic context should not be underestimated. Several studies point to the importance that information can have in an economic context – whether credible or fake news – and the evolution of companies, as we saw in the first chapter. There are many examples of misinformation intended to manipulate the market or a value. We can remember, for example, the *Associated Press*'s (the U.S. AFP) fake tweet in 2013, which caused panic on Wall Street. The tweet indicated that the White House had been the target of two explosions and that President Barack Obama had been wounded. The tweet was quickly relayed, causing, in just a few minutes, a $136 billion drop in Wall Street's market capitalization! This story reminds us of the impact that information can have.

However, the information distributed and misinformation or rumors in particular play a major role in the way people construct their economic expectations. This is particularly clear when looking at the evolution of the inflation rate or stock prices. Recent economic research is complex on this subject.

Michael Lamla and Sarah Lein (Lamla and Lein 2012), both researchers at the University of Zurich, analyze the content of information that allows individuals to anticipate the inflation rate. Individuals are in a Bayesian learning process that allows them to make predictions based on probabilities. These probabilities are established on the basis of information received by individuals (economists talk about signals). The behavior of individuals plays an important role in determining the rate of price growth.

The phenomenon is called "self-fulfilling prophecies": if people think that prices will increase, this can trigger early purchases, resulting in a feared increase in prices, which in turn triggers a spiral. The way people construct their expectations is therefore essential for conducting monetary policy. Central banks announce their monetary policy and publish it in the press. By communicating their monetary objectives, central banks reduce the information asymmetry between political authorities and individuals. By doing this, they reduce uncertainty and contribute to a reduction in price volatility. The central banks' communication policy therefore plays a major role in economic cycles.

Box 7.2. *Self-fulfilling prophecies*

The two researchers are working on a sample of 4,000 articles on the inflation rate over a 10-year period in Germany (1998–2007). The ability of individuals to establish expectations is measured by the difference between their own expectations and those made by professionals. The smaller the gap, the better the ability to anticipate is supposed to be. Lamla and Lein's study shows that capacity increases with the frequency of articles published on the subject. This means that a large volume of information is an element that promotes the understanding of economic processes and thus improves people's ability to anticipate. However, it also means that rumors, because of the extent to which they can quickly spread, are a very strongly destabilizing factor and can trigger major errors of anticipation.

However, if the volume is large, so is the nature of the information.

Yingying Xu and Zhixin Liu, from the University of Beihang, and Jaime Ortiz (Xu *et al.* 2018), from the University of Houston, are interested in the influence of the media on China's inflation rate. The article by the three researchers analyzes how information that is disseminated by central banks is relayed by the media, and how this information influences people's expectations. On the one hand, they study the influence of the volume of information and, on the other hand, that of information bias (here, in the sense of comments made by journalists on the announcement of monetary policy by the Governor of the Central Bank).

Regarding expectations, the research is based on questionnaires sent by the Central Bank of the People's Republic of China to 23,200 people each quarter, and on official inflation statistics. Concerning the media, the database used is that of the CNKI (China National Knowledge Infrastructure). The bias is calculated by identifying and accounting for papers announcing an increase in inflation and those forecasting a decrease, based on the same information released by the monetary authorities. The bias rate is measured by the ratio between increasing and declining papers. Before 2005, 10 publications released information about inflation. The number has since increased considerably: it stood at more than 200 in 2017. The results of the model and statistical tests are that the bias has more influence on expectations than the volume of information, in other words, the number of articles. If the informational bias is an announcement of increasing inflation, then the results of the questionnaires show an increase in upward expectations and vice versa. It can therefore be seen that the nature of economic information and the position taken by media have a significant influence on individuals.

We have already seen that there is an extensive study on the influence of the media on stock prices. It is only just developing. Indeed, the subject is important since it is a question of knowing to what extent information modifies individuals' expectations and therefore affects company valuations. It should be remembered that a company's stock price is an essential variable for three reasons: (1) savers invest their savings in shares, (2) companies can be the subject of a takeover bid if the value of the shares is low and (3) companies claim their good economic health via the value of the stock price, which reflects the conflict between supply and demand from investors, and therefore their opinion of it. A change in prices therefore has serious repercussions.

Among recent research, Paul Tetlock, a researcher at Columbia University, is interested in the influence of information according to its "freshness" and measures the impact of repeated information in the press (Tetlock 2011). According to the author, the accumulation of information in the media and its repetition leads to a strong reaction from investors, who modify their buying or selling strategy. The study covers articles in the *Wall Street Journal* and the *Dow Jones* news series and the S&P 500 Index[12]. It highlights the major influence of the press on investor behavior. However, the press is not the only source of information for market operators (traders). The latter, like many individual investors, regularly attend forums on which all types of information are constantly circulated, including rumors that operators are fond of.

There is a strong demand for information among traders, who are always looking for inside information on which to build their expectations. This explains the speed with which a stock price can be impacted by a rumor or fake news.

Many studies specifically focus on economic information in the press and its influence on prices, such as Gene Birtz's study (Birz 2017), which links press articles on unemployment to the evolution of the S&P 500 Index. In an earlier article and by a similar approach, Tetlock (Tetlock 2007) showed that the "tone" of press articles influences investors and therefore stock prices. Optimistic or pessimistic articles on economic developments play a role in the way investors construct their expectations. The study also included articles from the *Wall Street Journal*.

Manuel Ammann, Roman Frey and Michael Verhofen (Ammann *et al.* 2014), three researchers from the University of St. Gallen, are studying the possible correlation between the content of articles in one of Germany's leading financial newspapers, *Handelsblatt*, and the dynamics of company stock prices discussed in the articles of this journal. The study is being conducted between July 1989 and March 2011. It is based on an econometric

---

12 The Standard and Poor's 500 Index is an index that illustrates the stock price performance of the 500 largest listed companies in the United States. S&P is a financial rating company.

analysis established on a selection of representative words. The authors show that the articles anticipated the reversal of the main German stock market index, the DAX (which is calculated from the listing of the top 30 companies listed on the Frankfurt Stock Exchange). The authors conclude that the quality of information in this journal is very good, given that the journal publishes articles that make it possible to understand and anticipate the evolution of stock prices. They generalize this conclusion by referring to the usefulness of the press and suggest that future research be conducted on other stocks and other economic variables in order to confirm their findings.

Casey Dougal, Joseh Engelberg, Diego Garcia and Christopher Parsons (Dougal *et al.* 2012), four researchers at the University of North Carolina, are studying informational bias on the journalist's side. In particular, they are studying a section of the *Wall Street Journal* entitled "Abreast of the Market" for a 40-year period (1970–2007). Over this period, the editorial writers in charge of this section changed several times, especially given that a team of three journalists is required in order to supply the section. The authors record "increasing" or "decreasing" articles and compare them to the evolution of the Dow Jones Index (one of the indices representing stock market activity on the New York Stock Exchange). There is a relationship between the holding of articles and trend reversals, confirming Robert Shiller's famous statement about the tulip bubble in 1637: "the history of speculative bubbles begins roughly with the advent of newspapers" (The Economist, 2000)[13].

This approach is confirmed by the research of Alexander Hillert, Heiko Jacobs and Sebastian Müller, from the University of Mannheim. In an article published in 2014, they analyze the changes in stock market trends (momentum indicator) and check whether there is a correlation with comments made in the press. They conclude that the press is causing the "momentum", the very title chosen for their article. In order to do this, they compare the evolution of stock market indices in New York (NYSE Composite and NASDAQ) between 1989 and 2010 with the contents of articles in the *New York Times, USA Today, Wall Street Journal, Washington Post* and a few local newspapers via the LexisNexis database, in other words, 2.2 million articles covering 7,800 different companies.

---

13 The Economist (2000) Bubble bubble. The Economist. Available at: https://www.economist. com/finance-and-economics/2000/03/23/bubble-bubble.

The conclusion of all this research is that rumors, whether voluntary or involuntary fake news, are consubstantial with the digitization of information. One click is all it takes. It is essential to avoid the ravages of misinformation, media education and certification of information by a trusted third party. Here, the media and journalists regain their legitimacy by providing verified and secure information. This service therefore justifies a remuneration. Quality information and certification services are expensive and justify the development of professionally supported media brands.

8

Are Robots and AI
the Future of the Media?

In the fall of 2016, *Komoroid* and *Otonaroid*, two presenters in Japan, surprised their audience. Seemingly human and feminine, the two "journalists" were in fact robots who came to read the day's headlines at a conference at the National Museum of Science and Technology in Tokyo. One of them even stammered. These two androids were installed in order to collect human reactions when faced with machines, not to replace a television presenter.

That being said, in early 2018, the robot *Erica* was presented as the next star of a TV news program in Japan. According to the *Wall Street Journal* (Bellini 2018), the 23-year-old metal-made journalist, as per her creator Iroshi Ishuguro, director of the Intelligent Robotics Laboratory in Osaka, should be the first robot on the news. Iroshi Ishuguro even believes that his robot, which can express simple emotions, will soon have an independent conscience.

These examples illustrate the advances in the field of journalistic robots in recent years.

8.1. Robot journalists are already in action

On July 1, 2014, the Associated Press (AP) used the *Wordsmith*[1] robot platform for the first time in order to write articles on companies' quarterly financial results. Wordsmith then used the Zacks Investment database (Colford 2014). The AP explained that journalists had previously processed about 300 quarterly financial reports, but that the use of database processing and a robot could now allow 4,400 financial reports to be covered with short articles of 150 to 200 words. The AP points out that these are financial documents and that journalists remain the only ones with the ability to analyze these figures. The following year, in 2015, the AP extended this method of operation to sports information.

Furthermore, in 2014, the *Los Angeles Times* left its mark by publishing an article on an earthquake which was written automatically. The newspaper also uses robots to cover homicides. Robots collect the data, write the descriptive part of the article and forward it to the journalists who write the comments and analyses.

The Guardian, on the contrary, has robots writing longer articles for the weekend section called "The Long Good Read" (Moses 2014). The technology is based on two algorithms: one that extracts the data from the database, and another that uses this extraction to write an article.

During the 2015 regional elections in France, many sites such as *Le Monde*, *France Bleu* (Radio France), *Le Parisien* and *L'Express* used robots, or more precisely algorithms, in order to produce texts on the results city by city. One of the main advantages of these robots is that they can process a large amount of information in a short amount of time, which in this case was information on 36,000 municipalities, something that an army of journalists could probably not cover so quickly.

More than just raw data, the robot writers have produced short texts, which can also be referenced by Google. According to Syllabs, a French

---

1 Wordsmith is a solution developed by Automated Insights. From data to clear and insightful content, Wordsmith automatically generates narratives on a massive scale that sound like a person crafted each one. See https://automatedinsights.com.

company specializing in robotic journalists (which obtained €2 million in 2018), the cost of two election nights varied on average between €20,000 and €40,000, in other words, well below the cost of employing journalists for several months.

Some newspapers have gone even further. In Sweden, since 2017, the MittMedia press group has been experimenting with robots in order to enrich its content. Robots have taken an important place in the newsroom with articles on sports competition reports, stock market information and real estate information. "They are even our most efficient employees!", enthused Robin Govik, digital director of the group, who edits approximately 30 newspapers, as reported by Eric Scherer, Director of Forecasting at *France Télévisions*. Journalists would also be delighted to work with them. Robin Govik says:

> "Before, they were the robots [...]. With the 25% drop in the number of staff in Swedish newsrooms in recent years, the machines are producing the content that journalists have stopped providing but that people are demanding".

"Until now we thought that journalists, traditionally conservative, hated robots and considered them unreliable. In fact, this is not true", said Finnish journalist Hanna Tuulonen, a researcher at the University of Helsinki on information automation[2].

Specifically, the machines operate in several segments: the automatic publication of information with little journalistic added value directly on the Web, or the sending of messages to the editorial staff, who then choose whether or not to use it (information on road traffic, etc.).

According to Eric Scherer, a study conducted by MittMedia showed that more than a third of readers did not see any difference, even though the articles written by robots were indicated.

These examples remind us that in the space of a few years, the robotization of information has developed considerably.

---

2 See http://www.hannatuulonen.com/publications.html and http://immersiveautomation.com.

In April 2018, the Wordsmith Solution company (one of the main natural language generation platforms) announced more than 1.5 billion articles and suggested that its customers "make sense of the World's data". The process has five stages: data collection, data processing, article structuring, article writing and publication.

Box 8.1. *The five stages of automatically creating articles*

8.2. What is artificial intelligence?

Artificial intelligence (AI) will play an important role in the future. AI consists of using complex computer algorithms that mix large amounts of data to produce reasoning or learning (machine learning). This artificial intelligence can be incorporated into "machines" that are designed to perform tasks or provide assistance. Each of us already uses AI every day, such as in our mobile phones, which have a personal assistant that understands our voice, responds to our requests and can, in some cases, anticipate them.

Artificial intelligence can be "weak" or "strong".

"Weak" AI is what we are currently and increasingly dealing with more and more: a car that drives instead of us, a refrigerator that orders missing products online instead of us, a personal assistant like *Google Home* in our house, etc. The examples will multiply with the development of connected objects.

Intelligence is said to be "strong" when it is not limited to reproducing human intelligence faster or with less error, but when it develops consciousness and emotions. Recent developments in algorithms are based on the concept of biologically inspired "neural networks", hence the term bio-cybernetics, which is sometimes used. This evolution is also based on recent advances in quantum computing, which allows quantum computers to make calculations from the combinations of 0 and 1, just like a conventional computer that uses bits, as well as the superposition of 0 and 1 (called a qubit – a quantum bit). The superposition of layers multiplies computing capabilities. The possibility of a strong AI is discussed among scientists and raises major philosophical questions, as in Professor Jean-Gabriel Ganascia's book (Ganascia 2017). Since the future can only be a source of multiple questions, publications and essays are multiplying, developing within the context of a technophilic future or a technophobic apocalypse. All raise the point regarding the threat to humanity, as well as the hope of a trans-humanity, going so far as to declare the "death of death" (Alexandre 2011).

The "weak" AI promises us a *Smart Life*; in other words, to help our farmers optimize watering, to help individuals manage their waste or energy consumption, to help a doctor read an X-ray without error or to make a diagnosis, etc. A smart and green life. However, in the background, there is also the concern about robots making jobs disappear (Decanio 2017), in addition to a life where journalists could be replaced by robots producing articles for them.

8.3. Research on automatic journalism

2014 was the year of robotic journalism, and also the year of research on "automatic journalism" (Montal and Reich 2017). Although many articles on the role of algorithms in information production were published before this date, the research took a step forward following Philip Napoli's seminal article (Napoli 2014).

The research was initially more interested in the consequences of the explosion of mass data and took up the problem of content creation through the prism of *big data* and *data journalism* (Le Cam and Trédan 2017; Lewis 2015; Lewis and Westlung 2015; De Maeyer *et al.* 2015; Trédan 2014). The algorithm is therefore a technical tool that facilitates the journalist's work and allows them to say more interesting things about the quantitative data at their disposal, which them sometimes may have missed in the past due to the lack of easy and efficient analysis tools. The algorithm is often coupled with formatting tools that present digital information in the form of graphs or visuals that are enlightening, simplifying and attractive.

For Napoli, reflecting an article by Daniel Orr (Orr 1987) that presented the media as institutions with respect to their position in society, algorithms are institutions in the sense that they modify the production and consumption of information.

"Algorithms can, in many ways, embody the complex mix of human and non-human factors that is at the heart of the perspective of player-network theory on institutions" (Napoli 2014, p. 344).

8.3.1. *From quantitative journalism to robot journalism*

However, before the robots, there were several steps:

Mark Coddington (Coddington 2015) refers to the notion of quantitative journalism, that is, journalism that uses the processing of information in the form of data. Quantitative journalism is divided into three categories corresponding to three periods:

– computer-assisted journalism;

– data journalism;

– computational journalism.

The author retraces the main historical steps. Computer-assisted journalism is a "precision journalism" that was born in the 1950s with the arrival of office automation and the deployment of statistical tools for the general public. From the 2000s, the use of new technologies allowed the deployment of the data journalist, who mines[3] data in digitalized numbers (big data) and transforms the information that has been excavated from the databases by statistical processing into journalistic writing. The journalist's statistical ability gives him access to the new source of raw data.

The third step is computational journalism, which is seen as an evolution of computer-assisted journalism. This expression, which appeared in 2006, describes an increased significance of computer technology in the writing of articles, which nevertheless remain part of the initiative both in terms of the choice of subjects and in the editorial style of the journalist.

Sylvain Parasie, a researcher at the University of Paris-Est, and Eric Darigal, a researcher at the University of Paris René Descartes, speak about a

---

3 The expression *miner* is common in the world of bulk data processing. It describes an action consisting of diving into huge databases in order to extract information that was locked in them and that the miner's action brought to the surface of the database.

"journalist programmer" (Parasie and Darigal 2012). The boundaries between the three categories (quantitative, computer-assisted and computational) identified by social science researchers are permeable because journalistic practices are permeable too. This permeability means that the general public, and even researchers, use different expressions in different ways.

This confusion of terminology is due to the rapid changes in editorial practices and journalistic practices, as shown in the ICFJ (International Center for Journalists[4]) study published in October 2017. This is a survey of 2,000 journalists in 130 countries. The disparities between countries regarding the role of technologies are huge. In 82% of U.S. or European newsrooms, 18% of roles are dedicated to digital technology and a large part of them are occupied by computer specialists who specialize in databases or professionals in community management or multi-platform content distribution, most often without journalism training. Digital newsrooms are also resulting in a team of significantly younger people.

The most recent step, the fourth step in the evolution of article production, is the arrival of robots or automated (or automatic) journalism. Researchers classify journalistic robots into three categories according to the tasks they are assigned:

– robot 1.0 without narrative creation;

– robot 2.0 with narrative creation. These first two versions exist and are commonly used in the press;

– robot 3.0, which currently still remains a hypothetical version, but one that computer scientists are considering: it would have a narrative capacity exceeding financial or sports comments as in the case of a robot 2.0. This implies, on the one hand, that the robot is able to decide to process a subject and, on the other hand, has the analytical capacity as well as the editorial capacity to process it; in other words, it has the ability to judge.

---

4 See the site https://www.icfj.org. ICFJ is a think tank created 30 years ago by Tom and Liebe Winship, editors of the Boston Globe. The study can be downloaded at the following address: https://www.icfj.org/news/first-ever-global-survey-news-tech-reveals-perilous-digital-skills-gap.

8.3.2. *Do readers and advertisers enjoy articles that have been written automatically?*

There is a lot of research that tests the eligibility of articles for the public. In line with the famous Turing test, tests are performed with audiences divided into groups, who are given articles that have been written by both journalists and robots. The subjects covered are the same, but only the authors are different. The studies are relatively recent and date back to around mid-2010.

Christer Clerwall (Clerwall 2014) thus shows that the articles produced by the robot are considered to be more descriptive, sometimes even boring, but they are also more objective than the articles written by journalists. Andréas Graefe, from the University of Columbia, and Mario Haim, Bastian Haarmann and Hans-Bernd Brosius (Graefe *et al.* 2016) from LMU in Munich on the contrary show that it is very difficult to differentiate between the two types of articles. Mario Haim and Andreas Graefe (Haim and Graefe 2017) are interested in the expectations of readers who believe *a priori* that articles written by journalists have a better style and are of better quality than those written by robots; contrary to what they imagined, readers see little difference when reading between the two types of articles.

Yair Galily (Galily 2018) recounts the evolution of attitudes towards "automatic articles" in the field of sport. The author refers to "backtracking" because although readers are seduced by the speed of automated information, they still appreciate finding comments from journalists with whom they are familiar. As a result, journalists' personal blogs have been widely read, testifying to a "lack of humanity".

8.3.3. *The impact of robotization*

Elisabeth Blankespoor and Christina Zhu, Stanford researchers, and Ed Dehaan, from the Foster School of Business at the University of Washington, offer an economic analysis of automatic journalism (Blankespoor *et al.* 2017).

More precisely, the authors show that automatic journalism allows an increase in the number of articles on companies and that companies receive benefits in the form of changes in their share price. For this purpose, the authors study the case of Inventure Foods. They analyzed the company's financial results in 2015 after the Associated Press developed the first journalist robot system in 2014, increasing the production of articles on companies' financial results from 400 per quarter to 4,000. The company's case is interesting because it did not receive any media coverage until 2014. The authors monitored the evolution of the company's market capitalization through the Zacks database[5]. The time between the publication of results and the publication of automatic articles in the AP news feed is 2 hours 30 minutes. Once the article is in the AP news feed, it is immediately used by redistributive information platforms such as Yahoo Finance. The authors then used RavenPack[6], a content curation company, in order to verify that the financial information about the company was instantly published on CNBC, NBCNews.com[7] and Investor's Business Daily.

From this case, the authors extended their analysis to 4,292 listed companies between 2012 and 2015; 56% of them had press coverage within the AP before the transition to automated articles, which led the authors to refocus on the remaining 34% or 2268 companies. The results are an increase in trading volumes in corporate shares. Better known and more widely reported in the press, corporate shares have a more important place in investors' strategies and are better valued. The study is in line with the extensive research on the relationship between media and finance, which shows that the media improve the functioning of financial markets by informing investors and exposing fraud and rumors.

8.3.4. *What do human journalists think about it?*

An important issue regards the reasons that drive a newspaper to adopt robot journalists and the impact of adopting robot journalists on "human journalists".

---

5 See the site zacks.com. "Zacks is the leading investment research firm focusing on stock research, analysis and recommendations".

6 See the site RavenPack.com. "Content curation made simple". RavenPack makes mining for insights easy by gathering information relevant to a particular topic or area of interest. These insights can easily be downloaded in a variety of structured data formats.

7 CNBC (Consumer News and Business Channel) is a continuous financial information television channel. NBC News is a general-interest channel that broadcasts a continuous stream of financial information.

Two South Korean researchers, Daewon Kim and Seongcheol Kim, interviewed 42 leaders in 24 media groups (Kim and Kim 2017). The two authors indicate that the first time the term "robot journalist" was used was in 1998. The concept of a robot journalist relates to that of a "computational journalist". The difference between the two lies in the degree of autonomy. The robot journalist is a player that the authors describe as active in the production of information. Once the robot's programming is completed, the robot continues the role which it was programmed to do autonomously, without human intervention. The algorithm is the key to the process, as well as the database in which the algorithm can be used as a raw material. As a result, the human journalist is no longer the only producer of information and articles. Robots are currently mainly used when databases are objective (such as statistics on sports results) and for articles that need to be published quickly. The choice of using them depends on the willingness to reduce costs (decrease or remission in the number of human journalists), the type of information in the newspaper (rapid information against information with analysis) and the resistance of active journalists.

The very rapid development of robot journalists is causing great concern, leading some, such as Noam Latar, to question the end of human journalism (Latar 2015).

The two researchers from the University of Korea, then analyzed the attitudes of 47 journalists working in 17 newspapers in South Korea (Kim and Kim 2018). There were three types of reactions from journalists. Using the terms chosen by the authors of the article, the first type of journalist suffers from "Frankenstein syndrome", predicting a catastrophic future for journalists and the quality of information. The second type of journalist is called the "elitist", in other words, one who thinks that the robot has abilities far below those of a human journalist and that it cannot replace them, except very marginally. The third type is "neutral", in the sense that they can identify advantages and disadvantages with the arrival of robot journalists in the editorial offices. Human journalists' opposition to the implementation of robots is decreasing between the three groups, but remains strong even in the latter case. The concerns among journalists follow on from other concerns already felt during the deployment of data journalism, as Sylvain Parasie notes (Parasie 2015).

Journalists' concerns are all the more significant because they have been confronted with continuous technological innovations over the past 20 years.

Studies in this area are multiplying, reflecting the upheavals and concerns associated with the proliferation of robots in information production. Neil Thurman, Konstantin Doerr and Jessica Kunert, for example, interviewed 641 London journalists in several organizations such as the BBC, CNN, Trinity Miror and the Thomson Reuters agency, highlighting similar results by emphasizing that journalists are insisting on the necessary "human angle" in an article. Journalists also point out three consequences of the robotization of information (Thurman *et al.* 2017). Information is produced at a lower cost, at an accelerated speed and uses less journalist time (what some identify as a concern, which is related to the fear of a reduction in the number of journalists, and what others see as additional time to focus on other subjects or to investigate further).

Konstantin Dörr (Dörr 2017) discusses the ethical issues of automated journalism. While the author acknowledges that journalism has always been confronted with technological innovations, the arrival of algorithms and artificial intelligence is, according to the author, a different kind of change. Ethical issues related to technology are common, such as those related to automatic trading (robots that buy or sell financial shares on the stock markets). Dörr shows the specificity of the problem regarding the ethics of robot journalism by breaking it down into three sub-sets: media ethics, individual ethics (which he links to the attitude and morals of the journalist in his professional activity) and the ethics of the audience, which is part of the social sphere.

This creates ethical challenges for journalists. The main one is related to the shift in the focal point of responsibility within the media. With automated journalism, the human journalist is no longer the major moral player in the information production process. An essential subject that is not taken into account sufficiently is the undoubtedly growing relationship between the journalist and the coder.

In a 2017 paper, Jaemin Jung, Haeyeop Song, Youngju Kim, Hyunsuk Im and Sewook Oh, all researchers from Seoul, focus on analyzing the views of both readers and journalists regarding the work of robots (Jung *et al.* 2017). The paper recalls the strong criticism against journalists in South Korea following the scandal that was linked to a shipwreck in April 2014, when the public pointed to the media for their outrageous stories, in addition to accusations that they had partly hidden the truth. The credibility of the journalists was then questioned.

For their tests, the researchers selected an article on a baseball game completed by an algorithm developed in Korea, and another written on the same subject by a human. The study was conducted with 201 people: each person had to read both papers and rate them on several criteria (writing quality, clarity, credibility, etc.), without knowing the source. Verdict: the difference in perception is very small.

In a second step, another sample of 400 people was interviewed on both articles, but this time with the knowledge of who had written it (a human or a robot). The results here show that the public gives a higher rating to the article written by an algorithm when the article is presented as such. However, they are less positive about an article written by a robot, but which is indicated as being written by a journalist. Similarly, they give a high score to a paper made by a journalist but mentioned as being written by an algorithm. In other words, they prefer the work of "robots".

The researchers also conducted the test on a panel of journalists (164 professionals). Contrary to their initial hypotheses (imagining a certain resistance of journalists to robots), the researchers also show that journalists give a higher rating to algorithms than to their peers.

Nicholas Diakopoulos and Michael Koliska (Diakopoulos and Koliska 2016) analyze the reasons why it is difficult for journalists to improve their understanding of algorithms. To do this, they interviewed about 50 people, professionals (28) and academics (22), who were used to working in an environment with robots in order to gather their experiences. The result is that the understanding of algorithms is limited by two phenomena: the reservation of information from manufacturers and the large volume of complex information to be processed by users of algorithms.

Kevin Hamilton (Hamilton 2014) talks about the need for research on "interactions with the invisible".

However, the "robot" phenomenon goes beyond the media world.

Software suppliers, such as Arria[8], Narrative Science[9], Ax Semantics[10], Retresco and Automated Insights initially created tailor-made and media-specific products. In order to increase their market share and boost their business model, software manufacturers have developed a consumer offer that is easy to access via web interfaces, APIs[11] and plug-ins integrated into an Excel spreadsheet. The users concerned are in many economic sectors such as e-commerce and financial technology. For example, bank sites can install a media API to integrate with a news feed, such as the BBC's (the BBC API is called JUICER[12]), that scans multiple free sources of information in order to extract a list of articles.

---

8 "Arria NLG Studio is an advanced natural-language generation (NLG) tool that empowers journalists, writers, analysts, data scientists and developers alike to build their own NLG solutions". See https://www.arria.com.

9 "Narrative Science is humanizing data like never before, with technology that interprets your data, then transforms it into Intelligent Narratives at unprecedented speed and scale". See https://narrativescience.com. The tool developed by this company is called Quill.

10 "Ax Semantics add a new dimension to writing: anyone can automate copywriting". See https://www.ax-semantics.com/en. Ax Semantics is a German company, as is Retresco.

11 API = Application Programming Interface. An API is an IT solution that allows applications to communicate with each other and exchange services or data. For example, it would be difficult for an artist who wishes to sell their work online to write code that facilitated secure payments. Instead, the artist can integrate the PayPal API into their site to receive payments directly into their existing PayPal account.

12 See the website of the BBC Innovation Laboratory, BBCNewsLab.co.uk, from which the following text is extracted: "The JUICER is a news aggregation and content extraction API. It takes articles from the BBC and other news sites, automatically parses them and tags them with related DBpedia entities. The entities are grouped in four categories: people, places, organizations and things (everything that doesn't fall in the first three). [...]. BBC Juicer is a news aggregation 'pipeline'. It ingests news articles and extracts the best from them-well, just like a fruit juicer does. BBC Juicer pipeline is watching RSS feeds of news outlets. When a new article is published on one of these RSS feeds, BBC Juicer scrapes the news article, both raw text and metadata (e.g. date, time, title, news source ...). In the next step BBC Juicer identifies and tags concepts mentioned in the article text making them searchable and therefore useful for trend analysis. [...] At the moment, BBC Juicer monitors around 850 RSS feeds from international, national and local news outlets. We started with British and other English language sources and are expanding into other languages. Importantly the list of sources does not claim to be comprehensive nor does it claim to provide a representative set of sources. We do NOT ingest content that is behind a paywall. Any news outlet that does not provide news content for free will not be ingested in BBC Juicer".

8.4. How do these editorial algorithms work?

Everything is based on NLG (natural language generation) technology, in other words, automatic text-generation software.

Natural language generation (NLG) technology is a natural language processing (NLP) subsection. NLG software transforms structured data into a written narrative, which is written just as a human would write it, but at the speed of thousands of pages per second. NLG technology automates the writing of data such as financial reports, product descriptions, meeting notes, etc.

The Yseop[13] website, a company that markets NLG solutions, provides the following information: "The functionalities of NLG software vary from one software company to another. The simplest functionality is that of pre-written sentences, with spaces that are automatically filled in with the collected data".

For example, "The weather today in <<place>> is <<temperature>> degrees". These simple systems transform a few elements from a database into one sentence, but are limited to describing simple situations.

The next-generation NLG offers software that can summarize larger amounts of data and explain why numbers are what they are. These systems allow companies to generate back-office and front-office reports, because they write more than descriptive narrative.

Box. 8.2. *Natural language generation technology*

In an article in *Science* magazine published in 2015, Julia Hirschberg, a researcher in the Department of Computer Science at Columbia University, and Christopher Manning, in Language Department at Stanford University, point out that the NLG has made significant progress in recent years (Hirschberg and Manning 2015). Natural language processing uses computational techniques to learn, understand and produce content in human language. The first computational approaches to language research focused on automating the analysis of the linguistic structure of language, and developing basic technologies such as machine translation, speech recognition and speech synthesis. Today's researchers are refining and using

---

13 Yseop is a U.S.-based company with two offices in France (Paris, Lyon). See www.yseop. com.

these tools in more complex applications, such as simultaneous speech-to-speech translation systems, the use of information contained in social networks to extract health or financial information, or the identification of feelings and emotions towards products or services.

Bhargavi Goel (Goel 2017) summarizes the progress of NLP in three main periods. NLP emerged in the 1940s with Turing's work and saw the first period of structured research develop over the 1960s and 1970s. During this period, Joseph Weizenbaum of the MIT Artificial Intelligence Laboratory developed ELIZA, which simulates a conversation between a psychoanalyst and a patient. In addition, at MIT, Terry Wienigrad developed SHRDLU, which simulates a conversation with a computer regarding identification of various geometric shapes[14]. An important step was taken in the early 1980s with the development of algorithms that made predictions from data and the development of automatic learning. Automatic learning models are based on new probability processing models (hidden Markov models – HMM). The scientific advances of this period are particularly significant in Europe, in connection with the Eurotra research program that was funded by the European Community.

Research accelerated from the 2000s onwards, thanks to the development of the Internet and the digitalization of data, which gave access to an unlimited playground. Recent advances have focused on the ability to process multiple and complex data, in addition to taking the context into account. This requires powerful new statistical tools such as Word2vec, a two-layer neural network model developed by Google. There are five main NLP applications: information retrieval (IR), information extraction (IR) from one or more databases, question answering (QA) with a machine using a natural language, machine translation (MT) (which is the primary purpose of NLP) and automatic summarization (AS), which allows essential information to be extracted from a database. This technique involves providing the algorithm with abstraction capabilities, in other words, the ability to link information in the database to words that are not in the database.

Bhargavi Goel concludes his historical approach to NLP by making a prediction about the possibility of extracting a "permanent survey" of our political opinions or opinions about the products we consume.

---

14 The experimentation and dialog are described here: https://hci.stanford.edu/winograd/shrdlu/.

"In the coming years, NPL will have a major impact on the Big Data economy. The technology would no longer be limited to enriching the data, but could eventually predict the future. From understanding, the technology would become predictive. Through the advancement of related technologies such as cognitive computing and deep learning, the NPL will offer a competitive advantage to companies in the field of digital advertising, legal, media and medical science services. Price patterns could be predicted and advertising campaigns assessed by data mining. It would become possible to predict the appeal and performance of candidates in elections by searching political forums. Social networks could be examined to find indicators of influence and power. Medical forums could be studied to uncover common questions and misconceptions about patients and diseases, so that the information on the site could be improved" (p. 27).

David Caswell and Konstantin Dörr, both from the University of Zurich, are interested in the latest forms of automatic journalism, in other words, when a robot produces an article that goes beyond writing a few descriptive lines based on simple data such as sports results (Caswell and Dörr 2017). While the research massively focused on readers' impressions and showed that the reader generally makes little distinction between automatic articles and those produced by a journalist, as in the case of short articles, the researchers suggest changing the research framework by shifting the study of algorithm performance (do they work as well as a journalist can?) to the study of how databases are built.

In other words, algorithms are becoming increasingly efficient. However, the way in which they are supplied with raw materials has not been sufficiently studied. The issue that remains to be addressed is therefore that of the quality of the databases, which are now not only made up of texts, but also of sounds, images, videos, etc. This complexity makes them both rich and limited. An algorithm processes the data provided to it. The authors talk about algorithmic authority. Who provides the databases? How do the media choose the databases used? How about the platform they will use? The fields of analysis are therefore still vast.

Konstantin Dörr provides an economic description of the market for companies that offer NLG solutions (Dörr 2016). They are generally recent (the oldest one dates back to 2010) and, according to the author, of a limited number (the author counts 13 of significant size at the date of publication of the article, that is, 2017[15], in addition to the Chinese company called Tencent that is entering the market). The market is therefore not very competitive because the number of players is still small, but it is becoming bigger as companies are multiplying rapidly. Such an example is the recent company Urbs Media, with its remarkably ambiguous slogan: "written by a human, produced by a robot". This company specializes in automated local information[16] and is developing a new NLG tool with AP called RADAR (Reports and Data and Robots)[17]. It is financed by the Google Digital News Initiative program.

Lastly, researchers are interested in algorithms that are inaccessible because they are "proprietary". Proprietary algorithms cannot be searched because they are the core of the software or platform developer's business model. Algorithms are then highly protected and frequently modified, making them even more difficult to understand.

If artificial intelligence has not yet fulfilled expectations, the future remains open. The press must therefore accelerate its transformation and control its data in order to become a player that is capable of properly valuing its contribution to the digital economy.

Finally, to conclude, let us take up Eric Scherer's deliberately provocative question (Scherer 2017): what if the media were to become intelligent again?

---

15 There are four U.S.-based companies: Narrative Science, Automated Insights, OnlyBoth and Linguastat; five German companies: Retresco, Aexea, TEXT`ON, Textomatic and 2txt; three French companies: Syllabs, Labsense and Yseop (a French–American company); and one British company, Arria.

16 See the site Urbsmedia.com.

17 "Reports and Data and Robots (RADAR) is a global first in successfully combining humans and machine to scale up local news production." See https://www.pressassociation.com/radarwebinar/. Google funds it to the tune of €706,000 (July 2017).

References

Achtenhagen, L. (2016). Developing media management scholarship: A commentary to Picard and Lowe Essay. *Journal of Media Business Studies*, 13(2), 117–123.

Adary, A., Libaert T., Mas C. and Westphalen, M.-H. (2015). *Communicator*, 7th edition. Dunod, Paris.

Agirdas, C. (2015). What drives media bias? New evidence from recent newspaper closures. *Journal of Media Economics*, 28(3), 123–141.

Ahrend, R. (2002). Press freedom, human capital, and corruption. Delta Working Paper, No. 2002–11. Delta (Ecole normale supérieure), Paris.

Akerlof, G. (1970). The market for "lemons": Quality uncertainty and the market mechanism. *The Quarterly Journal of Economics*, 84(3), 488–500.

Akerlof, G. (1982). The economic consequences of cognitive dissonance. *American Economic Review*, 72, 307–19.

Albarran, A. (2002). *Media Economics: Understanding Markets, Industries and Concepts*. Iowa State Press.

Albarran, A. (2004). Media Economics. In *The SAGE Handbook of Media Studies*, Downing, J. *et al*. (eds). SAGE, London, 291–308.

Albarran, A. (2016). *Management of Electronic and Digital Media*, 6th edition. Cengage, US.

Albarran, A. and Chan-Olmsted, S. (eds) (1998). *Global Media Markets: Commercialization, Concentration and Integration of World Media Markets*. ISU Press.

Albarran, A., Chan-Olmsted, S. and Wirth, M. (2005). *Handbook of Media Management and Economics*. Routledge, London.

Albarran, A., Chan-Olmsted, S. and Wirth, M. (2008). *Handbook of Media Management and Economics*. Lawrence Erlbaum, London.

Albert, P. (2018). *Histoire de la presse*. PUF, Paris.

Alcaraz, M. (2005). Les robots journalistes de plus en plus nombreux dans les rédactions. *Les Echos*, December 17, 2005. Available at: https://www.lesechos. fr/17/12/2015/LesEchos/22089-105-ECH_les-robots-journalistes-de-plus-en-plus-nombreux-dans-les-redactions.htm.

Alcaraz, M. (2018a). Jean-Marie Charon : Slow info : "Les succès, ce sont souvent quelques milliers d'exemplaires". *Les Echos*, January 11, 2018.

Alcaraz, M. (2018b). Publicité : en vingt ans, les Gafa ont laminé les médias historiques. *Les Echos*, July 24, 2018.

Alexandre, L. (2011). *La Mort de la mort*. Jean-Claude Lattès Editeur, Paris.

Allcott, H. and Gentzkow, M. (2017). Social media and fake news in the 2016 election. *Journal of Economic Perspectives*, 31(2), 211–236.

Alloing, C. and Pierre, J. (2017). *Le web affectif : Une économie numérique des émotions*. INA Éditions, Paris.

Alloing, C. and Vanderbiest, N. (2018). La fabrique des Rumeurs Numériques. Comment la fausse Information circule sur Twitter ? *Le temps des Médias*, 30, 105–123.

Ammann, M., Frey, R. and Verhofen, M. (2014). Do newspaper articles predict aggregate stock returns? *The Journal of Behavioral Finance*, 15, 195–2013.

An, S., Jin, H. and Simon, T. (2006). Ownership structure of publicity traded newspaper companies and their financial performance. *Journal of Media Economics*, 19(2), 119–136.

Anderson, S., Stromberg, D. and Waldfogel, J. (2015). *Handbook of Media Economics*. North Holland, Elsevier, London.

Andrès, L., Zentner, A. and Zentner, J. (2016). Measuring the effect of internet adoption on paper consumption. Policy Research working Paper, no. 6965, World Bank Group, Washington.

Ansolabehere, S., Lessem, R. and Snyder, J. (2006). The orientation of newspaper endorsements in U.S: elections, 1940–2002. *Quarterly Journal of Political Science*, 1, 393–404.

Antheaume, A. (2016). *Le journalisme numérique*. Presse de Science Po, Paris.

Athey, S. and Mobius, M. (2017). The impact of news aggregators on internet news consumption: The case of localization. Working paper no. 3353, Stanford Graduate School of Business.

Aubert-Tarby, C., Escobar, O. and Rayna, T. (2018). The impact of technological change on employment: The case of press digitalization. *Technological Forecasting & Social Change*, 128, 36–45.

Augey, D. and Rebillard, F. (2009). La Dimension Economique du Journalisme. *Les Cahiers du Journalisme*, 20, 10–20.

Augey, D., De Barnier, V. and Sonnac, N. (2010). Economie de l'attention: le cas de la presse en ligne. *Revue Gestion 2000*, 2(10), 115–126.

Augey, D., De Barnier, V. and Jammot, A. (2013). Le Management du Changement dans la presse : le cas du passage au bi-média. In *La Communication Numérique demain*, Scouarrec, A. (ed). Editions MPE, Paris, 117–135.

Bakir, V. and McStay, A. (2018). Fake News and the economy of emotions: Problems, causes and solutions. *Digital Journalism*, 6(2), 154–175.

Bakker, P. (2002). Free daily newspapers: Business model and strategies. *International Journal on Media Management*, 4(3), 180–187.

Balkin, J. (1999). How mass media simulate political transparency. *Cultural Values*, 3(4), 393–413.

Balle, F. (2017). *Les médias*. PUF, Paris.

Ban, P., Fouirnaies, A., Hall, A. and Snyder, J. (2018). How newspapers reveal political power. *Political Science Research and Methods*, 1–18, doi.org/10.1017/psrm.2017.43.

Barbera, P. (2015). How social media reduces mass political polarization. evidence from Germany, Spain, and the U.S. Working paper. Available at: http://pablobarbera.com/static/barbera polarization APSA.pdf [Accessed 5 March 2018].

Barbera, P. and Rivero, G. (2015). Understanding the political representativeness of Twitter users. *Social Science Computer Review*, 33(6), 721–729.

Barraud, B. (2016). L'analyse économique du droit. In *La recherche juridique, Sciences et pensées du droit*, Barraud, B. (ed.). L'Harmattan, Paris, 141–152.

Barrera, O., Guriev, S., Henry, E. and Zhuravskaya, E. (2017). Facts, alternative facts and fact checking in times of post-truth politics. Working paper, PSE. Available at: https://www.parisschoolofeconomics.eu/docs/barrera-rodriguez-oscar-david/ssrn-id3004631.pdf [Accessed 5 January 2018].

Bassoni, M. and Joux, A. (2014). *Introduction à l'économie des médias*. Armand Colin, Cursus, Paris.

Bauer, J. and Latzer, M. (2016). The economics of the internet: An overview. In *Handbook on the Economics of Internet*, Bauer J. and Latzer, M. (eds). Edward Elgar Publishing, London, 6–14.

Bellini, J. (2018). The Robot Revolution: Humanoid Potential, *Wall Street Journal*, January 29, 2018. Available at: https://www.wsj.com/articles/the-robot-revolution-humanoid-potential-moving-upstream-1517221862.

Benzoni, L. and Bourreau, M. (2001). Mimétisme ou contre-programmation : un modèle de concurrence entre programmes pour la télévision en clair. *Revue d'Economie Politique*, 111(6), 885–908.

Benzoni, L. and Clignet, S. (2017). Internet advertising: an economy of dominance. Working paper. Available at: http://dx.doi.org/10.2139/ssrn.3082761 [Accessed 17 December 2017].

Besley, T. and Prat, A.A. (2006). Handcuffs for the grabbing hand: media capture and government accountability. *American Economic Review*, 96(3), 720–736.

Besley, T. and Burgess, R. (2001). Political agency, government responsiveness and the role of the media. *European Economic Review*, 45, 629–640.

Besley, T. and Burgess, R. (2002). The political economy of government responsiveness: theory and evidence from India. *The Quarterly Journal of Economics*, 117(4), 1415–1451.

Bhattacharrya, S. and Holder, R. (2015). Media freedom and democracy in the fight against corruption. *European Journal of Political Economy*, 39, 13–24.

Bignon, V., Miscio, A. (2009). Media bias in financial newspapers: evidence from early twentieth century France. *European Economic History*, 14(3), 383–432.

Birz, G. (2017). Stale economic news, media and the stock market. *Journal of Economic Psychology*, 61, 87–102.

Blandin, C., Delporte, C. and Robinet, F. (2016). *Histoire de la presse en France : 20ème et 21ème siècle*. Armand Colin, Paris.

Blankespoor, E., Dehaan, E. and Zhu, C. (2017). Capital market effects of media synthesis and dissemination: evidence from robo-journalism. *Review of Accounting Studies*, 23(1), 1–36.

Blasco, A., Pin, P. and Sobbrio, F. (2016). Paying positive to go negative: advertisers' competition and media reports. *European Economic Review*, 83, 243–261.

Boltz, P. (1996). Economics and the media. *Quarterly Review of Economics and Finance*, 36, 161–168.

Bond, R. and Messing, S. (2015). Quantifying social media's political space: Estimating ideology from publicly revealed preferences on Facebook. *American Political Science Review*, 109(1), 62–78.

Bouckaert, B. and De Geest, G. (eds) (2000). *Encyclopedia of Law and Economics, Volume I, II, III and IV*. Edward Elgar, Cheltenham.

Bouquillion, P. (2005). La constitution des pôles des industries de la culture et de la communication. Entre "coups" financiers et intégration de filières industrielles. *Réseaux*, 131, 111–144.

Bovitz, G., Druckman, J. and Lupia, A. (2002). When can news organisation lead public opinion? Ideology versus market forces in decision to make News. *Public Choice*, 113(1–2), 127–155.

Boxell, L., Gentzkow, M. and Shapiro, J. (2017). Is the internet causing political polarization? Evidence from Demographics. NBER Working paper, no. 23258.

Boyer, M. (2006). The impact of media attention: Evidence from the automobile insurance industy. *Journal of Media Economics*, 19(3), 193–220.

Bregman, D. (1989). La fonction d'agenda : une problématique en devenir. *Revue Hermès*, 1(4), 191–202.

Broyelle, C. and Passa, J. (2018). *La loi Bichet sur la Distribution de la Presse 70 ans après*. Editions Panthéon-Assas, Paris.

Brunetti, A. and Weder, B. (2003). A free press is bad news for corruption. *Journal of Public Economics*, 87(7–8), 1801–1824.

Bruns, A. (2014). Media innovations, user innovations, societal innovations. *Journal of Media Innovation*, 1(1), 13–27.

Bruns, C. and Himmler, O. (2016). Mass media, instrumental information, and electoral accountability. *Journal of Public Economics*, 134, 75–84.

Burger, M., Thornborrow, J. and Fitzgerald, R. (2017). *Discours des réseaux sociaux*. De Boeck, Brussels.

Cagé, J., Hervé, N. and Viaud, M.-L. (2017). *L'information à tout prix*. INA Editions, Paris.

Cagé, J. (2016). *Sauver les médias: capitalisme, financement participatif et démocratie*. La République des Idées, Paris.

Cagé, J. and Godechot, O. (2017). Qui possède les médias? Une analyse de l'actionnariat des médias. Rapport du LIEPP, Paris. Available at: https://spire. sciencespo.fr/hdl:/2441/5ej8oq8p589tbq524jeiieb7cl/resources/media-independance-project-finalreport.pdf?_ga=2.138658544.2125989818.1531381695-2025662808. 1531381695 [Accessed 12 March 2018].

Calabresi, G. (1970). *The Cost of Accidents: A Legal and Economic Analysis*. Yale University Press, New Haven.

Calvert, R. (1985). The value of biased information: A rational choice model of political advice. *The Journal of Politics*, 47, 530–555.

Carr, N. (2018). *The Shallows: What the Internet Is Doing to Our Brains*. W. W. Norton & Company, New York.

Casas, A., Fawaz, Y. and Trindade, A. (2016). Surprise me if you can: the influence of newspaper endorsements in US Presidential elections. *Economic Inquiry*, 54(3), 1484–1498.

Castaneda, A. and Martinelli, C. (2018). Politics, entertainment and business: a multisided model of media. *Public Choice*, 174, 239–256.

Caswell, D. and Dörr, K. (2017). Automated Journalism 2.0: Event-driven Narratives. *Journalism Practices*. Available at: http://dx.doi.org/10.1080/17512786.2017.1320773 [Accessed 22 December 2017].

Cazares, F. (2017). Facebook va bloquer les revenus des sites de 'fake news'. *Les Echos*. Available at: https://www.lesechos.fr/29/08/2017/lesechos.fr/010198518 493_facebook-va-bloquer-les-revenus-des-sites-de---fake-news--.htm.

Chamoux, J.-P. (ed.) (2018). *The Digital Era 1*. ISTE Ltd, London, and Wiley, New York.

Champlin, D. and Knoedler, J. (2002). Operating in the public interest or in pursuit of private profits? News in the age of media consolidation. *Journal of Economic Issues*, 36(2), 459–468.

Charon, J.-M. (2016). *La presse d'information multi-supports*. UPPR Editions, Toulouse.

Charon, J.-M. (2014). *Les médias en France*. PUF, Paris.

Cherubini, F. and Graves, L. (2016). The rise of fact-checking sites in Europe. Rapport Reuters Institute. Available at: http://reutersinstitute.politics.ox.ac.uk/our-research/rise-fact-checking-sites-europe [Accessed 10 October 2017].

Cherubini, F. and Nielsen, R. (2016). Editorial analytics: How news media are developing and using audience data and metrics. *Reuters Institute for the Study of Journalism*. Available at: http://reutersinstitute.politics.ox.ac.uk [Accessed 10 October 2017].

Chiang, C-F. and Knight, B. (2011). Media bias and influence: Evidence from newspaper endorsements. *Review of Economic Studies*, 78, 795–820.

Chiou, L. and Tucker, C. (2013). Paywall and the demand for news. *Information Economics and Policy*, 25(2), 61–69.

Chiou, L. and Tucker, C. (2015). Content aggregation by platforms: the case of the news media. NBER Working paper, no. 21404.

Cho, D., Smith, M. and Zentner, A. (2016). Internet adoption and the survival of print newspapers: a country-level examination. *Information Economics and Policy*, 37, 13–19.

Chung, M. (2017). Not just numbers: the role of social media metrics in online news evaluations. *Computers in Human Behavior*, 75, 949–957.

Chupin, I., Hube, N. and Kaciaf, N. (2013). *Histoire Politique et Economique des Médias en France*. La Découverte, Paris.

Clerwall, C. (2014). Enter the robot journalist: Users' perceptions of automated content. *Journalism Practice*, 8(5), 519–531.

Coase, R. (1974). The market for goods and the market for ideas. *American Economic Review*, 64(2), 384–391.

Coase, R. (1977). Advertising and free speech. *Journal of Legal Studies*, 6(1), 1–34.

Coddington, M. (2015). Clarifying journalism's quantitative turn. *Digital Journalism*, 3(3), 331–348.

Coddington, M. (2015). The wall becomes a curtain: revisiting journalism's news-Business Boundary. In *Boundaries of Journalism: Professionalism, Practices and Participation*, Carlson, M. and Lewis, S. (eds). Routledge, London, 67–82.

Colford, P. (2014). A leap forward in quarterly earnings stories. *Associated Press*. Available at: https://blog.ap.org/contributor/paul-colford [Accessed 21 April 2016].

Conover, M., Goncalves, B., Flammini, A. and Menczer, F. (2012). Partisan asymmetries in online political activity. *EPJ Data Science*, 1(1), 1–19.

Corden, W-M. (1952–1953). The maximization of profit by a newspaper. *The Review of Economic Studies*, 20(3), 181–190.

Corneo, G. (2006). Media capture in a democracy: The role of wealth concentration. *Journal of Public Economics*, 90, 37–58.

Cox, J. and Goldman, A. (1996), Speech, truth and the free market for ideas. *Legal Theory*, 2, 1–32.

Cunningham, S., Flew, T. and Swift, A. (2015). *Media Economics*. Palgrave Macmillan, New York.

Cunningham, S. and Flew, T. (2015). Reconsidering media economics: From orthodoxies to heterodoxies. *Media Industries Journal*, 2(1), 1–18.

D'Almeida, F. and Delporte, C. (2010). *Histoire des médias en France*. Flammarion, Paris.

Dahan, R., Leboeuf, N., Lenne, O., Pelouard, L., Reffait, N. (2018). Médias et Publicité en ligne, Transfert de valeur et nouvelles pratiques. Report, BearingPoint, Paris.

Davenport, T. (2002). *The Attention Economy: Understanding the New Currency of Business*. McGraw-Hill, New York.

Davis, N. and Dunaway, J. (2016). Party polarization, media choice, and mass partisan-ideological sorting. *Public Opinion Quarterly*, 80(1), 272–297.

De Baynast, A. and Landrevie, J. (2014). *Publicitor*, 8th edition. Dunod, Paris.

De Biaf, L. (2015). *Journalisme 2.0*. L'Harmattan, Paris.

De Corniere, A. and Sarvary, M. (2018). Social media and news: Attention capture via content building, TSE, Working paper. Available at: https://www.tse-fr.eu [Accessed 10 July 2018].

De Laubier, C. (2000). *La presse sur internet*. PUF, Paris.

De Leon, F. (2016). Endorse or not to endorse: Understanding the determinants of newspapers' likelihood of making political recommendations. *Scottish Journal of Political Economy*, 63(4), 357–376.

De Maeyer, J., Libert, M., Domingo, D., Heinderyckx, F. and Le Cam, F. (2015). Waiting for data journalism. *Digital Journalism*, 3(3), 432–446.

De Rochegonde, A. and Sénéjoux, R. (2017). *Médias, les nouveaux empires*. First Document, Paris.

De Rochegonde, A. (2018). Le Monde face à la pression économique. *Strategies*, July 18, 2008. Available at: http://www.strategies.fr/actualites/medias/4015889W/le-monde-face-a-la-pression-economique.html.

Decanio, S. (2017). Robots and humans – complements or substitutes? *Journal of Macroeconomics*, 49, 280–291.

Degand, A. and Grevisse, B. (2012). *Journalisme en ligne*. De Boeck, Brussels.

Della Vigna, S. and La Ferrare, E. (2016). Economic and social impacts of the media. NBER Working paper, no. 21360.

Demeulemeester, J.-L. and Diebolt, C. (2006). Cliométrie et gestion : vers une nouvelle alliance ? *Revue Française de Gestion*, 9(168–169), 359–367.

Dertouzos, J. and Trautman, W. (1990). Economic effects of media concentration: estimates from a model of newspaper firm. *Journal of Industrial Economics*, 39(1), 1–14.

Deslandes, G. (2008). *Le Management des médias*. La Découverte, Paris.

Devito, M. (2017), From editors to algorithms: a values-based approach to understanding story selection in the Facebook news feed. *Digital Journalism*, 5(6), 753–773.

Devito, M.A., Gergle, D.R. and Birnholtz, J.P. (2017). "Algorithms ruin everything": #RIPTwitter, Folk Theories, and Resistance to Algorithmic Change in Social Media. In *Proceedings of the 2017 CHI Conference on Human Factors in Computing Systems*, G. Mark, and S. Fussell (eds.). ACM, 3163–3174.

Dewenter, R., Dulleck, U. and Thomas, T. (2016). Does the 4th estate deliver? Toward a more direct measure of political media bias. Discussion Paper, DICE, Dusseldorf University Press.

Diakopoulos, N. and Koliska, M. (2016). Algorithmic transparency in the news media. *Digital Journalism*, 5(7), 809–828.

Ditella, R. and Franceschelli, I. (2009). Government advertising and media coverage of corruption scandals. *American Economic Journal: Applied Economics*, 3(4), 119–51.

Djankov, S., McLiesh, C., Nenova, T. and Shleifer, A. (2003). Who owns the media? *The Journal of Law and Economics*, 46(2), 341–382.

Doguel, L. (2014). What is so special about media innovations? A characterization of the field. *Journal of Media Innovation*, 1(1), 52–69.

Dörr, K. (2016). Mapping the field of algorithmic journalism. *Digital Journalism*, 4(6), 700–722.

Dörr, K. (2017). Ethical challenges of algorithmic journalism. *Digital Journalism*, 5(4), 404–419.

Dougal, C., Engelberg, J., Garcia, D. and Parsons, C. (2012). Journalists and the stock market. *Review of Financial Studies*, 25(4), 639–679.

Downs, A. (1957). *An Economic Theory of Democracy*. Harper and Row, New York.

Doyle, G. (2013). *Understanding Media Economics*. Sage, London.

Drago, F., Nannicini, T. and Sobbrio, F. (2014). Meet the press: How voters and politicians respond to newspaper entry and exit. *American Economic Journal: Applied Economics*, 6(3), 159–188.

Drake, D. (2017). The invisible hand of the unaccountable algorithm: How Google, Facebook and other tech companies are changing journalism. In *Digital Technology and Journalism, An International Comparative Perspective*, Tong, J. and Lo, S.-H. (eds.). Palgrave McMillan, New York, 25–46.

Dyck, A. and Zingale, S.L. (2002). Bubble and the media. In *Corporate Governance and Capital Flows' in a Global Economy*, Cornelius, P. and Kogut, B. (eds). Oxford University Press, New York.

Dyck, A. and Zingales, L (2003). The media and asset price's. NBER and CEPR. Working paper, University of Chicago.

Dyck, A., Volchkova, N. and Zingales, L. (2008). The corporate governance role of the media: evidence from Russia. *The Journal of Finance*, 73(3), 1093–1135.

Elligsen, S. and Hernaes, O. (2015). The impact of commercial television on turnout and public policy: Evidence from Norwegian local politics. *Journal of Public Economics*, 159, 1–15.

Ellman, M. and Germano, F. (2009). What do the papers sell? *The Economic Journal*, 119 (537), 680–704.

Eniklopov, R., Petrova, M. and Zhuravskaya, E. (2011). Media and political persuasion: Evidence from Russia. *American Economic Review*, 101(7), 3253–3285.

Eniklopov, R., Petrova, M. and Sonin, K. (2018). Social media and corruption. *American Economic Journal: Applied Economics*, 10(1), 150–174.

Eom, S.-J., Hwang, H. and Kim, J.-H. (2018). Can social media increase government responsiveness? A case study of Seoul, Korea. *Government Information Quarterly*, 35, 109–122.

Eraslan, H. and Özertürk, S. (2017). Information gatekeeping and media bias. Working paper. Available at: https://economics.rice.edu/file/2691/download?token=sEJ52cd4 [Accessed 6 January 2018].

Eveno, P. (2017). *La Presse*. PUF, Paris.

Eveno, P. (2017). *100 ans à travers les Unes de la presse*. Larousse, Paris.

Falkinger, J. (2007). Attention Economics. *Journal of Economic Theory*, 133, 266–294.

Farrell, H. (2012). The internet's consequences for politics. *Annual Review of Political Science*, 15, 35–52.

Fengler, S. and Russ-Mohl, S. (2008). The crumbling hidden wall: Towards an economic theory of journalism. *Kyklos*, 61(4), 520–524.

Fergusson, L. (2014). Media markets, special interests and voters. *Journal of Public Economics*, 109, 13–26.

Filistrucchi, L. and Trucker, C. (eds.) (2012). The economics of digital media markets. *Information Economics and Policy*, 24(1), 1–2.

Fogel, J.-F. and Patino, B. (2007). *La presse sans Gutenberg*. Points, Paris.

Fotorino, E. (ed.) (2017). *Les Médias sont-ils dangereux ? Comprendre les mécanismes de l'Information*. Philippe Rey Editeur, Paris.

Freibel, G. and Heinz, M. (2014). Media slant against foreign owners: Downsizing. *Journal of Public Economics*, 120, 97–106.

Freille, S., Haque, E. and Kneller, R. (2007). A contribution to the empirics of press freedom and corruption. *European Journal of Political Economy*, 23, 838–862.

Friedrichsen, M. and Mühl-Benninghaus, W. (2017). The social media management chain, how social media influences traditional media. In *Handbook of Social Media Management*, Friedrichsen M., Mühl-Benninghaus W. (eds.). Springer, 3–6.

Gabszewicz, J., Sonnac, N. (2013). *L'industrie des médias à l'ère numérique*. La Découverte, Paris.

Gabszewicz, J., Laussel, D. and Sonnac, N. (2001). Press advertising and the accent of the "Pensée Unique". *European Economic Review*, 45, 641–651.

Gabszewicz, J., Laussel, D. and Sonnac, N. (2002). Press advertising and the political differentiation of newspapers. *Journal of Public Economic Theory*, 4(3), 317–334.

Gabuthy, Y. (2013). Analyse économique du Droit : Présentation générale. *Economie et Prévisions*, 202–203, 1–8.

Gal-Or, E., Giliani, T. and Yildirim, T-P. (2012). The impact of advertising on media bias. *Journal of Marketing Research*, 49, 92–99.

Galily, Y. (2018). Artificial intelligence and sports journalism: is it a sweeping change. *Technology in Society*, 54, 47–51.

Galperti, S. and Trevino, I. (2017). Coordination motives and competition for attention in information markets. Working paper. San Diego University. Available at: https://pdfs.semanticscholar.org [Accessed 22 October 2017].

Galvis, A., Snyder, J. and Song, B. (2016). Newspaper market structure and behavior: partisan coverage of political scandals in the United States from 1870 to 1910. *The Journal of Politics*, 78(2), 368–381.

Gambaro, M. (2014). Some economics of new media content production and consumption and strategic implication for media companies. In *Handbook of Social Media Management*, Friedrichsen M. and Mühl-Benninghaus W. (eds.). Springer, 49–59.

Gambaro, M. and Puglisi, R. (2015). What do ads buy? Daily coverage of listed companies on the Italian press. *European Journal of Political Economy*, 39, 41–57.

Ganascia, J.-G. (2017). *Le mythe de la Singularité. Faut-il craindre l'Intelligence Artificielle ?* Le Seuil, Paris.

Garcia Pires, A. (2013). Media plurality and the intensity of readers' political preferences. *Journal of Media Economics*, 26(1), 41–55.

Garcia Pires, A. (2014). Media diversity, advertising, and adaptation of news to readers'political preferences. *Information Economics and Policy*, 28, 28–38.

Garcia-Arenas, J. (2016). The impact of free media on regime change: Evidence from Russia. Working paper. Available at: www.amse-aixmarseille.fr/en/event/javier-garcia-arenas [Accessed 12 October 2017].

Garcia-Uribe, S. (2016). Multidimensional media slant: Complementarities in news reporting by US newspapers. Working Paper, University of Hamburg.

Garz, M. (2015), Research Network Economics of Media Bias. Available at: www.hamburgmediaschool.com/fileadmin/user_upload/Dateien/Forschung/Media_Bias/network_media_bias_web_description.pdf

Garz, M., Sood, G., Stone, D. and Wallace, J. (2018). What drives demand for media slant? SSRN Working paper.

Gehlbach, S. and Sonin, K. (2014). Government control of the media. *Journal of Public Economics*, 118, 163–171.

Gentzkow, M. (2016). Polarization in 2016. Toulouse Network for Information Technology Whitepaper.

Gentzkow, M. and Shapiro, J. (2006). Media bias and reputation. *Journal of Political Economy*, 114(2), 280–316.

Gentzkow, M. and Shapiro, J. (2010). What drives media slant? Evidence from US daily newspapers. *Econometrica*, 78(1), 35–71.

Gentzkow, M. and Shapiro, J. (2011). Ideological segregation on Line and off line. *Quarterly Journal of Economics*, 126(4), 1799–1839.

Gentzkow, M. and Shapiro, J. (2015). Ideology and online news. In *Economic Analysis of the Digital Economy*, Golfarb, A., Grennstein, S. and Tucker, C. (eds.). NBER, University of Chicago Press.

Gentzkow, M., Glaeser, E. and Goldin, C. (2006). The rise of the fourth estate: How newspapers became informative and why it mattered in corruption and reform. In *Lessons from America's Economic History*, Glaeser E. and Goldin C. (eds.). NBER, University of Chicago Press.

Gentzkow, M., Kelly, B. and Taddy, M. (2018). Text as data. NBER Working paper.

Gentzkow, M., Petek, N., Shapiro, J. and Sinkinson, M. (2015). Do newspapers serve the State? Incumbent party influence on the US Press, 1986–1928. *Journal of European Economic Association*, 13(1), 29–61.

Gentzkow, M., Shapiro, J. and Stone, D. (2016). Media bias in the marketplace: theory. In *Handbook of Media Economics*, Anderson, S., Stromberg, D. and Waldfogel, J. (eds.). North Holland, London, 2.

Gentzkow, M. and Kamenika, E. (2017). Competition in persuasion. *Review of Economic Studies*, 84, 300–322.

Gentzkow, M., Shapiro, J. and Sinkinson, M. (2014). Competition and ideological diversity: Historical evidence from US newspapers. *American Economic Review*, 104(10), 3073–3114.

George, L. and Hogendorn, C. (2013). Local news online: Aggregators, geo-targeting and the market for local news. Economics Working paper, Hunter College.

George, L. and Waldfogel, J. (2003). Who affects whom in daily newspaper markets? *Journal of Political Economy*, 111(4), 765–784.

Gilbert, A. (2016). 36% des Français sont équipés d'un adblock. Ipsos, IAB Barometer France, December 2, 2016. Available at: https://www.ipsos.com/frfr/36-des-francais-sont-equipes-dun-adblock.

Gillespie, T. (2014). The relevance of algorithms. In *Media Technologies: Essays on Communication, Materiality, and Society*, Boczkowski P. and Foot K. (eds.). MIT Press, 167–193.

Goel, B. (2017). Developments in the field of natural language processing. *International Journal of Advanced Research in Computer Science*, 8(3), 23–28.

Goel, R., Nelson, M. and Naretta, M. (2012). The internet as an indicator of corruption awareness. *European Journal of Political Economy*, 28, 64–75.

Graefe, A., Haim, M., Haarmann B. and Brosius, H.-B. (2016). Readers' perception of computer-generated news: Credibility, expertise, and readability. *Journalism*, 19(5), 595–610.

Granovetter, M. (2000). *Le marché autrement. Les réseaux dans l'économie.* Desclée de Brouwer, Paris.

Groseclose, T. and Milyo, J. (2005). A measure of media bias. *The Quarterly Journal of Economics*, 120(4), 1191–1237

Guilbert, G., Rebillard, F. and Rochelandet, F. (2016). *Médias, culture et numérique : approches socio-économiques.* Armand Colin, Paris.

Haim, M. and Graefe, A. (2017). Automated news, better than expected. *Digital Journalism*, 5(8), 1044–1059.

Haim, M., Graefe, A. and Brosius, H.-B. (2017). Burst of the filter bubble? Effects of personalization on the diversity of Google news. *Digital Journalism*, 6(3), 330–343.

Hamilton, K. (2014). A path to understanding the effects of algorithm awareness. Available at: Doi.org/10.1145/2559206.2578883 [Accessed 18 October 2017].

Hang, M. (2006). The history and development of media economics research in China. *Journal of Media Business Studies*, 3(2), 23–39.

Haupert, M. (2017). The impact of cliometrics on economies and history. *Revue d'Economie Politique*, 27(6), 1051–1089.

Hayek, F. (1945). The uses of knowledge in society. *American Economic Review*, 35(4), 519–530.

Heinz, M. and Swinnen, J. (2015). Media slant in economic news: a factor 20. *Economic Letters*, 132, 18–20.

Hirschberg, J. and Manning, C. (2015). Advances in natural language processing. *Science*, 349(6245), 261–266.

Ho, B. and Liu, P. (2015). Herd journalism: investment in novelty and popularity in market for news. *Information Economics and Policy*, 31, 33–46.

Hong, S. (2012). Online news on TWITTER: newspapers' social media adoption and their online readership. *Information Economics and Policy*, 24, 69–74.

Innis, H. (1942). The newspaper in economic development. *Journal of Economic History*, 2, 1–33.

Jackson, M. (2014). Networks in the understanding of economic behaviors networks in the understanding of economic behaviors. *Journal of Economic Perspectives*, 28(4), 3–22.

Jackson, M., Rogers, B. and Zenou, Y. (2016). Networks: an economic perspective. CEPR Discussion Papers no. 11452.

Jeanne-Perrier, V. (2018). *Les journalistes face aux réseaux sociaux*. MkF Editions, Paris.

Jeanneney, J.-N. (2015). *Histoire des médias, des origines à nos jours*. Editions Points Histoire, Paris.

Jeon, D.-S. and Nars, N. (2016). News aggregators and the competition among newspapers on the internet. *American Economic Journal: Microeconomics*, 8(4), 91–114.

Jia, M., Ruan, H. and Zhang, Z. (2016). How rumors fly. *Journal of Business Research*, 72, 33–45.

Jla, C.-K. and Sarangi, S. (2017). Does social media reduce corruption? *Information Economics and Policy*, 39, 60–71.

Jung, J., Song, H., Kim, Y., Im, H., Oh, S. and Kim, Y. (2017). Intrusion of software robots into journalism: The public's and journalists' perceptions of news written by algorithms and human journal. *Computers in Human Behavior*, 71, 291–298.

Kalifa, D., Regnier, P., Therenty, M-E. and Vaillant, A. (eds) (2011). *La civilisation du journal. Histoire culturelle et littéraire de la presse française au 19ème siècle*. Nouveau Monde Editions, Paris.

Kantar Media (2018). BUMP 2018 : Baromètre Unifié du Marché Publicitaire, Le Marché Publicitaire 2017, IREP, France Pub and Kantar Media.

Kayser, M. and Peress, M. (2015). The media, the economy and the vote. Working paper.

Kennedy, P. and Prat, A. (2018). Where do people get their news? Working paper.

Kim, D. and Kim, S. (2017). Newspaper companies' determinants in adopting robot journalism. *Technological Forecasting & Social Change Review*, 117, 184–195.

Kim, D. and Kim, S. (2018). Newspaper journalists' attitudes towards robot journalism. *Telematics and Informatics*, 35, 340–357.

Kind, H., Schjelderup, G. and Stahler, F. (2013). Newspaper differentiation and investments in journalism: the role of tax policy. *Economica*, 80, 131–148.

Koschat, M. and Putsis, W. (2000). Who wants you when you're old and poor? Exploring the economics of media pricing. *Journal of Media Economics*, 13(4), 215–232.

Kshetri, N. and Voas, J. (2017). The economics of fake news. *IT* Professional, 19(6), 8–12.

Küng, L. (2008). *Strategic Management in the Media*. Sage, London.

Küng, L. (2015). *Innovators in Digital News*. Tauris Eds, Oxford.

Küng, L. (2016). Why is media management research so difficult and what can scholars do to overcome the field's intrinsic challenges? *Journal of Media Business Studies*, 13(4), 276–282.

Küng, L. (2017). Reflection on the ascendancy of technology in the media and its implications for organisations and their leaders. *Journal of Media Innovation*, 4(1), 77–81.

Lancelin, A. (2018). *La pensée en otage*. Les liens qui libèrent, Paris.

Lamla, M. and Lein, S. (2012). The Role of media for consumers' inflation expectation formation. Working paper.

Larcinese, V., Puglisi, R. and Snyder, J. (2011). Partisan bias in economic news: evidence on the agenda-setting behavior of U.S. newspapers. *Journal of Public Economics*, 95, 1178–1189.

Latar, N. (2015). The robot journalist in the age of social physics: The end of human journalism? In *The New World of Transition Media*, Einav G. (ed.). Springer Publishing, London.

Latham, O. (2015). Lame duck and the media. *The Economic Journal*, 125, 1918–1951.

Le Cam, F. and Trédan, O. (2017). Journalisme et données: de l'investigation à la robotisation. In *Les big data à découvert*, Bouzeghoub, M. and Mosseri, R. (eds.). CNRS Editions, Paris.

Le Cam, F. and Ruellan, D. (2017). *Émotions de journalistes : sel et sens du métier*. PUG, Grenoble.

Le Champion, R. (ed.) (2012). *Journalisme 2.0*. La Documentation française, Paris.

Le Flock, P. and Sonnac, N. (2000). *L'industrie des médias*. La Découverte, Paris.

Le Flock, P. and Sonnac, N. (2013). *L'économie de la presse à l'ère numérique*. La Découverte, Paris.

Lee, N., Kim, Y. and Sang, Y. (2017). How do journalists leverage Twitter? Expressive and consumptive use of Twitter. *The Social Science Journal*, 54, 139–147.

Letteron, R. (2017). *La liberté de la presse au 21ème siècle*. CNRS Editions, Paris.

Levy, G., Moreno de Barreda, I. and Razin, R. (2016). Persuasion with correlation neglect: media power via correlation of news content. *Discussion Paper 836*, Department of Economics, Oxford University.

Lewis, S. (2015). Journalism in the area of big data. *Digital Journalism*, 3(3), 321–330.

Lewis, S. and Westlung, O. (2015). Big data and journalism: Epistemology, expertise, economics, and ethics. *Digital Journalism*, 3(3), 447–466.

Liang, C.-Y. and Nordin M. (2012). The internet, news consumption and political attitudes. Working paper no. 2012–14.

Lim, C. (2015). Media influence on courts: evidence from civil case adjudication. *American Law and Economics Review*, 17(1), 87–126.

Lim, C., Snyder, J. and Stromberg, D. (2015). The judge, the politician, and the press: newspaper coverage and criminal sentencing across electoral systems. *American Economic Journal: Applied Economics*, 7(4), 103–135.

Lischka, J. (2016). Innovators in digital news. *The Journal of Media Innovation*, 3(2), 88–91.

Liu, B. and McConnel, J. (2013). The role of the media in corporate governance: Do the media influence manager's capital allocation decisions? *Journal of Financial Economics*, 110, 1–17.

Lokot, T. and Diakopoulos, N. (2015). News bots: automating news and information dissemination on Twitter. *Digital Journalism*, 4(6), 682–699.

Lott, J. and Hassett, K. (2014). Is newspaper coverage of economic events politically biased? *Public Choice*, 160, 65–108.

Luo, X. (2017). Collective mass media bias, social media, and non-partisans. *Economics Letters*, 156, 78–81.

Maigret, E. (2015). *Sociologie de la communication et des médias*. Armand Colin, Paris.

Maigret, E. and Rebillard F. (2015). La nécessaire rencontre des *cultural studies* et de l'économie politique de la communication. *Réseaux*, 4(192), 9–43.

Magis, C. (2016). Économie politique de la communication et théorie critique des médias. *Revue Réseaux*, 5(199), 43–70.

Malka, L. (2016). *Les journalistes se slashent pour mourir, la Presse face aux défis du numérique*. Robert Laffont, Paris.

Martin, G. and Yurukiglu, A. (2017). Bias in cable news: Persuasion and polarization. *American Economic Review*, 107(9), 2565–2599.

Mariet, F (2017). Livre blanc. Valeurs de la presse: ses audiences, sa data. Ipsos, Weborama, Paris.

Martin, J., Abbas, D. and Martins, R. (2016). The validity of global press ratings: Freedom House and Reporters sans Frontières, 2002–2014. *Journalism Practice*, 10(1), 93–108.

Mas, V. and Petit, C. (2014). *La presse sur tablette. Les journaux et magazines de demain.* CFPJ Editions, Paris.

Mata, T. (2011). Fractals in economic journalism. *History of Political Economy*, 43(2), 379–385.

Mathien, M. (2003). *Economie générale des médias.* Ellipses, Paris.

Mattelart, A. and Neveu, E. (2003). *Introduction aux cultural studies.* La Découverte, Paris.

Mauro, P. (1995). Corruption and growth. *Quarterly Journal of Economics*, 110(3), 681–712.

Mayer, A. (2009). Online social networks in economics. *Decision Support System*, 47, 169–184.

McChesney, R. and Schiller, D. (2003). The political economy of international communications: foundations for the emerging global debate about media ownership and global regulation. United Nations Research Institute for Social Development, Programme paper no. 11.

McCluskey, J., Swinnen, J. and Vandemoortele, T. (2015). You get what you want: A note on the economics of bad news. *Information Economics and Policy*, 30, 1–5.

McCombs, M. and Shaw, D. (1972). The agenda-setting function of mass media. *Public Opinion Quarterly*, 36(2), 176–87.

MediaPart (2008). Le Projet. *MediaPart.* Available at: https://presite.mediapart.fr/contenu/le-projet.html.

Menager, L. (2006). Connaissance commune et consensus. *Revue d'économie industrielle*, 114(115), 41–66.

Mercier, A. and Pignard-Cheynel, N. (2018). *#info : Commenter et partager l'actualité sur TWITTER et FACEBOOK.* Editions de la Maison des Sciences de l'Homme, Paris.

Miege, B. (2004). L'Économie Politique de la Communication, *Revue Hermès*, 38, 46–54.

Milgrom, P. (1981). Good news and bad news: representation theorems and application. *Bell Journal of Economics*, 12(2), 380–391.

Miller, G. (2006). The press as a watchdog for accounting fraud. *Journal of Accounting Research*, 44(5), 1001–1033.

Mings, S. and White, P. (2000). Profiting from online news: the search for viable business models. In *Internet Publishing and Beyond*, Kahin, B. and Varian, H. (eds). MIT Press, Boston.

Ministère de la culture et de la communication (2015). Tableaux statistiques de la presse, Presse écrite 2015. Report, Direction générale des médias et des industries culturelles, Paris.

Montal, T. and Reich, Z. (2017). I, robot. You, journalist. Who is the author? Authorship, bylines and full disclosure in automated journalism. *Digital Journalism*, 5(7), 829–849.

Moses, L. (2014). The Guardian's robot newspaper comes to the U.S. *Digiday*. Available at: https://digiday.com/media/guardian-robot-newspaper/ [Accessed 15 October 2017].

Mueller, D. (2010). *Choix Publics, Analyse Economique des décisions publiques*. De Boeck, Brussels.

Mulhmann, G. (2017). *Du journalisme en démocratie*. Payot, Paris.

Mullainathan, S. and Shleifer, A. (2002). Media bias. NBER Working paper, no. 9295.

Mullainathan, S. and Shleifer, A. (2004). Market for news. *American Economic Review*, 95(1), 1031–1053.

Nair, T. (2003). Growth and structural transformation of newspaper industry in India: an empirical investigation. *Economic and Political Weekly*, 38(39), 4182–4189.

Napoli, P. (2014). Automated media: An institutional theory perspective on algorithmic media production and consumption. *Communication Theory*, 24, 340–360.

Neveu, E. (2013). *Sociologie du journalisme*. La Découverte, Paris.

Newman, N., Fletcher, R., Kalogeropoulos, A., Levy, D. and Nielsen, R. (2017). Reuters Institute Digital News Report. Available at: https://reutersinstitute. politics.ox.ac.uk/sites/default/files/Digital%20News%20Report%202017%20we b_0.pdf. Page 34 onwards.

Newman, N., Fletcher, R., Kalogeropoulos, A., Levy, D. and Nielsen, R. (2018). Reuters digital news report. Reuters Institute for the study of Journalism. Available at: http://www.digitalnewsreport.org/survey/2018/overview-key-findings-2018/.

Niskanen, W. (1975). Bureaucrats and politicians. *Journal of Law and Economics*, 18, 617–44.

Oborne, P. (2015). Why I have resigned from the Telegraph. *Open Democracy*, February 17, 2015. Available at: https://www.opendemocracy.net/ourkingdom/peter-oborne/why-i-have-resigned-from-telegraph.

Oliveros, S. and Vardy, F. (2015). Demand for slant: How abstention shapes voters' choice of news media. *The Economic Journal*, 125, 1327–1368.

Orr, D. (1987). Notes on the mass media as economic institution. *Public Choice*, 53, 79–95.

O'Sullivan, J. Fortunati, L. Taipale, S. and Barnhurst, K. (2017). Innovators and innovated: Newspapers and the postdigital future beyond "death of print". *Information Society*, 33(2), 89–95.

Ozertürk, S. (2018). Choosing a media outlet when seeking public approval. *Public Choice*, 174(1–2), 3–21.

Parasie, S. (2015). Data-driven revelation? Epistemological tensions in investigative journalism in the age of 'big data'. *Digital Journalism*, 3(3), 364–380.

Parasie, S. and Darigal, E. (2012). Data-driven journalism and the public good: "Computer-assisted-reporters" and "programmer-journalists" in Chicago. *New Media & Society*, 15(6), 853–871.

Pariser, E. (2011). *The Filter Bubble: What the Internet is Hiding from You*. Penguin Books London.

Pearsall, J. (2002). *Oxford English Dictionary*, 2nd edition. Oxford University Press, Oxford, UK.

Persson, T. and Tabellini, G, (2000). *Political Economics: Explaining Economic Policy*. MIT Press, Boston.

Petrova, M. (2008). Inequality and media capture. *Journal of Public Economics*, 92(1–2), 183–212.

Petrova, M. (2012). Mass media and special interest groups. *Journal of Economic Behavior and Organization*, 84, 17–38.

Petrova, M. and Enikolopov, R. (2016). Media capture: Empirical evidence. In *Handbook of Media Economics*, Anderson, S., Waldfogel, J. and Strömberg, D. (eds.). North-Holland, 687–700.

Picard, R. (1996). The rise and fall of communication empires. *Journal of Media Economics*, 9(4), 23–40.

Picard, R. (1998). A note on relationship between circulation size and advertising rates. *Journal of Media Economics*, 11(2), 47–55.

Picard, R. (2015). Journalists'perceptions of the future of journalistic work, Reuters Institute Report for the Study of Journalism.

Picard, R. and Lowe, G. (2016). Questioning media management scholarship: Four parables about how to better develop the field. *Journal of Media Business Studies*, 13(2), 61–72.

Picard, R. and Wildman, S. (2015). *Handbook on the Economics of the Media.* Edward Elgar Publishing, London.

Picard, R. (2000a). Changing business models of online content service. *International Journal on Media Management*, 2(11), 60–68.

Picard, R. (2000b). The structure of newspaper industry. In *The Media and Entertainment Industries*, Greco, A. (ed.). Allyn and Bacon, Boston.

Picard, R. (2001a). Effects of recessions on advertising expenditures: an explanatory study of economic downturns in nine developed nations. *Journal of Media Economics*, 14(1), 1–14.

Picard, R. (2001b). Strategic responses to free distribution daily newspapers. *International Journal on Media Management*, 2(3), 167–172.

Pignard-Cheynel, N. and Sebbagh, B. (2012). La presse quotidienne régionale sur les réseaux sociaux : Etude de la présence des titres français sur Facebook et Twitter. *Sciences de la Société*, 84–85, 171–191.

Pinker, S. (2005). *Comprendre la nature humaine.* Odile Jacob, Paris.

Pires, A. (2016). Plurality: private versus mixed duopolies. *Journal of Public Economic Theory*, 18(6), 942–960.

Pitoura, E., Tsaparas, T., Flouris, G., Fundulaki, I., Papadakos, P., Abiteboul, S. and Weikum, G. (2017). On measuring bias in online information. *ACM SIGMOD Record*, 46(4). Available at: https://sigmodrecord.org/2018/01/27/onmeasuring-bias-in-online-information/ [Accessed 10 February 2018].

Pogorelski, K. and Shum, M. (2017). Sharing and voting on social networks: An experimental study. Available at: https://papers.ssrn.com/sol3/papers.cfm?abstract_id=2972231 [Accessed 4 may 2018].

Posner, R. (1972). *Economic Analysis of Law.* Little Brown, Boston.

Prashanth, V., Vosoughi, S., Yuan, A. and Roy, D. (2017). TweetVista: An AI-powered interactive tool for exploring conversations on Twitter. *Proceedings of the 22nd International Conference on Intelligent User Interfaces Companion*, ACM, 145–148.

Prat, A. and Stromberg, D. (2005). Commercial television and voter information. Working paper.

Prat, A. (2015). Media capture and media power. In *Handbook of Media Economics*, Anderson, S., Stromberg, D. and Waldfogel, J. (eds). North Holland, London, 669–685.

Prat, A. (2018). Media Power. *Journal of Political Economy*, 126(4), 1747–1783.

Prat, A. and Stromberg, D. (2013). The political economy of mass media. In *Advances in Economics and Econometrics*, Acemoglu, D., Arellano, M. and Dekel, E. (eds). Cambridge University Press, New York.

Puglisi, R. (2011). Being The New York Times: the political behaviors of a newspaper. *Journal of Economic Analysis and Policy*, 11(1), 1–34.

Puglisi, R. and Snyder, J. (2011). Newspaper coverage of political scandals. *The Journal of Politics*, 73(3), 931–950.

Puglisi, R. and Snyder, J (2015). The balanced US press. *Journal of the European Economic Association*, 13(2), 240–264.

Qin, B., Stromberg D. and Wu, Y. (2017). Why does China allow free social media? Protests versus surveillance and propaganda. *Journal of Economic Perspectives*, 31(1), 117–140.

Rallet, A. (2006). Une économie de la communication. *Revue Hermès*, 44, 169–171.

Ravanello, O. (2016). Une histoire à part. *Explicite*. Available at: https://www.explicite.info/about-us/story.

Rebillard, F. (2011). Création, contribution, recommandation : les strates du journalisme participatif. *Les Cahiers du Journalisme*, 22(23), 28–40.

Reddaway, B. (1963). The Economics of Newspapers. *The Economic Journal*, 33, 201–218.

Reinikka, R. and Svensson, J. (2003). The Power of Information: Evidence from a Newspaper Campaign to Reduce Capture. World Bank Publications, Washington DC.

Reinikka, R. and Svensson, J. (2011). The power of information in public services: Evidence from education in Uganda. *Journal of Public Economics*, 95, 956–966.

Reuter, J. and Zitzewitz, E. (2006). Do Ads influence editors? Advertising and bias in the financial market. Working paper.

Rosse, J. (1967). Daily newspapers, monopolistic competition and economies of scale. *American Economic Review*, 57(2), 522–533.

Roumeen, I., Djankov, S. and McLeish, C. (2002). The Right to Tell: the Role of Mass Media in Economic Development. WBI development studies: The World Bank, Washington, D.C.

Ruellan, D. (2011). *Nous, journalistes : déontologie et identité*. PUG, Grenoble.

Russ-Mohl, S. (2006). The economics of journalism and the challenge to improve journalism quality: A research manifesto. *Studies in Communication Sciences*, 6(2), 189–208.

Salmon, N. (2017). Donald Trump takes credit for inventing the word 'fake'. *The Independent*. Available at: https://www.independent.co.uk/news/world/americas/donald-trump-takes-credit-for-inventing-the-word-fake-a7989221.html.

Scherer, E. (2011). *A-t-on encore besoin des journalistes ? Manifeste pour un journalisme augmenté*. PUF, Paris.

Scherer, E. (2018). Des robots journalistes déjà bien meilleurs que les vrais! *Méta-Media*, March 15, 2018. Available at: https://www.meta-media.fr/2018/03/15/des-robots-journalistes-deja-bien-meilleurs-que-les-vrais.html.

Scherer, E. (2017). Et si les Médias redevenaient Intelligents. *Revue Méta-Média*, 13, Spring-Summer.

Schnakenberg, K. (2017). The downsides of information transmission and voting. *Public Choice*, 173, 43–59.

Schulhofer-Whol, S. and Garrido, M. (2013). Do newspapers matter? Short-run and long-run evidence from the closure of The Cincinnati Post. *Journal of Media Economics*, 26(2), 60–81.

Schwartzenberg, E. (2007). *Spéciale dernière : Qui veut la mort de la presse quotidienne française*? Calman-Levy, Paris.

Sen, A. (1984). Food battles: Conflicts in the access to food. *Food and Nutrition*, 10(1), 81–89.

Shiller, B., Waldfogel, J. and Ryan, J. (2018). The effect of Ad blocking on website traffic and quality. *RAND Journal of Economics*, 49(1), 43–63.

Shiller, R. (2017). Narrative Economics. *American Economic Review*, 107(4), 967–1004.

Shrihari, S. and Srinasaraghavan, S. (2015). Is online newspaper advertising cannibalizing print advertising? *Quantitative Marketing and Economics*, 13(4), 283–318.

Siegel, D. (3013). Social network and the mass media. *The American Political Science Review*, 107(4), 786–805.

Simonov, A. and Rao, J. (2017). Demand for (un)biased news: Government control in online news markets. Working paper, Department of Economics, Chicago University.

Smyrianos, N. (2015). Google and the algorithmic infomediation of news. *Media Field Journal*, 10, 1–10.

Snyder, J. and Stromberg, D. (2010). Press coverage and political accountability. *Journal of Political Economy*, 118(2), 355–408.

Sobbrio, F. (2014). Citizen-editors'endogenous information acquisition and news accuracy. *Journal of Public Economics*, 113, 43–53.

Sommer, C. (2018). Market orientation of news startups. *Journal of Media Innovations*, 4(2), 34–54.

Song, B.K. (2018). Did television reduce the effect of partisan press on electoral politics? *American Politics Research*. doi.org/10.1177/1532673X18786722.

Sonnac, N. (2000). Readers' attitudes toward press advertising: Are they Ad-lovers or Ad-averse? *Journal of Media Economics*, 13(4), 249–259.

Sonnac, N. (2001). L'économie des Magazines. *Réseaux*, 105, 79–100.

Steiner, P. (1952). Program patterns and preferences, and the workability of competition in radio broadcasting. *Quarterly Journal of Economics*, 66, 194–223.

Stromberg, D. (2001). Mass media and public policy. *European Economic Review*, 45, 652–663.

Stromberg, D. (2002). Distributing news and political influence. In *The Media's Right to Tell*, Djankov, S. (ed.). The World Bank, Washington D.C.

Stromberg, D. (2004). Mass media competition, political competition and public policy. *Review of Economic Studies*, 71(1), 265–284.

Suen, W. (2004). The self-perpetuation of biased beliefs. *The Economic Journal*, 114, 377–396.

Sutter, D. (2001). Can the media be so liberal? The economics of media bias. *Cato Journal*, 20, 431–451.

Sutter, D. (2002). Advertising and political bias in the media: the market for criticism of the market economy. *American Journal of Economics and Sociology*, 61(3), 725–745.

Tetlock, P. (2007). Giving content to investor sentiment: the role of media in the stock market. *The Journal of Finance*, 72(3), 1139–1168.

Tetlock, P. (2011). All the news that's fit to reprint: do investors react to stale information? *Review of Financial Studies*, 24(5), 1481–1512.

Thurman, N., Doerr, K. and Kunert, J. (2017). When reporters get hands-on with robot-riting: Professionals consider automated journalism's capabilities and consequences. *Digital Journalism*, 5(10), 1240–1259.

Tirole, J. (2016). *Economie du bien commun*. PUF, Paris.

Toussaint-Desmoulin, N. (1996). *Economie des médias*. PUF, Paris.

Trédan, O. (2014). Quand le journalisme se saisit du web : l'exemple du data journalisme. In *Changements et permanences du journalisme*, Le Cam, F., Ruellan, D. (eds). L'Harmattan, Paris, 199–214.

UNESCO (2007). Liberté de la presse et développement : une analyse des corrélations entre la liberté de la presse et le développement, la pauvreté, la gouvernance et la paix. Report.

Vadlamannati, K. and Cooray, A. (2016). Do freedom of information laws improve bureaucratic efficiency? An empirical investigation. *Oxford Economic Papers*, 68(4), 968–993.

Van Damme, S. (2004). Comprendre les *Cultural Studies : une approche d'histoire des savoirs*. *Revue d'histoire moderne et contemporaine*, 51–4bis, 48–58.

Vara-Miguel, A. and Díaz-Espina, C. (2014). Paid news versus free news: evolution of the wsj.com business model from a content perspective (2010–2012). *Communication and Society*, 27(2), 147–167.

Varian, H. and Shapiro, C. (1999). *Information Rules: A Strategic Guide to the Network Economy*. Harvard Business Review Press, Boston.

Vos, T. and Singer, J. (2016). Media discourse about entrepreneurial journalism: Implications for journalistic capital. *Journalism Practice*, 10(2), 143–159.

Vosoughi, S., Roy, D. and Aral, S. (2018). The spread of true and false news online. *Revue Science*, 359(6380), 1146–1151.

Waldfogel, J. (2017). How digitalization has created a Golden Age of music, movies, books and television. *The Journal of Economic Perspectives*, 31(3), 195–204.

Wallace, J. (2018). Modelling contemporary gatekeeping, the rise of individuals, algorithms and platforms in digital news dissemination. *Digital Journalism*, 6(3), 274–293.

Wallich, H. (1972). Economics and the press. *American Economic Review*, 62(1–2), 384–386.

Weber, M. and Kosterich, A. (2018). Coding the news: The role of computer code in the distribution of news media. *Digital Journalism*, 6(3), 310–329.

Westerman, D., Spence, P. and Van Der Heide, B. (2012). A social network as information: The effect of system generated reports of connectedness on credibility on Twitter. *Computers in Human Behavior*, 28, 199–206.

White, D. (1950). The gate keeper: a case study in the selection of news. *Journalism Quarterly*, 27, 383–90.

Xiang, Y. and Savart, M. (2007). News Consumption and Media Bias. *Marketing Science*, 26(5), 611–628.

Xu, Y., Liu, Z. and Ortiz, J. (2018). The relationship between media bias and inflation expectations in P.R. China. *Research in International Business and Finance*, 45, 402–412.

Yazaki, Y. (2017). Newspapers and political accountability: evidence from Japan. *Public Choice*, 172, 311–331.

Yuan, H. (2016). Measuring media bias in China. *China Economic Review*, 38, 49–59.

Zeller, F. and Hermida, A. (2015). When tradition meets immediacy and interaction. The integration of social media in journalists' everyday practices. *Sur le journalisme*, 4, 106–119.

Index

A, B, C

adblock, 76
agenda, 109, 132
  setting, 42
algorithm, 102, 109, 115, 133,
  164, 174
artificial intelligence, 164
attention economy, 79
automated (automatic) journalism,
  165, 167
automatic articles, 169
bad news, 153
bias of negativity, 152
Big Data, 165, 176
bureaucracy, 43
capture, 54
citizen journalism, 132
cliometrics, 58
cognitive dissonance, 40, 54, 110
collusion, 24, 60
commercial bias, 82
computational journalism, 166
computer-assisted journalism, 166
consciousness, 164
conspiracy theories, 140
corruption, 19
credibility, 35
crisis, 71

D, E, F

data, 106, 120, 166, 177
  journalism, 165, 166, 170
  scientists, 92
digitization, 101
disinformation, 149
diversification, 108
economic analysis of public
  decisions, 28, 52
economic analysis of the law, 65
embedded values, 134
externalities, 122
fact-checking, 142, 152
fake news, 139
fall of the wall, 104

G, H, I

GAFA, 120
game theory, 26, 49, 126, 150
governance, 22
human journalism, 170
ideological bias, 26, 78
industrial economy, 30
information
  economy, 6
  production, 171
informational bias, 38, 156

J, M, N

jobs, 101
journalist programmer, 167
media management, 14
newspaper owners, 48
NLG (natural language generation), 174
NLP (natural language processing), 175

P, Q, R

polarization, 103, 128
political power, 58
post truth, 143
press freedom, 17, 64
public choice, 29

pure player, 98
quantitative journalism, 166
recommendation, 147
risk aversion, 154
robot
    journalism, 161, 169–171
    writers, 162
rumor, 145, 150

S, T, W

social networks, 146
start-up, 104
two-sided, 38
watchdog, 57

Other titles from

in

Information Systems, Web and Pervasive Computing

2018

ARDUIN Pierre-Emmanuel
Insider Threats
(Advances in Information Systems Set – Volume 10)

CARMÈS Maryse
Digital Organizations Manufacturing: Scripts, Performativity and
Semiopolitics
(Intellectual Technologies Set – Volume 5)

CARRÉ Dominique, VIDAL Geneviève
Hyperconnectivity: Economical, Social and Environmental Challenges
(Computing and Connected Society Set – Volume 3)

CHAMOUX Jean-Pierre
The Digital Era 1: Big Data Stakes

DOUAY Nicolas
Urban Planning in the Digital Age
(Intellectual Technologies Set – Volume 6)

FABRE Renaud, BENSOUSSAN Alain
The Digital Factory for Knowledge: Production and Validation of Scientific
Results

GAUCHEREL Cédric, GOUYON Pierre-Henri, DESSALLES Jean-Louis
Information, The Hidden Side of Life

GAUDIN Thierry, LACROIX Dominique, MAUREL Marie-Christine, POMEROL Jean-Charles
Life Sciences, Information Sciences

GAYARD Laurent
Darknet: Geopolitics and Uses
(Computing and Connected Society Set – Volume 2)

IAFRATE Fernando
Artificial Intelligence and Big Data: The Birth of a New Intelligence
(Advances in Information Systems Set – Volume 8)

LE DEUFF Olivier
Digital Humanities: History and Development
(Intellectual Technologies Set – Volume 4)

MANDRAN Nadine
Traceable Human Experiment Design Research: Theoretical Model and Practical Guide
(Advances in Information Systems Set – Volume 9)

PIVERT Olivier
NoSQL Data Models: Trends and Challenges

ROCHET Claude
Smart Cities: Reality or Fiction

SAUVAGNARGUES Sophie
Decision-making in Crisis Situations: Research and Innovation for Optimal Training

SEDKAOUI Soraya
Data Analytics and Big Data

SZONIECKY Samuel
Ecosystems Knowledge: Modeling and Analysis Method for Information and Communication
(Digital Tools and Uses Set – Volume 6)

2017

BOUHAÏ Nasreddine, SALEH Imad
Internet of Things: Evolutions and Innovations
(Digital Tools and Uses Set – Volume 4)

DUONG Véronique
Baidu SEO: Challenges and Intricacies of Marketing in China

LESAS Anne-Marie, MIRANDA Serge
The Art and Science of NFC Programming
(Intellectual Technologies Set – Volume 3)

LIEM André
Prospective Ergonomics
(Human-Machine Interaction Set – Volume 4)

MARSAULT Xavier
Eco-generative Design for Early Stages of Architecture
(Architecture and Computer Science Set – Volume 1)

REYES-GARCIA Everardo
The Image-Interface: Graphical Supports for Visual Information
(Digital Tools and Uses Set – Volume 3)

REYES-GARCIA Everardo, BOUHAÏ Nasreddine
Designing Interactive Hypermedia Systems
(Digital Tools and Uses Set – Volume 2)

SAÏD Karim, BAHRI KORBI Fadia
Asymmetric Alliances and Information Systems:Issues and Prospects
(Advances in Information Systems Set – Volume 7)

SZONIECKY Samuel, BOUHAÏ Nasreddine
Collective Intelligence and Digital Archives: Towards Knowledge Ecosystems
(Digital Tools and Uses Set – Volume 1)

2016

BEN CHOUIKHA Mona
Organizational Design for Knowledge Management

BERTOLO David
Interactions on Digital Tablets in the Context of 3D Geometry Learning
(Human-Machine Interaction Set – Volume 2)

BOUVARD Patricia, SUZANNE Hervé
Collective Intelligence Development in Business

EL FALLAH SEGHROUCHNI Amal, ISHIKAWA Fuyuki, HÉRAULT Laurent,
TOKUDA Hideyuki
Enablers for Smart Cities

FABRE Renaud, in collaboration with MESSERSCHMIDT-MARIET Quentin,
HOLVOET Margot
New Challenges for Knowledge

GAUDIELLO Ilaria, ZIBETTI Elisabetta
Learning Robotics, with Robotics, by Robotics
(Human-Machine Interaction Set – Volume 3)

HENROTIN Joseph
The Art of War in the Network Age
(Intellectual Technologies Set – Volume 1)

KITAJIMA Munéo
Memory and Action Selection in Human–Machine Interaction
(Human–Machine Interaction Set – Volume 1)

LAGRAÑA Fernando
E-mail and Behavioral Changes: Uses and Misuses of Electronic
Communications

LEIGNEL Jean-Louis, UNGARO Thierry, STAAR Adrien
Digital Transformation
(Advances in Information Systems Set – Volume 6)

NOYER Jean-Max
Transformation of Collective Intelligences
(Intellectual Technologies Set – Volume 2)

VENTRE Daniel
Information Warfare – 2nd edition

VITALIS André
The Uncertain Digital Revolution
(Computing and Connected Society Set – Volume 1)

2015

ARDUIN Pierre-Emmanuel, GRUNDSTEIN Michel, ROSENTHAL-SABROUX Camille
Information and Knowledge System
(Advances in Information Systems Set – Volume 2)

BÉRANGER Jérôme
Medical Information Systems Ethics

BRONNER Gérald
Belief and Misbelief Asymmetry on the Internet

IAFRATE Fernando
From Big Data to Smart Data
(Advances in Information Systems Set – Volume 1)

KRICHEN Saoussen, BEN JOUIDA Sihem
Supply Chain Management and its Applications in Computer Science

NEGRE Elsa
Information and Recommender Systems
(Advances in Information Systems Set – Volume 4)

POMEROL Jean-Charles, EPELBOIN Yves, THOURY Claire
MOOCs

SALLES Maryse
Decision-Making and the Information System
(Advances in Information Systems Set – Volume 3)

SAMARA Tarek
ERP and Information Systems: Integration or Disintegration
(Advances in Information Systems Set – Volume 5)

2014

DINET Jérôme
Information Retrieval in Digital Environments

HÉNO Raphaële, CHANDELIER Laure
3D Modeling of Buildings: Outstanding Sites

KEMBELLEC Gérald, CHARTRON Ghislaine, SALEH Imad
Recommender Systems

MATHIAN Hélène, SANDERS Lena
Spatio-temporal Approaches: Geographic Objects and Change Process

PLANTIN Jean-Christophe
Participatory Mapping

VENTRE Daniel
Chinese Cybersecurity and Defense

2013

BERNIK Igor
Cybercrime and Cyberwarfare

CAPET Philippe, DELAVALLADE Thomas
Information Evaluation

LEBRATY Jean-Fabrice, LOBRE-LEBRATY Katia
Crowdsourcing: One Step Beyond

SALLABERRY Christian
Geographical Information Retrieval in Textual Corpora

2012

BUCHER Bénédicte, LE BER Florence
Innovative Software Development in GIS

GAUSSIER Eric, YVON François
Textual Information Access

STOCKINGER Peter
Audiovisual Archives: Digital Text and Discourse Analysis

VENTRE Daniel
Cyber Conflict

2011

BANOS Arnaud, THÉVENIN Thomas
Geographical Information and Urban Transport Systems

DAUPHINÉ André
Fractal Geography

LEMBERGER Pirmin, MOREL Mederic
Managing Complexity of Information Systems

STOCKINGER Peter
Introduction to Audiovisual Archives

STOCKINGER Peter
Digital Audiovisual Archives

VENTRE Daniel
Cyberwar and Information Warfare

2010

BONNET Pierre
Enterprise Data Governance

BRUNET Roger
Sustainable Geography

CARREGA Pierre
Geographical Information and Climatology

CAUVIN Colette, ESCOBAR Francisco, SERRADJ Aziz
Thematic Cartography – 3-volume series
Thematic Cartography and Transformations – Volume 1
Cartography and the Impact of the Quantitative Revolution – Volume 2
New Approaches in Thematic Cartography – Volume 3

LANGLOIS Patrice
Simulation of Complex Systems in GIS

MATHIS Philippe
Graphs and Networks – 2nd edition

THERIAULT Marius, DES ROSIERS François
Modeling Urban Dynamics

2009

BONNET Pierre, DETAVERNIER Jean-Michel, VAUQUIER Dominique
Sustainable IT Architecture: the Progressive Way of Overhauling Information Systems with SOA

PAPY Fabrice
Information Science

RIVARD François, ABOU HARB Georges, MERET Philippe
The Transverse Information System

ROCHE Stéphane, CARON Claude
Organizational Facets of GIS

2008

BRUGNOT Gérard
Spatial Management of Risks

FINKE Gerd
Operations Research and Networks

GUERMOND Yves
Modeling Process in Geography

KANEVSKI Michael
Advanced Mapping of Environmental Data

MANOUVRIER Bernard, LAURENT Ménard
Application Integration: EAI, B2B, BPM and SOA

PAPY Fabrice
Digital Libraries

2007

DOBESCH Hartwig, DUMOLARD Pierre, DYRAS Izabela
Spatial Interpolation for Climate Data

SANDERS Lena
Models in Spatial Analysis

2006

CLIQUET Gérard
Geomarketing

CORNIOU Jean-Pierre
Looking Back and Going Forward in IT

DEVILLERS Rodolphe, JEANSOULIN Robert
Fundamentals of Spatial Data Quality

Printed and bound by CPI Group (UK) Ltd, Croydon, CR0 4YY